BRITISH BUSINESS HISTORY

A BIBLIOGRAPHY

British Business History

A Bibliography

Edited by

Stephanie Zarach

Second Edition

First edition (entitled *Debrett's Bibliography of Business History*) 1987

Second edition published 1994 by
THE MACMILLAN PRESS LTD
Houndmills, Basingstoke, Hampshire RG21 2XS
and London
Companies and representatives
throughout the world

ISBN 0–333–59287–5

A catalogue record for this book is available
from the British Library.

Printed in Great Britain by
Ipswich Book Co Ltd
Ipswich, Suffolk

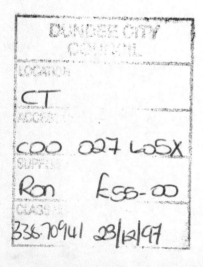

Contents

Acknowledgements

This bibliography is dedicated to Theo Barker, Professor Emeritus of Economic History at the University of London, whose astonishing energy in writing books and articles, taping radio programmes and arranging conferences and seminars never ceases to amaze me. Sometimes controversial, occasionally mischievous and always perceptive in his analyses, Theo does much to promote the cause of business history to businessmen and academics alike. My thanks go to him for his friendship and bottomless ability to enjoy life.

Tenacious ferreting by Gordon Phillips, archivist and business historian, has done much to ensure that titles missing from the first edition – as well as titles produced since – have been included in this bibliography. His task was an arduous one and I thank him for his efforts.

Finally, I would also like to use this book to thank numerous friends in the field of business history, both the authors with whom I have worked and the firms for whom I have organised and produced histories. The number and variety of subjects – law, artificial limbs, banking, building, transport, medicine, public utilities – has been fascinating; above all, I learned that the process of writing the history of a firm can forge lasting and close friendships and provide a great deal of fun.

June 1993   STEPHANIE ZARACH

Introduction

Six years on since the first edition and it is surprisingly more, rather than less, difficult to amass a comprehensive bibliography of business history. For one thing, there is a considerable increase in the number of titles, which makes cataloguing them in a limited space impossible: for another, new publications are so hard to find, partly because many are still being privately printed and only come to light by accident and an efficient grapevine. Even when they are published, very recent titles can disappear like needles in a haystack amongst the 60,000 odd books published each year and listed in Whitaker's *Books in Print*. Whitaker certainly divides titles into subjects, but there is no all-encompassing category called business history; and even if there were, it would not automatically follow that a book on, for example, Sandeman's port, would be seen first as a 'business history' and be placed in that category. So, to be absolutely accurate, I really should have pored over every Whitaker's entry since *Books in Print* began: an impossible task in the time available.

The sources of information on books in this field have remained much the same as they were six years ago. The Business Archives Council continues to do sterling work in collating material and has been the chief source of extra information; moreover, their library collection of business histories must be one of the best there is in the UK. *A Bibliography of British Business Histories*, edited by Francis Goodall and published by Gower in 1987, did much to fill in the gaps in my first edition; Francis is currently working on an international bibliography of selected business histories, due to be published in 1994. Other sources have included *Business History* and *The Bookseller*. One very ambitious project has come to fruition under the auspices of St James's Press: the *International Directory of Company Histories* is a multi-volumed effort which gives potted biographies of the biggest companies in the world. It is a mine of information. Books which have been published will be easily found in the catalogues of the copyright libraries. Titles which have been privately printed are more difficult, but the Business Archives Council will be the main source, as well as the Guildhall Reference Library and university libraries. The companies themselves are often very happy to help either by providing *bona fide* researchers with copies of their histories or at least offering the loan of them.

Business history has blossomed in the last six years, with more universities setting up specialist departments in the field. Companies and professional firms have come to recognise the use and importance of having their histories documented and, delightfully, many have also seen the wisdom of actually publishing them so that they are available to the public at large. As both a business historian and a publisher of business histories, I have seen the relationship between authors and companies from both sides. There is now a much better understanding between them – a splendid improvement which has augured well for current students of the subject seeking to gain experience in the field. Companies and firms are beginning to see that no matter how small their histories, if they are properly researched and written in a readable style, perhaps with pictures and illustrations, they will contribute more pieces to the jigsaw that goes to make British industrial history through the centuries.

The previous format for this bibliography was well received, so I have retained it and classified companies under their relevant subjects; the index provides an alphabetical list of individual companies. The overwhelming number of titles would have become unwieldy without some sort of fixed criteria; I had to be wickedly ruthless in excluding any titles under 50 pages and this decision may mean that some gems have been missed, though there were very few instances of companies having to be left out entirely as a result. An equally ruthless and potentially a much more controversial decision has been to omit categories which have been well covered elsewhere. These include cooperatives, railways, tramways and the press. I am unrepentant; I could not possibly, for example, have done justice to the number of publications on railways without regurgitating George Ottley's comprehensive bibliography in its entirety. Similarly, although I have included a section on shipping, I am aware that it is inadequate and that readers would be better by far to refer to the general titles listed at the start of the shipping section. Indeed, the section on 'Books for General Use to the Business Historian' on page 310 is a must.

As in the previous edition, books are confined to this century and biographies have been excluded unless they are extremely relevant to a company. I have not included articles and journals, on the assumption that books suggested in the general sections have very useful bibliographies and source references of their own which will take a reader further. Once again, I have not attempted to pass judgement on the histories; my intention is to show the range of publications that have been produced this century and, in so doing, provide a historical snapshot of the business of writing company history.

I hope that this bibliography enables you to gain knowledge of the wonderful variety of commercial enterprise in which men and women have set about the business of earning a living.

Stephanie Zarach

Accountancy

General

Kitchen, J. and Parker, R. H., *Accounting Thought and Education: Six English Pioneers* (Institute of Chartered Accountants in England and Wales, 1980).

Littleton, A. C. and Yamey, B. S. (eds), *Studies in the History of Accounting* (Sweet & Maxwell, 1956).

Parker, R. H., *Management Accounting: An Historical Perspective* (Macmillan, 1969).

Parker, R. H., *British Accountants: A Biographical Sourcebook* (New York: Arno Press, 1980).

Pryce-Jones, J., *Accounting in Scotland: A Historical Bibliography* (Edinburgh: Institute of Chartered Accountants in Scotland, 1976) 2nd edition, 107 pp.

A guide to the records of firms of chartered accountants in England and Wales, sponsored by the Institute of Chartered Accountants, is to be published in September 1993.

Arthur Andersen & Co.

—— *The First Fifty Years 1913–1963* (Chicago: Library of Congress, 1963). 201 pp.

Begbie, Robinson, Cox & Knight

—— *A Hundred Years of Accountancy 1837–1937* (1938).

Coopers & Lybrand

Cooke, John, *A History of Cooper Bros & Co. 1854–1954* (Batsford for Coopers, 1954). xi 116 pp.

Hopkins, L., *The Hundredth Year* (MacDonald & Evans, 1980). vii 168 pp.

1

Deloitte Haskins & Sells

Kettle, Sir R., *Deloitte & Co., 1845–1956* (privately printed for Deloitte Plender Griffiths & Co. at the Oxford University Press, 1958). 171 pp.

Ernst & Whinney (now Ernst & Young)

Edwards, J. R. and Baker, C., *Ernst and Ernst 1903–1960: A History of the Firm* (Cleveland, 1960).

Jones, Edgar, *Accountancy and the British Economy 1840–1980: The Evolution of Ernst & Whinney* (Batsford, 1981). 288 pp.

Foulks Lynch & Co. Ltd

—— *Seventy Years of Progress in Accountancy Education* (1955). 63 pp. [Now Chart Foulks Lynch Ltd.]

Grace, Darbyshire & Todd

—— *A Short History of Grace, Darbyshire & Todd: Chartered Accountants of Bristol 1818–1957* (The Company, 1957).

Haskins & Sells: *see* Deloitte Haskins & Sells

The Institute of Chartered Accountants in England & Wales

Hein, L. W., *History of the Institute of Chartered Accountants in England and Wales 1870–1965* (Heinemann, 1966).

Howitt, Sir Harold, *The History of the Institute of Chartered Accountants in England and Wales 1870–1965: and of its Founder Accountancy Bodies 1870–1880 – The Growth of a Profession and its Influence on Legislation and Public Affairs* (Heinemann, 1966). 269 pp.

Magnus, Philip, *The History of the Institute of Chartered Accountants in England and Wales 1880–1959* (1959). (Unpublished typescript.)

The Institute of Chartered Accountants in Scotland

Hein, L. W., *History of the Chartered Accountants of Scotland from the Earliest Times to 1954* (Edinburgh, 1954).

McDougall, E. H. V., *Fifth Quarter-Century: Some Chapters in the History of the Chartered Accountants of Scotland* (Institute of Chartered Accountants of Scotland, 1980). xv 101 pp.

Stewart, J. C., *Pioneers of a Profession* (Edinburgh: The Institution, 1977). xii 181 pp.

The Institute of Municipal Treasurers and Accountants

—— *A Short History* (London, 1960).

Mann Judd Gordon & Co.

—— *Interim Account of a Going Concern: Some Essays on the Firm of Mann Judd Gordon & Company . . .* (Glasgow: The Firm, 1967). 57 pp.

Morris Gregory & Co.

—— *A History of One Hundred Years of Accountancy Practice, 1852–1952* (Manchester, 1953).

Peat Marwick Mitchell & Co.

Dawe, D. and Oswald, A. *11 Ironmonger Lane: The Story of a Site in the City of London* (Hutchinson, 1952).

Wise, T. A., *Peat Marwick Mitchell & Co., 85 Years* (New York: Published by The Firm, 1982).

Pike Russell & Co.

—— *Pike Russell & Co., An Account of a London Firm of Chartered Accountants 1903–1973* (The Firm, 1973). [Now called Russell Limebeer.]

Price Waterhouse & Co.

DeMond, Chester W., *Price Waterhouse in America: A History of a Public Accounting Firm* (New York, 1951). (Reprinted New York: Arno Press, 1980.)

Jones, H. E., *The Memoirs of Edwin Waterhouse: A Founder of Price Waterhouse* (Batsford, 1988). 248 pp.

Society of Incorporated Accountants

Garratt, A. A., *History of the Society of Incorporated Accountants 1885–1957* (Oxford University Press, 1961). 360 pp.

Thomson McLintock & Co.

Winsbury, R., *Thomson McLintock & Co – The First Hundred Years 1877–1977* (Seeley Service, 1977). 164 pp. [The firm is now known as KMG Thomson McLintock.]

Touche Ross & Co.

Richards, Archibald B., *Touche Ross & Co. 1899–1981: The Origins and Growth of the United Kingdom Firm* (Touche Ross & Co., c.1981). xiii 145 pp.

Advertising

General

National Archive for the History of Advertising, founded on a grant by the Leverhulme Trust, 1982, based at Raveningham, Norfolk.

Dunbar, D. S., *Almost Gentlemen: The Growth and Development of the Advertising Agent 1875–1975* (privately printed by the J. Walter Thompson Co., 1976). 76 pp.

Elliot, B. B., *A History of English Advertising* (1962). 247 pp.

Nevett, T. R., *Advertising in Britain* (London: Heinemann, 1982). (On behalf of The History of Advertising Trust.) xiii 231 pp.

Advertiser's Weekly

Advertiser's Weekly, 1913–1963: A Half-Century in the Service of Advertising (The Firm, 1983). 168 pp.

Allen (David) & Sons Ltd

Gould, R., *David Allens 1857–1957* (John Murray, 1957). xii 57 pp.

F. H. Brown Ltd

Halstead, Allan, *F. H. Brown, 40 Years: Advertising Special* (Burnley, 1969).

Crawford (W. S.)

Mills, G. H. S., *There is a Tide . . . The Life and Work of Sir William Crawford* (Heinemann, 1954). viii 197 pp.

Lintons

Sharpe, Len (compiler), *The Lintons Story: Impressions and Recollections* (The Firm, 1964). vii 112 pp.

Ogilvy & Mather Ltd

Ogilvy, D., *Blood, Brains and Beer* (Hamilton, 1978). 118 pp.

Piggott, Stanley, *OBM: A Celebration: One Hundred and Twenty-Five Years in Advertising* (The Firm, 1975). 84 pp.

Saatchi & Saatchi

Fallon, E., *The Brothers: The Rise and Rise of Saatchi & Saatchi* (1988).

Agricultural Industries

General

The Institute of Agricultural History, Museum of English Rural Life at the University of Reading can provide excellent bibliographies and archival information in this field.

Bomford & Evershed & Co. Ltd

Sherwen, Theo, *The Bomford Story: A Century of Service to Agriculture* (The Company, 1979). 104 pp.

Fordson

Bate, D. M. and Cordle, A. T., *A Fordson Dealer's Portfolio* (Willenhall, Cordle Publications, 1984). 75 pp.

Fowler (John) & Co. (Leeds) Ltd

Davis, Theo., *John Fowler and the Business he Founded* (The Company, 1951).

Howie (Robert) & Sons

—— *Things I Remember: The Story of Robert Howie & Sons 1850–1978: The Memoirs of James M. Howie* (The Company, 1978). 52 pp.

May Horticulture

—— *Seventy Years in Horticulture* (Cable Printing, 1928). 92 pp.

Rochford's Nurseries

Allan, M., *Tom's Weeds: The Story of Rochford's and their House Plants* (Faber, 1970). 220 pp.

Strutt & Parker Farms

Gavin, W., *Ninety Years of Family Firms . . . Strutt & Parker Farms* (Hutchinson, 1967). 246 pp.

Wright Stephenson

Irving, J. C., *A Century's Challenge 1861–1961* (Wellington: The Firm, 1961). 297 pp.

Architects, Chartered Surveyors, Estate Companies and Estate Agents

General

A biography of British Architects, 1834–1914 has been set up as an online database source at the British Architectural Library (66 Portland Place, W1N 4AS).

Thompson, F. M. L., *Chartered Surveyors: The Growth of a Profession* (Routledge & Kegan Paul, 1968). 416 pp.

Artizan's and General Properties Company

—— *Artizans Centenary 1867–1967* (The Firm, 1967). 67 pp.

Baxter, Payne and Lepper

—— *Baxter, Payne and Lepper, 1760–1985: A Chronicle of the Period*, (The Firm, 1986). 60 pp.

Bradford Property Trust

—— *History of the Bradford Property Trust Limited 1928–1978* (The Firm, 1978). viii 55 pp.

Bridgewater Estates plc

Grayling, Christopher, *The Bridgewater Heritage: The Story of Bridgewater Estates* (The Company, 1983).

Campbell Smith & Co. Ltd

Campbell, K. L. G., *Campbell Smith & Company 1873–1973: A Century of Decorative Craftsmanship* (The Company, 1973). ix 77 pp.

Drivers Jonas

Barty-King, Hugh, *Scratch a Surveyor* (Heinemann, 1975). 273 pp.

Ellis (Richard)

Wainwright, David, *Richard Ellis 1773–1973* (Hutchinson Benham, 1973). 71 pp.

Gresham House Estate Co. Ltd

—— *Gresham House Estate Company Ltd 1857–1957: Centenary Review by the Chairman* (privately printed, 1956).

Humberts

Barber, D., *Humberts into the Eighties: A History of Humberts, Chartered Surveyors 1842–1980* (The Firm, 1980). 103 pp.

Knight Frank & Rutley

Jenkins, A., *Men of Property. Knight Frank & Rutley: The Building of a Partnership* (Quiller Press, 1986). 232 pp.

Martyn (H. H.) & Co.

Whitaker, J., *The Best: A History of H. H. Martyn & Co.: Carvers in Wood, Stone and Marble* (The author, 1985). xiii 360 pp.

Matthews & Goodman

King, J. E., *Matthews & Goodman: A Short History, 1866–1974* (The Firm, 1974). 170 pp.

Royal Institute of British Architects

Mace, R., *The Royal Institute of British Architects: A Guide to its Archive and History* (Mansell, 1986). xliv 378 pp.

St Quintin

Carter, A., *The History of St Quintin Chartered Surveyors 1831–1981* (privately published, 1981). 62 pp. (Reprinted 1984.)

Savills

Watson, J. A. F., *Savills: A Family as a Firm 1652–1977* (Hutchinson Benham, 1977). 173 pp.

Slough Estates

Cassell, M., *Long Lease! The Story of Slough Estates, 1920–1991* (Pencorp Books, 1991). 200 pp.

Sugden & Son

Lovenbury, G. A., *The Sugdens of Leek: Brief History of a Family Business* (1975). 19 pp.

Arms for War and Peace

General

Blackmore, H. I., *A Dictionary of London Gunmakers, 1350–1850*
   (Phaidon Christie's, 1986). 224 pp.

Armstrong (Sir W. G.) Whitworth & Co.: *see also in* 'Engineering'
(p. 106) *and in* 'Shipping and General Merchants' as
Vickers-Armstrong (p. 274)

Dougan, D., *The Great Gunmaker* (Frank Graham, 1971).

Warren, K., *Armstrongs of Elswick: Growth in Engineering and
   Armaments to the Merger with Vickers* (Macmillan, 1989). 302 pp.

Forsyth & Co.

Neal, W. K. and Back, D. H., *Forsyth & Co., Patent Gunmakers*
   (Bell, 1969). xix 280 pp.

Holland & Holland

King, Peter, *The Shooting Field* (Quiller, 1986). 176 pp.

Imperial Chemical Industries plc: *see also in* 'Chemical Industries' (p. 70)

—— *The History of Nobel's Explosives Company Limited and Nobel
   Industries Limited, 1871–1926,* volume 1: *ICI Ltd and its Founding
   Companies* (ICI, 1938). xii 240 pp.

Miles, F. D., *A History of Research in the Nobel Division of ICI*
   (The Firm, 1955). 210 pp.

Manton (J. & J.)

Neal, W. K. and Back, D. H., *The Mantons, Gunmakers* (Jenkins, 1967).
   xv 300 pp.

Purdey (James) & Sons

Beaumont, R., *Purdey's: The Guns and the Family* (David & Charles, 1984). 248 pp.

Vickers plc: *see also in* 'Engineering' (p. 136) *and* **Vickers-Armstrong** *in* 'Shipping and General Merchants' (p. 274)

Richardson, A., *Vickers Sons & Maxim Ltd: Their Works and Manufactures* (1902). 200 pp.

Trebilock, R. C., *The Vickers Brothers: Armaments and Enterprise 1884–1914* (Europa, 1977). 181 pp.

Webley & Scott

Dowell, W. C., *The Webley Story: A History of Webley Pistols and Revolvers . . .* (Skyrne, 1962). 337 pp.

Westley, Richards

Taylor, L. B., *A Brief History of the Westley Richards Firm, 1812–1913* (The Firm, 1913). 94 pp.

Art Dealers and Auctioneers

Ackermann

Ford, J., *Ackermann 1783–1983: The Business of Art* (Ackermann, 1983). 256 pp.

Agnew (Thomas) & Sons

Agnew, Geoffrey, *Agnew's 1817–1967* (Barry & Jenkins, 1967). 90 pp.

Christie's Fine Art Auctioneers

Colson, P., *A Story of Christie's* (The Firm, 1950). 206 pp.

Marillier, H. C., *Christie's 1766 to 1925* (1926). 311 pp.

Colnaghi (P. & D.) & Co. Ltd

—— *Art Commerce Scholarship: A Window on to the World 1760–1984* (Colnaghi's, 1984).

Duveen

Duveen, J. H., *The Rise of the House of Duveen* (1957). 252 pp.

Fine Art Society Ltd

—— *1876–1976 Centenary Exhibition Catalogue* (The Firm, 1976).

Mitchell's Auction Co. Ltd

—— *Centenary 1873–1973 of Mitchell's Auction Company Limited* (privately printed, 1973).

Parker (Thomas H.) Ltd

—— *An Introduction to the Parker Gallery* (1950). 56 pp.

—— *A Visit to the Parker Gallery* (1961). 71 pp.

—— *Looking Back 200 Years: The House of Parker Bi-Centenary 1750–1950* (1950).

Sotheby's

Faith, N., *Sold: The Rise and Fall of the House of Sotheby* (Macmillan, 1985). vii 269 pp.

Herrmann, Frank, *Sotheby's: A Portrait of an Auction House* (Chatto, 1980). xvi 468 pp.

Stevens' Auction Rooms Ltd

Allingham, E. C., *A Romance of the Rostrum: Being the Business Life of Henry Stevens* (1924). 333 pp.

Tattersalls

Orchard, V. R., *Tattersalls: Two Hundred Years of Sporting History* (1953). 312 pp.

Aviation

General

Edwards, R. S. and Townsend, H.(eds), *Business Growth* (Macmillan, 1966). xxiv 410 pp.

Penrose, H., *British Aviation: The Pioneer Years 1903–1914* (Putnam, 1967). viii 309 pp.

Penrose, H., *British Aviation: The Great War and Armistice 1915–1919* (Putnam, 1969).

Penrose, H., *British Aviation: The Adventuring Years, 1920–1929* (Putnam, 1973). 727 pp.

Penrose, H., *British Aviation: Widening Horizons 1930–1934* (HMSO, 1979). viii 340 pp.

Penrose, H., *British Aviation: The Ominous Skies 1935–1939* (HMSO, 1980). viii 318 pp.

Reader, W. J., *Architect of Air Power: The Life of the First Viscount Weir 1877–1959* (Collins, 1968). 351 pp.

Airspeed

Middleton, D. H., *Airspeed: The Company and its Aeroplanes* (Terence Dalton, 1982). ix 206 pp.

Avro Aircraft

Jackson, A. J., *Avro Aircraft Since 1908* (Putnam, 1965).

Birmingham International Airport plc

Negus, G., *Happy Landings: A Celebration of Birmingham International Airport plc 1939–1989* (The Firm, 1989). 62 pp.

Blackburn Aircraft Ltd: *see* **Hawker Siddeley Group.**

Bristol Aeroplane Co.

Barnes, C. H. G. B., *Bristol Aircraft Since 1910* (Putnam, 1964). 415 pp.

Green, G., *Bristol Aeroplane Since 1910* (The Author, 1985). 127 pp.

Pudney, J. S., *Bristol Fashion: Some Aircraft of the Earlier Days of Bristol Aviation* (Putnam, 1960). 102 pp.

Britannia Airways

Cuthbert, G., *Flying to the Sun: A Quarter Century of Britannia's Airways* (Hodder & Stoughton, 1987). 160 pp.

British Aerospace

Tapper, O., *Roots in the Sky: A History of British Aerospace Aircraft* (IPC, 1980). 96 pp.

British Aircraft Corporation

Adams, A. R., *Good Company: The Story of the Guided Weapons Division of British Aircraft Corporation* (Stevenage: The Firm, 1976). 220 pp.

Gardner, Charles, *The British Aircraft Corporation: A History* (Batsford, 1981). 320 pp.

Knight, G., *Concorde: The Inside Story* (Weidenfeld & Nicolson, 1976). ix 147 pp.

Owen, K., *Concorde: New Shape in the Sky* (James, 1982). 292 pp.

Wilson, A., *The Concorde Fiasco* (Harmondsworth: Penguin, 1973). 157 pp.

British Airways

Corke, A., *British Airways. The Path to Profitability* (Pinter, 1986).
145 pp.

Edwards, R. S. and Townsend, H. (eds), *Business Growth* (Macmillan,
1966). [Chapter entitled 'Development and Organization of British
Airways 1949 to 1960'.]

May, Gary, *The Challenge of BEA: The Story of A Great Airline's First
25 Years* (Wolfe, 1971).

Smith, D. C., *British Airways: Struggle for Take Off* (Coronet, 1986). viii
327 pp.

British Caledonian Airways

Thomson, A., *High Risk: The Politics of the Air* (Sidgwick & Jackson,
1990). x 590 pp.

British Overseas Airways Corporation

Pudney, J. S., *The Seven Skies: A Study of BOAC and its Forerunners
Since 1919* (The Firm, 1959). 320 pp.

Cambrian Airlines

Staddon, T. G., *History of Cambrian Airways, the Welsh Airline from
1935–1976* (Hounslow, Airline Publications & Sales, 1979). 111 pp.

de Havilland

Sharp, C. and Martin, D. H., *A History of de Havilland* (Airlife, 1982).
487 pp.

Dowty Group Ltd

Edwards, R. S. and Townsend, H. (eds), *Studies in Business Organisation*
(Macmillan, 1966). [Chapter entitled 'Development and Organisation
of the Dowty Group Ltd'.]

Rolt, L. T. C., *The Dowty Story* (Newman Neame for private circulation, 1962). vi 90 pp.

Fairey Aviation Co.

Taylor, H. A., *Fairey Aircraft Since 1915* (Pitman, 1974).

Handley Page

Barnes, C. H. G. B., *Handley Page Aircraft since 1907* (Putnam, 1976). viii 664 pp.

Ramsden, J. M. (ed), *Handley Page 60th Anniversary* (The Firm, 1969).

Hawker Siddeley Group plc [formerly Blackburn Aircraft Ltd]

—— *Blackburn Aircraft Ltd: The Blackburn Story 1909–1959* (1960) 51 pp.

Jackson, A. F., *Blackburn Aircraft Since 1909* (1968). 555 pp.

Edwards, R. S. and Townsend, H. (eds), *Business Growth* (Macmillan, 1966). [Chapter entitled 'Development and Organisation of Hawker Siddeley Group Ltd'.]

Imperial Airways

Brittain, Sir H., *By Air* (Hutchinson, 1933). xiv 294 pp.

Laker Airways

Barks, H., *The Rise and Fall of Freddie Laker* (Faber, 1982). 155 pp.

Eglin, R. and Ritchie, B., *Fly Me, Oh Freddie!* (Weidenfeld & Nicolson, 1980). 238 pp.

Martin Baker Aircraft

—— *The Story of an Enterprise 1929–1955* (Higher Denham, 1955). 80 pp.

Jewell, J., *Engineering for Life: The Story of Martin Baker*
(Higher Denham, 1979). 108 pp.

Power Jets Ltd

Whittle, Sir Frank, *Jet: The Story of a Pioneer* (London, 1953).
[Sir Frank Whittle was the owner of Power Jets Ltd.]

Rolls-Royce: *see also* **Rolls-Royce** *in* 'Motor Cars' (p. 211)

Harker, R. W., *The Engines were Rolls-Royce: An Informal History of
that Famous Company* (Collier-Macmillan, 1979). xxi, 202 pp.

Donne, M., *Leaders of the Skies: Rolls-Royce: The First Seventy-Five
Years* (Muller, 1981). 158 pp.

Lloyd, I., *Rolls-Royce: The Merlin at War* (Macmillan, 1978). xvii
188 pp.

Harker, R. W., *Rolls-Royce from the Wings: Military Aviation 1925–1971*
(Oxford Illustrated Press, 1976). viii 168 pp.

Short Brothers

Taylor, M. J. H., *Shorts the Planemakers* (Janes, 1984). 160 pp.

Vickers plc: *see also* 'Engineering' (p. 125) *and* 'Arms for War and
Peace' (p. 13).

Andrews, Charles F., *Vickers Aircraft since 1908* (Putnam, 1969).

Scott, J. D., *Vickers: A History* (Weidenfeld & Nicolson, 1963). xxiii
416 pp.

Scrope, H. E., *Golden Wings: The Story of Fifty Years of Aviation by the
Vickers Group of Companies 1908–1958* (The Firm, 1960). 90 pp.

Westland plc

Linklater, M. and Leigh, D., *Not With Honour: The Inside Story of the
Westland Scandal* (Sphere, 1986). 218 pp.

Taylor, J. W. R. and Allward, M. F. *Westland 50* (Shepperton: Ian Allen, 1965). 216 pp.

White (J. Samuel) & Co.

Goodall, M. H., *The White Aircraft: The History of the Aviation Department of J. Samuel White and Co. Ltd, 1913–1919* (Gentry, 1973). 194 pp.

Banking and Finance

General

Anderson, B. L. and Cottrell, P. L., *Money and Banking in England: The Development of the Banking System 1694–1914* (David & Charles, 1974).

Chapman, Stanley D., *The Rise of Merchant Banking* (Allen & Unwin, 1984). xi 224 pp. (Reprinted 1992 by Gregg Revivals.)

Checkland, S. G., *Scottish Banking, A History, 1695–1973* (Collins, 1975). xxvi 785 pp.

Clay, C. J. J. and Wheble, B. S., *Modern Merchant Banking: A Guide to the Workings of the Accepting Houses of the City of London and Their Service to Industry and Commerce* (Woodhead-Faulkner, 1976).

Ferris, P., *Gentlemen of Fortune: The World's Merchant and Investment Bankers* (Weidenfeld & Nicolson, 1984). 260 pp.

Goodhart, C.A.E., *The Business of Banking 1891–1914* (Weidenfeld & Nicolson, 1972). ix 628 pp.

Green, E., *Banking: An Illustrated History* (Phaidon, 1989). 160 pp.

Jones, G., *Banks as Multinationals* (Routledge, 1990). xii 301 pp.

Mottram, R. H., *Miniature Banking Histories* (Chatto, 1930).

Orbell, M. J. and Pressnell, L. S., *A Guide to the Historical Records of British Banking* (Gower Press, 1985). (Published in association with the Business Archives Council.) 156 pp. (Revised edition in preparation.)

Pressnell, L. S., *Country Banking in the Industrial Revolution* (Clarendon Pess, 1956).

Sampson, Anthony, *The Money Lenders* (Hodder & Stoughton, 1981).

Wechsberg. J., *The Merchant Bankers* (Weidenfeld & Nicolson, 1967).

Aberdeen Banking Company

Munn, C. W., *The Scottish Provincial Banking Companies 1747–1864* (Edinburgh: John Donald, 1981). 306 pp.

Aberdeen Savings Company

—— *Aberdeen Savings Bank: Its History from 1815–1965* (Aberdeen University Press, 1967). 123 pp.

Jaffrey, T., *The Aberdeen Savings Bank: Its History, Development and Present Position* (The Bank, 1896). 64 pp.

Airdie Savings Bank

Blake, G., *The Romance of the Airdie Savings Bank: Centenary Souvenir* (Airdie, Baird & Hamilton, 1935). 67 pp.

Knox, J., *The Triumph of Thrift: The Story of the Savings Bank of Airdie, Instituted 1835* (Airdie, Baird & Hamilton, 1927). 382 pp.

Ashton-under-Lyne & District Savings Bank

—— *1829–1911* (Ashton-under-Lyne, 1911).

Bahr Behrend & Co.

Behrend, Arthur, *Portrait of a Family Firm, 1793–1945* (Liverpool, 1970). 205 pp.

Balfour Williamson & Co.

Forres, Lord, *Balfour Williamson & Company and Allied Firms: Memoirs of a Merchant House* (The Firm, 1929). vii, 100 pp.

Hunt, W., *Heirs of Great Adventure; The History of Balfour Williamson and Company Limited 1851–1951* (Balfour Williamson, 1951–1960). Two volumes.

The Bank of Bermuda Limited

Phillips, Gordon, *First, One Thousand Miles ... Bermudian Enterprise and The Bank of Bermuda* (Granta Editions, 1992). xii, 242 pp.

Bank of Commerce and Credit International

Truell, P. and Gurwin, L., *BCCI: The Inside Story of the World's Most Corrupt Financial Empire* (Bloomsbury, 1992). (In preparation as of November 1992.)

Bank of England

Acres, W. M., *The Bank of England From Within, 1694–1900* (Oxford University Press, 1931). (Two volumes.)

Andreades, A. M., *History of the Bank of England, 1640–1903* (1924). 455 pp. (2nd edition Cass, 1966.)

Bowman, W. D., *The Story of The Bank of England from its Foundations in 1694 until the Present Day* (Herbert Jenkins, 1937). 312 pp.

Clapham, Sir J. H., *The Bank of England: A History* (Cambridge University Press, 1944). (Two volumes: volume 1 1694–1797; volume 2 1797–1914.)

Fay, S., *Portrait of the Old Lady: Turmoil in the Bank of England* (Harmondsworth: Viking, 1987). 208 pp.

Fforde, John, *The Bank of England and Public Policy 1941–58* (Cambridge University Press, 1992). 861 pp.

Giuseppi, John, *The Bank of England: A History from its Foundations in 1694* (Evans Bros, 1966). xii 224 pp.

Hennessy, E., *A Domestic History of the Bank of England 1930–1969* (Cambridge University Press, 1992). 449 pp.

Mackenzie, A. D., *The Bank of England Note: A History of its Printing* (Cambridge University Press, 1953). x 163 pp.

Rosenberg, K. and Hopkins, R. T., *The Romance of the Bank of England* (Thornton Butterworth, 1933). 228 pp.

Saw, R., *The Bank of England 1694–1944 and its Buildings Past and Present* (Harrap & Co., 1944). 164 pp.

Sayers, R. S., *Bank of England Operations 1890–1914* (King, 1936). xxiv 142 pp.

Sayers, R. S., *The Bank of England, 1891–1944* (Cambridge University Press, 1976). (Three volumes).

Stockdale, E., *The Bank of England in 1934* (The Firm, 1967). 316 pp.

Warren, H., *The Story of the Bank of England* (Jordan, 1903). 251 pp.

Zeigler, D., *Central Bank, Peripheral Industry: The Bank of England in the Provinces, 1826–1913* (Leicester University Press, 1990). 162 pp.

Another history of the Bank of England is currently in preparation.

Bank of Ireland

Lyon, F. S. (ed.), *Bicentenary Essays. Bank of Ireland 1783–1983* (1983). 222 pp.

Bank of Scotland

Malcolm, C. A., *The Bank of Scotland 1695–1945* (R. & R. Clark, 1948). viii 322 pp.

Bank of West Africa: *see* **Standard Chartered Bank**

Bankers' Clearing House

Matthews, P. W., *The Bankers' Clearing House; What it is and What it Does* (1921). vii 168 pp.

Barclays Bank plc

A history of Barclays Bank is currently being prepared by Les Hannah.

Matthews, P. W. and Tuke, A. W. (eds), *A History of Barclays Bank Ltd* (Blades, East & Blades Ltd, 1926). xiv 441 pp.

—— *Barclays Bank Ltd, Manchester Road, Burnley: 70th Anniversary 1929; A Brief History* (1959).

Tuke, A. W. and Gillman, R. J. H., *Barclays Bank Ltd, 1926–1969* (Barclays Bank, 1972). 167 pp.

Barclays Bank (Dominion, Colonial & Overseas) Ltd

—— *A Banking Centenary, Barclays Bank (Dominion, Colonial & Overseas) 1836–1936* (Plymouth, 1938). 269 pp.

Crossley, Sir J. and Blandford, J., *The DCO Story: A History of Banking in Many Countries 1925–1971* (The Firm, 1975). 366 pp.

Baring Bros & Co. Ltd

Hidy, R. W., *The House of Baring in American Trade and Finance 1763–1861* (New York: Russell & Russell, 1970). xxiv 631 pp. (1st edition 1949).

Orbell, M. J., *Baring Brothers & Co. Limited: A History to 1939* (The Firm, 1985). 93 pp.

Ziegler, P., *The Sixth Great Power: Barings 1763–1929* (Collins, 1988). 430 pp.

Belfast Bank

Ollerenshaw, P., *Banking in Nineteenth Century Ireland: The Belfast Bank 1825–1914* (Manchester University Press, 1987). 263 pp.

Simpson, N., *The Belfast Bank 1827–1970* (1975).

Birmingham Municipal Savings Bank

Hilton, J. P., *Britain's First Municipal Saving Bank: The Romance of Great Achievement* (Blackfriars Press, 1927). xvii 1, 251 pp.

Blackburn Savings Bank

Shaw, J. G., *House of the Blackburn Savings Bank, 1831–1931: Record of a Century of Progress* (Blackburn, 1931).

Blyth, Greene & Jourdain & Co. Ltd

Muir, Augustus, *Blyth, Greene, Jourdain & Company Limited, 1810–1960* (Neame, 1961). 55 pp.

Bradford Old Bank Ltd

—— *Bradford Old Bank Ltd. Centenary Souvenir 1803–1903* (1903). 52 pp.

Bradford Savings Bank

Lougee, F. G., *From East Morley and Bradford Savings Bank to York County Savings Bank. A Brief Account of 150 Years of the Bradford Savings Bank 1818–1968* (Bradford, 1969).

Brandt's (William) Sons & Co.

—— *The House of Brandt* (1956). [Merchant Bankers.]

The British Bank of the Middle East

Jones, G., *Banking and Empire in Iran; Banking and Oil: The History of the British Bank of the Middle East* (Cambridge University Press, 1986/7). Two volumes.

British Linen Bank

Malcolm, C. A., *The History of The British Linen Bank* (Edinburgh, 1950). xii 253 pp. (Privately printed.)

Brown, Shipley & Co. Ltd

Brown, J. C., *A Hundred Years of Merchant Banking: A History of Brown Brothers & Co., Brown Shipley & Co.* (1909). 374 pp.

Ellis, A., *Heir of Adventure: The Story of Brown Shipley Merchant Bankers, 1810–1960* (London, 1960). vi 165 pp.

Perkins E. J., *Financing Anglo-American Trade: The House of Brown, 1800–1880* (Harvard University Press, 1975). xi 323 pp.

Bury Trustees Savings Bank

—— *Trustees Savings Bank: An Account* (Bury, 1924).

Butterfield (N. T.) & Son (Bermuda) Ltd

Butterfield. Harry C., *Five Generations in Bermuda* (Hamilton, Bermuda, 1958). 112 pp.

Chartered Institute of Public Finance & Accountancy

Sowerby, T., (ed.), *The History of the Chartered Institute of Public Finance and Accountancy 1885–1985* (1985). 123 pp.

Charterhouse Group

Dennett, Laurie, *The Charterhouse Group 1925–1979* (Gentry Books, 1979). 175 pp.

Child's Bank

Clarke, P., *The First House in the City: An Excursion into the History of Child & Co. to Mark its 300th Year of Banking at the Same Address* (Child's Bank, 1973). 67 pp.

Price, F. G. H., *The Marygold of Temple Bar: Being a History of the Site now Occupied by No. 1 Fleet Street, the Banking House of Messrs Child & Co.* (Quaritch, 1902). 202 pp.

Chorley Savings Bank

Walker, John, *The Story of the Chorley Savings Bank, Established 1845* (Leyland, 1930).

—— *The Story of the Chorley Savings Bank and a Short History of Croston & Rufford Trustee Savings Bank* (Leyland, 1945). (Continued from 1930 publication.)

Clydesdale Bank Ltd

Munn, C. W., *Clydesdale Bank: The First One Hundred and Fifty Years* (Collins, 1988). 353 pp.

Reid, J. M., *The History of the Clydesdale Bank, 1838–1938* (Blackie, 1938). ix 299 pp.

Commercial Bank of Scotland Ltd

—— Our Bank: *The Story of the Commercial Bank of Scotland Ltd 1810–1946* (Nelson, 1946) (2nd edition). 94 pp.

Anderson, J. L., *The Story of the Commercial Bank of Scotland During its Hundred Years from 1810 to 1910* (The Firm, 1910). 113 pp.

Coutts & Co.

Coleridge, E. H., *The Life of Thomas Coutts, Banker* (John Lane, 1920). Two volumes.

Healey, E., *Coutts & Co. 1692–1992: The Portrait of a Private Bank* (Hodder & Stoughton, 1992). 488 pp.

Richardson, R., *Coutts & Co., Bankers, Edinburgh and London: Being the Memoirs of a Family Distinguished for its Public Services in England and Scotland* (Elliot Stock, 1901). 166 pp.

Robinson, R. M., *Coutts, The History of a Banking House* (Murray, 1929). xii 189 pp.

District Bank

Mottram. R. H., *The District Bank Ltd* (Manchester, 1929).

Drummonds Bank

Bolitho, H. H. and Peel, D., *The Drummonds of Charing Cross* (Allen & Unwin, 1967). 232 pp.

Dundee Savings Bank

—— *Dundee Savings Bank: Its Origins, Progress and Present Position 1900* (The Firm, 1901). 85 pp.

Edinburgh Savings Bank

McCulloch, J. H. and Stirling, K. I., *The Edinburgh Savings Bank: A Review of its Century of Service 1836–1936* (The Firm, 1936). xiv 120 pp.

Finlay (James) & Co.

Brogan, C., *James Finlay & Co., 1750–1950* (Glasgow, 1951). 276 pp.

Fleming (R.) & Co. Ltd

Gilbert, J. C., *A History of Investment Trust in Dundee, 1873–1938* (1939).

Gibbs (Antony) & Sons Ltd

Gibbs, J. A., *The House of Antony and Dorothea Gibbs . . . The Early Years of the House of Antony Gibbs and Sons* (The Firm, 1922). xvi 509 pp.

Mathew, William M., *The House of Gibbs and the Peruvian Guano Monopoly* (Royal Historical Society, 1981). xii 281 pp.

Maude, Wilfred, *Antony Gibbs & Sons Ltd, Merchants & Bankers 1808–1958* (privately printed, 1958). 136 pp.

Gilletts Brothers Discount Co. Ltd

Sayers, Richard S., *Gilletts in the London Money Market, 1867–1967* (Clarendon Press, 1968). x, 204 pp.

Taylor, Audrey M., *Gilletts – Bankers at Banbury and Oxford: A Study in Local Economic History* (Claredon Press, 1964). xiv 247 pp.

Glyn, Mills & Co.

Fulford, R., *Glyn's, 1753–1953: Six Generations in Lombard Stree*t (Macmillan, 1953). 266 pp.

Gore-Browne, Sir Eric, *The History of the House of Glyn, Mills & Co.* (privately printed, 1933). 200 pp.

Price, Hilton, *The Marygold by Temple Bar* (1902). xliii 202 pp.

Grindlays Bank Group

Aldington, Lord, *Grindlays 1828–1978* (The Firm, 1978). 161 pp.

Tyson, G. W., *100 Years of Banking in Asia and Africa, 1863–1963* (National & Grindlays Bank, 1963). xii 246 pp.

Guinness Mahon

Jones, I. F., *The Rise of a Merchant Bank* (printed by Cahill & Co., 1974). 63 pp.

McGrandle, Leith, *Two Centuries of Lewis & Peat 1775–1975* (Guinness Peat Group, 1975). 64 pp. [Became Guinness Peat Group and in 1972 they merged with the Merchant Bank of Guinness Mahon.]

Hambros Bank Ltd

Bramsen, B. D. and Wain, K. M., *The Hambros, 1779–1979* (Michael Joseph, 1979). 457 pp.

Ferris, P., *Gentlemen of Fortune: The World's Merchant and Investment Bankers* (Weidenfeld & Nicolson, 1984). 260 pp.

Hoare (C.) & Co.

Hoare, H. P. R., *Hoare's Bank, A Record, 1672–1932* (1932). xi 87 pp.

Hoare, H. P. R., *Hoare's Bank, a Record, 1672–1955: The Story of a Private Bank* (Collins, 1955). x 116 pp.

Hodge Group

—— *A Short History of Gwent and the Hodge Group* (The Firm, 1963).

Hongkong and Shanghai Banking Corporation

Collis, Maurice, *Wayfoong: The Hongkong and Shanghai Banking Corporation* (Faber & Faber, 1965). 269 pp.

King, Frank H. H., (ed.), *Eastern Banking: Essays in the History of the Hongkong and Shanghai Banking Corporation* (Athlone Press, 1983). xvi 791 pp.

King, F. H. H., and others, *The History of the Hongkong and Shanghai Banking Corporation* (Cambridge University Press, 1988). Volume 2: 1919–1945, 743 pp.

Institute of Bankers

—— *The First Fifty Years of the Institute of Bankers, 1879–1929* (Blades, East & Blades, 1929). 69 pp.

Green, Edwin, *Debtors to their Profession: A History of The Institute of Bankers, 1879–1979* (Methuen, 1979). xxi 245 pp.

International Bank for Reconstruction and Development

—— *The International Bank, 1946–1953* (1954). 273 pp.

Johnson Matthey Bankers Ltd: *see* **Johnson Matthey & Co. Ltd** *in* 'Metals' (p. 194).

Knowles & Foster

Foster, W. F., *Richard Foster* (Eyre & Spottiswoode, 1914). vi 160 pp.

—— *The History of Knowles & Foster, 1828–1948* (Knowles & Foster, 1948). 92 pp.

Lancashire & Yorkshire Bank Ltd

McBurnie, J. M., *The Story of the Lancashire and Yorkshire Bank Ltd, 1872–1922* (Manchester, 1922). 108 pp.

Lewis & Peat

McGrandle, L., *Two Centuries of Lewis & Peat 1775–1975* (The Firm, 1975). 65 pp.

Lloyds Bank plc

—— *'Twixt Lombard Street and Cornhill* (1930). 69 pp.

Allison, E., *Fruitful Heritage: A History of the Lloyd Family Including Charles Lloyd the Banker* (Roy Lee, 1952). 131 pp.

—— *At the Sign of the Black Horse* (1954).

Jones, K. R., *The Cox's of Craig's Court and Hillingdon* (1969). 58 pp. (Typewritten script.)

Lloyd, S., *The Lloyds of Birmingham with Some Account of the Founding of Lloyds Bank (Cornish, 1908).* 271 pp. (3rd edition.)

Sayers, R. S., *Lloyds Bank in the History of English Banking* (Clarendon Press, 1957). 381 pp.

Winton, J. R., *Lloyds Bank 1918–1969* (Oxford University press, 1982). viii 203 pp.

Martins Bank Ltd

Byron, K. (comp.), *Catalogue of Archives of Martins Bank Limited* (Martins Bank, 1970). (Typewritten script.)

Chandler, G., *Four Centuries of Banking: As Illustrated by the Banker's Customers and Staff Associated with the Constituent Banks of Martins Bank Ltd* (Batsford, 1964–8). Two volumes: volume 1: *The Grasshopper and the Liver-Bird – Liverpool and London;* volume 2: *The Northern Constituent Banks.*

Mercantile Credit Company Ltd

Wood, M., *'Have a Nice Weekend': The Story of Mercantile Credit Company Limited* (The Firm, 1986). 240 pp.

Midland Bank plc

Crick, W. F. and Wadsworth, J. E., *A Hundred Years of Joint Stock Banking* (Hodder & Stoughton, 1936). 464 pp. (3rd edition 1958.)

Froom, F. J., *A Site in Poultry: The Historical background to the Midland Bank Building* (Watnoughs, 1950). ix 113 pp.

Green, Edwin, *The Making of a Modern Banking Group: A History of the Midland Bank Since 1900* (privately printed, 1979). 116 pp.

Holmes, A. R. and Green, Edwin, *Midland. 150 Years of Banking Business* (Batsford, 1986). xvi, 352 pp.

Wadsworth, J. E., *Counter Defensive, Being the Story of a Bank in Battle* (Hodder & Stoughton, 1946). 106 pp.

Morgan Grenfell & Co. Ltd

Burk, K., *Morgan Grenfell 1838–1988: The Biography of a Merchant Bank* (Oxford University Press, 1989). xv 348 pp.

Chernow, R., *The House of Morgan* (Simon & Schuster 1990) 524 pp.

Hobson, D., *The Pride of Lucifer: Morgan Grenfell 1838–1988: The Unauthorised Biography of a Merchant Bank* (Hamish Hamilton, 1990). 482 pp.

Hoyt, E. P., *The House of Morgan* (Muller, 1968). xix 428 pp.

National Bank Ltd

Slattery, M., *The National Bank 1835–1970* (privately printed, 1972).

National Bank of Scotland

—— *National Bank of Scotland Ltd: Centenary 1825–1925 and a Short History of the Bank* (The Bank, 1925/1947). Two volumes.

National Provincial Bank Ltd

Leighton-Boyce, J. A. S. L., *Smiths the Bankers, 1658–1958* (National Provincial Bank, 1958). xiii, 337 pp. [Smith amalgamated with the Union Bank of London in 1902 and these merged with the National Provincial Bank in 1918.]

Withers, H., *National Provincial Bank, 1833–1933* (National Provincial Bank, 1933). 90 pp.

National Westminster Bank plc

Gregory, Sir Theodore E. G. and Henderson, A., *The Westminster Bank Through a Century* (Oxford University Press, 1936). Two volumes.

Reed, Richard, *National Westminster Bank: A Short History* (National Westminster, 1983). 56 pp.

—— *Three Banks in Bristol, Corn Street, 1750–1980* (1980).

North of Scotland Bank Ltd

Keith, A., *The North of Scotland Bank Ltd 1836–1936* (Aberdeen Journals, 1936). viii 188 pp.

Perth Savings Bank

A Brief Sketch of the . . . Savings Bank of the Country and City of Perth: Centenary 1815–1915 (The Firm, 1915). 108 pp.

Ralli Bros Ltd

—— *Ralli Brothers Ltd* (1951). 56 pp

—— *History and Activities of the Ralli Trading Group* (The Firm, 1979). 80 pp.

Rothschild (N. M.) & Sons Ltd

Ayer, J., *A Century of Finance, 1804–1904. The London House of Rothschild* (1905). 135 pp.

Davis, R. W., *The English Rothschilds* (Collins, 1983). 272 pp.

Ferris, P., *Gentlemen of Fortune: The World's Merchant and Investment Bankers* (Weidenfeld & Nicolson, 1984). 260 pp.

Palin, R., *Rothschild Relish* (Cassell, 1970). 192 pp.

Rothschild, Lord, *The Shadow of a Great Man* (privately printed, 1982). 62 pp.

Royal Bank of Scotland plc

Groat, W., *See Under My Counter* (Paul Harris Publishing, 1980). 97 pp.

Munro, N., *The History of the Royal Bank of Scotland, 1727–1927* (Clark, 1928). xviii 416 pp. (Privately printed.)

—— *The Royal Bank of Scotland 1727–1977* (The Firm, 1977). 55 pp.

The Royal Mint

Craig, Sir, John, *The Royal Mint* (Oxford University Press, 1953). xvii 450 pp.

Savings Bank of Glasgow

Henderson, T., *The Savings Bank of Glasgow: One Hundred Years of Thrift* (The Firm, 1936). xii 91 pp.

Schroder Wagg (J. Henry) & Co. Ltd

Fraser, W. I., *All to the Good* (Heinemann, 1963). x 275 pp. (Autobiography of the Chairman of Herbert Wagg.)

Roberts, Richard, *Schroders: Merchants and Bankers* (Macmillan, 1992). 640 pp.

Scottish American Investment Co. Ltd

Weir, B., *A History of the Scottish American Investment Company Ltd 1873–1973* (Edinburgh, 1973).

Scottish Provincial Banking Companies

Munn, C. W., *'The Scottish Provincial Banking Companies'*, Glasgow University, 1976. (Unpublished PhD thesis.)

Sheffield Banking Co.

Leader, R. E., *The Sheffield Banking Co. Ltd: An Historical Sketch 1831–1916* (The Firm, 1916). 144 pp.

Leader, R. E., *A Century of Thrift: An Historical Sketch of the Sheffield Savings Bank 1819–1919* (The Firm, 1920). vii 87 pp.

Slater Walker Securities

Row, C., *Slater Walker: An Investigation of a Financial Phenomenon* (Deutsch, 1977). 368 pp.

Slater, J., *Return to Go: My Autobiography* (Weidenfeld & Nicolson, 1977). vi 278 pp.

Smith, Payne & Smiths

Easton, H. T., *The History of a Banking House* (Blades, 1903). xvi
   127 pp.

Leighton-Boyce, J. A. S. L., *Smiths The Bankers, 1658–1958* (National
   Provincial Bank, 1958).

Solomon Brothers

Sobell, R., *Advancing to Leadership: Solomon Bros 1910–1985*
   (The Firm, 1986). 240 pp.

Standard Chartered Bank Ltd

Amphlett, G. T., *History of the Standard Bank, 1862–1913* (MacLe-
   house, 1914). xiii 251 pp.

Anderson, H. C. P., *Three Quarters of a Century of Banking in
   Rhodesia* (1967).

Fry, R. H., *Bankers in West Africa: The Story of the Bank of British West
   Africa Limited* (Hutchinson Benham, 1976). xviii, 270 pp. (Reissued in
   part of the history of The Standard Chartered Bank, 1979.)

Henry, J. A., and Siepmann, H. A., (ed.), *The First Hundred Years of the
   Standard Bank* (Oxford University Press, 1963). ix 371 pp. (Reissued
   as part of the history of The Standard Chartered Bank, 1979.)

MacKenzie, Sir, E. M. Compton, *Realms of Silver: One Hundred Years of
   Banking in the East* (Routledge, 1954). 338 pp. [This is a history of
   Standard Chartered Bank of India, Australia and China, now part of the
   Standard Chartered Bank.]

Sewell, V., *Standard Chartered Bank Ltd. A Story Brought up to Date*
   (Standard Chartered, 1983). 99 pp.

Steel Brothers & Co. Ltd

—— *Calling to Mind: Being Some Account of the First Hundred Years
   (1870–1970) of Steel Brothers and Company Ltd* (Pergamon Press,
   1975). 151 pp.

Stockport Savings Bank

A Century of Thrift: An Historical Sketch of the Stockport Savings Bank, 1824–1924 (Stockport, 1925).

Austin, A. V., *A Brief History of the Trustee Savings Bank Movement and the Stockport Savings Bank* (Stockport, 1960).

Stuckey's Banking Co. Ltd

Saunders, P. T., *Stuckey's Bank* (Taunton: Barnicott & Pearce, 1926). 116 pp.

Tozer, Kemsley & Millbourn (Holdings) Ltd

—— *Tozer, Kemsley & Millbourn Ltd 1899–1949: Fifty Years of Service* (1949). 66 pp. (Mainly illustrations.)

Trustee Savings Bank

Horne, H. O., *A History of Savings Banks* (The Firm, 1947). xii 407 pp.

Trustee Savings Bank of Yorkshire and Lincoln

Hebden, C. D., *The Trustee Savings Bank of Yorkshire and Lincoln: The Story of the Formation* (The Firm, 1981). 382 pp.

Ulster Bank

Knox, W. J., *Decades of the Ulster Bank 1836–1964* (The Firm, 1965). xiii 274 pp.

Union Bank of Scotland

Rait, R. S., *Union Bank of Scotland, History* (Glasgow, 1930). xviii 392 pp.

Tamaki, Norio, *The Life Cycle of the Union Bank of Scotland 1830–1954* (Aberdeen University Press, 1983).

Union Discount Co.

Cleaver, G. and P., *The Union Discount: A Centenary Album* (The Company, 1985). 128 pp.

Warrington, Runcorn & District Savings Bank

Hatton, Frank, *The Warrington, Runcorn and District Savings Bank: An Address to the Rotary Club* (Warrington, 1943).

Warrington Savings Bank

—— *150th Anniversary Luncheon Invitation Menus* (1968). (Includes historical notes.)

Williams Deacon's Bank Ltd

Allman, A. H., *Williams Deacon's Bank, 1771–1970* (Williams Deacon's Bank, 1971). xi 180 pp.

Yorkshire Bank

Broomhead, L. J., *The Great Oak: A Story of the Yorkshire Bank* (The Firm, 1981). 100 pp.

Beverages and Soft Drinks

Assam Co. Ltd

Antrobus, H. A., *A History of the Assam Company 1839–1953* (privately printed, 1957). xv 501 pp.

Brooke Bond Group plc: *see also* **Brooke Bond Oxo plc** *in* 'Food' (p. 129)

Wainwright, D., *Brooke Bond – A Hundred Years* (Newman Neame, 1969). 72 pp.

Cadbury: *see* **Cadbury** *in* 'Confectionery' (p. 86) and **Schweppes** below.

Coca-Cola

Bayley, Stephen, *Coke: Designing a Whole Brand* (Conran Foundation, 1986). 95 pp.

Hoy, A. H., *Coca-Cola: The First Hundred Years* (Atlanta: The Firm, 1986). 159 pp.

Kahn, E. J., *The Big Drink: An Unofficial History of Coca-Cola* (Reinhardt, 1960). ix 179 pp.

Jewsbury & Brown Ltd

—— *Centenary 1826–1926: A Hundred Years of Progress* (Leeds, 1926).

—— *The Jewsbury and Brown Story* (1957).

Lipton

Lipton, Sir Thomas, *Leaves from the Lipton Bags* (1931). 278 pp.

Waugh, A., *The Lipton Story* (Cassell, 1961). 277 pp.

There is a section on **Lipton** in P. Mathias, *The Retailing Revolution* (Longmans, 1967).

Lyons (J.) & Co. Ltd (now **Lyons-Tetley**)

—— *Lyons: The Tea Diary, Special Reserve Edition* (The Firm, 1989). 136 pp.

Lyons (J.) & Co. Ltd *see also* **Allied-Lyons** in 'Food' (p. 128)

Mennell (Tuke) & Co. Ltd and **Mennell (R. C.) & Co. Ltd**

—— *Tea: An Historical Sketch Based on the History of the Firms* (1926). 63 pp.

Nestlé

Heer, Jean, *World Events 1866–1966: The First Hundred Years of Nestlé* (Switzerland, 1966). 277 pp. [Translated by A. Braley, G. Heath, Peter Walding.]

Schweppes

Simmons, Douglas A., *Schweppes. The First 200 Years* (Springwood Books, 1983). 160 pp. [Schweppes has now merged with Cadbury to become Cadbury Schweppes.]

Tetley Joshua & Co. Ltd

Lackey, C., *Quality Pays . . . The Story of Joshua Tetley & Son* (Springwood Books, 1985). 160 pp.

Twining (R.) & Co. Ltd

Twining, S. H., *The House of Twining 1706–1956: A History of the Firm* (1956). xi 115 pp.

Typhoo

Williams, K., *The Story of Typhoo [and the Birmingham Tea Industry]* (Quiller Press, 1990). viii 132 pp.

Bookselling, Newsagents and Stationers

General

Mumby, F. A., *Romance of Bookselling: A History from the Earliest Times to the Twentieth Century* (Chapman Hall, 1910). 491 pp.

Plant, M., *The English Book Trade* (Allen & Unwin, 1974). 518 pp.

Dean & Co. (Stockport) Ltd

Dean, J. N., *A Brief History of Deans* (1954).

Ellis

Smith, G. and Berger, F., *The Oldest London Bookshop: A History of Two Hundred Years (Ellis's, New Bond Street, 1728–1928)* (1928). 141 pp.

Foyle (W. and G.) Ltd

Fabes, G. H., *The Romance of a Bookshop 1904–1929* (1929). 56 pp.

Fabes, G. H., *The Romance of a Bookshop 1904–38* (1938). 64 pp. (2nd edition).

Menzies (John) & Co. Ltd

—— *The House of Menzies: John Menzies & Co. Ltd: 123 Years of Bookselling* (The Firm, 1958). 76 pp.

Gardiner, L., *The Making of John Menzies* (The Firm, 1983). 96 pp.

Graham, H., *The Menzies Group* (1965). 63 pp.

Millers

—— *The Millers of Haddington, Dunbar & Dunfermline: A record of Scottish Bookselling* (T. Fisher Unwin, 1914). 319 pp.

Smith (W. H.) & Son Ltd

Clear, G., *The Story of W. H. Smith & Son* (1949). viii 221 pp.

—— *The Story of W. H. Smith & Son* (The Firm, 1955). 242 pp.

Fraser, Lady Antonia, *The Pleasure of Reading* (Bloomsbury, 1992). 252 pp.

Pocklington, G. R., *The Story of W. H. Smith & Son* (privately printed, 1932). vii 152 pp.

Wilson, Charles, *First With The News: The History of W. H. Smith 1792–1972* (Cape, 1985). 510 pp.

Stevens (B. F.) & Brown Ltd

Fenn, G. M., *Memoir of Benjamin Franklin Stevens* (1903). iv 310 pp.

Turner (H.) & Son Ltd

Farnsworth, K., *The Turner Story: Bringing the News to Sheffield [Centenary of H. Turner & Son Ltd, newsagents]* (Henry Melland, 1991). 204 pp.

Waterstone (George) & Sons

—— *Bi-centenary History: George Waterstone & Sons Limited, 1752–1952* (The Firm, 1952). 54 pp.

—— *Two Hundred and Twenty Five Years: A History of George Waterstone & Sons Ltd, 1752–1977* (The Firm, 1977). 69 pp.

Brewing

General

Barber, N., *Where Have All the Breweries Gone? A Directory of British Brewery Companies* (Richardson, 1980).

Brown, J., *Steeped in Tradition: The Malting Industry in England Since The Railway Age* (Reading University, Institute of Agricultural History, Museum of Rural Life, 1983).

Conran, H. S., *A History of Brewing* (David & Charles, 1975).

Donnachie, Ian, *A History of the Brewing Industry in Scotland* (John Donald, 1979). xi 287 pp.

Dunn, M., *Traditional Breweries and their Ales* (Robert Hale, 1986). 249 pp.

Faulkner, N., *A Long Life: A Directory of Ancestor Breweries* (Allied Breweries, 1988). 152 pp.

Hawkins, K. and Pass, C. L., *The Brewing Industry: A Study in Industrial Organisation and Public Policy* (Heinemann, 1979). ix 169 pp.

Mathias, P., *The Brewing Industry in England 1700–1830* (Cambridge University Press, 1959). xxviii 596 pp.

Osborne, K., *Bygone Breweries, Also Depicting Beer Labels* (Rochester Press, 1982). 64 pp.

Richmond, L., and Turton, A., T*he Brewing Industry: A Guide to Historical Records* (Manchester University Press, 1990). 485 pp.

Vaizey, J. E., *The Brewing Industry 1886–1951: An Economic Study* (Isaac Pitman, 1960). 173 pp.

Alloa Brewery Co.

McMaster, C., *Alloa Ale: A History of the Brewing Industry in Alloa: Sponsored to Commemorate 175 Years of Brewing in Alloa* (The Firm, 1985). 70 pp.

Barclay, Perkins & Co. Ltd

—— *Anchor Magazine: The House Organ of Barclay Perkins & Co. Ltd: Commemorating the 150th Anniversary of the Firm* (The Firm, 1931). 111 pp.

The Barnsley Brewery Co. Ltd

—— *The Barnsley Brewery Co. Ltd* (privately printed, 1958).

Crampton, Y., *Seventy Years and More: The Story of the Barnsley Brewery* (Newman Neame, 1960).

Bass Charrington

Hawkins, K. H., *A History of Bass Charrington* (Oxford University Press, 1978). 228 pp.

Birkenhead Brewery

—— *The First Hundred Years* (1965).

Boddington's Breweries plc

Jacobson, Michael., *The Story of Boddingtons 1778–1978: 200 Years of Beer* (1978). 96 pp.

Brakspear (W. H.) & Sons plc

Sheppard, Francis H. W., *Brakspear's Brewery, Henley on Thames 1779–1979* (The Company, 1979). viii 103 pp.

Bristol Brewery Georges & Co.

—— *144 Years of Brewing: 1788–1932* (The Firm, 1938). 99 pp.

Burtonwood Brewery

—— *Burtonwood Brewery, 1867–1967* (The Firm, 1967). 120 pp.

Charrington & Co. Ltd

Strong, L. A. G., *A Brewer's Progress 1757–1957: A Survey of Charrington's Brewery on the Occasion of its Bicentenary* (privately printed, 1957). viii 88 pp.

Courage plc

—— *The Story of the Star Brewery* (Eastbourne, 1936).

—— *150 Years of Brewing* (Georges Bristol Brewery, 1938).

—— *Yorke Crampton, Seventy Years and More* (Barnsley Brewery Co., 1960).

Corley, T. A. B., *The Road to Worton Grange: Simonds and Courages Brewery, Reading 1785–1980* (1981).

Hardinge, G. N., *The Development and Growth of Courage's Brewery 1787–1932* (1932). 54 pp.

Hardinge, G. N., *To Celebrate the 150th Anniversary of Courage's Brewery 1787–1937* (The Firm, 1937). 52 pp.

Pudney, John Sleigh, *A Draught of Contentment: The Story of the Courage Group* (New English Library, 1971). 152 pp.

Crown Cork Company

Strong, S., *The Romance of Brewing* (Review Press for the Crown Cork Company, 1951). 120 pp.

Davenport (John) & Sons

—— *Fifty Years of Progress: Being a Description of the House of Davenport* (The Firm, 1935). 56 pp.

Distillers: *see* **Guinness plc,** *below*: *see also* **Distillers Co. Ltd** *in* 'Chemical Industries' (p.69)

Dutton's Blackburn Brewery Ltd

—— *150 Years of the House of Dutton 1799–1949* (Blackburn, 1949).68 pp.

Greenall Whitley & Co. Ltd

Slater, J. Norman., *A Brewer's Tale: The Story of Greenall Whitley & Co. Ltd Through Two Centuries* (The Company, 1980). 230 pp.

Greene King & Sons plc

Page, K., *Greene King Biggleswade Brewery 1764–1984* (The Firm, 1984). 51 pp.

Wilson, Richard G., *Greene King: A Business and Family History* (Heinemann, 1983). xii 337 pp.

Greengate Brewery

—— *The Greengate Brewery Near Manchester* (1944).

Guinness plc

—— *St James's Gate Brewery: A History* (1935). 110 pp.

—— *Guinness, Dublin* (The Firm, 1952). 70 pp.

Brown, J. F., *Guinness and Hops* (Arthur Guinness & Son & Co. (Park Royal) Ltd, 1980). xv 264 pp.

Lynch, P. and Vaizey, J., *Guinness's Brewery in the Irish Economy, 1759–1876* (Cambridge University Press, 1960). 278 pp.

Pugh, P., *Is Guinness Good For You? The Bid from Distillers, the Inside Story* (Financial Trading Publications, 1987). 175 pp.

—— *The Guinness Book of Guinness 1935–1985* (The Firm, 1988). 546 pp.

Saunders, J., *Nightmare: The Ernest Saunders Story* (Hutchinson, 1989). 288 pp.

Sibley, B., *The Book of Guinness Advertising* (Guinness Books, 1985). 224 pp.

Hall & Woodhouse Ltd

Janes, Hurford, *Hall & Woodhouse 1777–1977: Independent Family Brewers* (Melland, 1977). 80 pp.

—— *Badger Beer Country* (Blandford Forum: The Firm, 1982). 72 pp.

Hardys & Hansons plc

Bruce, George, *Kimberley Ale: The Story of Hardys & Hansons, Kimberley 1932–1982* (Melland, 1982). 128 pp.

Harvey & Son

Jenner, M. A., *Harvey & Son, Bridge Wharf Brewery, Lewes: A Bicentenary Year* (Lewes: The Firm, 1990). 102 pp.

Heineken

Mayle, P., *Thirsty Work: Ten Years of Heineken Advertising* (Macmillan, 1983). 121 pp.

Higsons Brewery

Cook, N., *Higsons Brewery, 1780–1980* (Kershaw Press Service, 1981). 51 pp.

Holt (Joseph) & Co.

Grayling, C., *Manchester Ales and Porter: The History of Holt's Brewery* (The Firm, 1985). 68 pp.

Hull Brewery

—— *Illustrated History of the Hull Brewery Company Ltd* (1960). 76 pp.

Barnard, R., *Barley, Mash and Yeast: A History of the Hull Brewery Company, 1782–1985* (Beverley: Hutton Press, 1990). 60 pp.

Hyde's Anvil Brewery Ltd

—— *Hyde's Anvil Brewery Ltd* (1985).

Institute of Brewing

Bird, W. H., *A History of the Institute of Brewing* (IB, 1955). ix 139 pp.

Mann, Crossman & Paulin Ltd.

Janes, H. H., *Albion Brewery 1808–1958: The Story of Mann, Crossman & Paulin Ltd* (Harley Publishing Co., 1958). 115 pp.

Mansfield Brewery Company

Bristow, Philip, *The Mansfield Brewery* (Navigator Publishing, 1976). 188 pp.

Mitchells & Butlers

—— *Fifty Years of Brewing 1879–1929* (Smethwick: The Firm, 1929). 120 pp.

St Austell Brewery Co. Ltd

Hockin, C., *St Austell Brewery, Established 1851* (The Firm, 1979?). 52 pp.

Shepherd Neame Ltd

—— *Shepherd Neame Ltd* (1948).

Steward & Patterson

Gourvish, T., *Norfolk Beers from English Barley: A History of Steward & Patterson 1793–1963* (Norwich: Centre of East Anglia Studies, 1987). 206 pp.

Tennent Caledonian Breweries

McMaster, C. and Ritherford, T., *The Tennent Caledonian Breweries* (Edinburgh: Scottish Brewing Archive, 1985). 100 pp.

Scottish Brewing Archive, *Tennent Caledonian Breweries Ltd: Tennent's Archives 1550–1988* (Edinburgh: The Archive, 1988). 104 pp.

Tetley Walker Ltd

—— *Tetley's: A Review of a Hundred Years, 1823–1923* (1923). 64 pp.

Tollemache & Cobbold

Jacobson, Michael, *The Cliff Brewery 1723–1973* (Tollemache & Cobbold, 1973). 59 pp.

—— *Tolly Cobbold: Brewers of Fine Suffolk Ales Since 1723* (Martlet, 1983).

Truman Hanbury Buxton & Co. Ltd

Birch, J. E. L., *The Story of Beer* (Truman Hanbury Buxton & Co. Ltd, 1965). 95 pp. (2nd edition, 1st edition 1951.)

Birch, L., *Truman Hanbury Buxton & Co.* (The Firm, 1957). 96 pp.

—— *Trumans The Brewers: The Story of Truman Hanbury Buxton & Co. Ltd* (Neame, 1966). 62 pp.

Watney Mann & Truman Ltd

Serocold, W. P., *The Story of Watneys* (Watney, Combe, Reid & Co., 1949). 130 pp.

Janes, H., *The Red Barrel: A History of Watney Mann* (John Murray, 1963). 226 pp.

—— *Crowley's Brewery 1766–1963* (1963).

Whitbread & Co. Ltd

—— *Whitbread's Brewery* (1947). 53 pp.

—— *Whitbread's Brewery, Incorporating the Brewer's Art* (The Firm, 1951). 92 pp.

—— *West Country Brewery: 200 Years of Brewing in the West Country* (1960).

—— *The Story of Whitbreads* (Whitbreads, 1964). 54 pp.

Fulford, R., *Samuel Whitbread 1764–1815: A Study in Opposition* (Macmillan, 1967). xiii 336 pp.

Hill, B., *Whitbread's Brewery* (The Firm, 1951). 92 pp.

Monkton, H. A., *Whitbread Breweries, A Chronological Survey* (1984). 56 pp.

Morgan, D., *Whitbread's Entire* (1978). (Reissued.)

Nevile, S. O., *Seventy Rolling Years* (Faber, 1958). 288 pp.

Redman, N. B., *The Story of Whitbread plc, 1742–1990* (The Firm, 1991). 88 pp.

Ritchie, B., *An Uncommon Brewer: The Story of Whitbread 1742–1992* (James & James, 1992). 144 pp.

Younger (William) & Co. Ltd

Keir, David, *The Younger Centuries: The Story of William Younger & Co. Ltd 1749–1949* (McLagan, 1951). vi 110 pp.

Youngs & Co. Brewery Ltd

—— *Coronation Souvenir Brochure* (The Firm, 1936). 100 pp.

—— *Youngs & Co.'s Brewery Ltd* (1974).

Building and Construction

[Includes Asbestos, Asphalt, Cement, Building Firms etc.]

General

Bowley, Marian, *The British Building Industry: Four Studies in Response to Resistance and Change* (Cambridge University Press, 1969). [Covers twentieth century.]

Christian, R., *Butterfly Brick; 200 Years in the Making* (1990). 256 pp.

Earle, J. B. F. *Black Top. A History of the British Flexible Roads Industry* (Blackwell, 1974). xiii 269 pp.

Kingsford, P. W., *Builders and Building Workers* (Arnold, 1973).

Middlemas, R. K., *The Master Builders: Thomas Brassey, Sir John Air, Lord Cowdray, Sir John Norton-Griffiths* (1963). 328 pp.

Powell, C. G., *An Economic History of the British Building Industry 1815–1979* (Methuen, 1980).

Richardson, H. W. and Aldcroft, D. H., *Building in the British Economy between the Wars* (Allen & Unwin, 1968). 355 pp.

The Construction History Society is hoping to produce a bibliography of construction history: for further information please contact Peter Harlow, CHS, c/o The Chartered Institute of Building, Englemere, Kings Ride, Ascot, Berkshire SL5 8BJ.

Acrow

—— *Twenty-Eight Years of Progress 1936–1964* (The Firm, 1964). 95 pp.

—— Acrow: *The Success Story of Achievement Through Team Spirit: 40 years On, 1936–1975* (The Firm, 1975). 108 pp.

Anelay (William) Ltd

Stapleton, H. E. C. and others, *A Skilful Master-Builder: The Continuing Story of a Yorkshire Family Business* (The Firm, 1975). viii 72 pp.

Associated Portland Cement Ltd: see **Blue Circle Industries plc**

Atkins (W. S.) Ltd

Atkins, Sir William, *Partners: Fifty Years of WSA & P* (The Firm, 1988). viii 129 pp.

Balfour Beatty & Co. Ltd

Scott, A. T., *Balfour Beatty: 50 Years* (1959). 78 pp.

White, Valerie, *Balfour Beatty 1909–1984* (Balfour Beatty, 1984). 83 pp.

Bamford (J. C.)

Irwin, M. D. J., *JCB 1945–1980* (Condie Publications, 1980). 64 pp.

Hume, D., *40 Years of JCB* (J. M. Pearson, 1985). 64 pp.

The Bath & Portland Group plc

Bezzant, Norman, *Out of the Rock* (Heinemann, 1980). xii 244 pp.

Baxendale & Co. Ltd

—— *A Fifty Years' Record* (1913?).

Onlooker, An (pseud.), *A Fifty Years' Chapter of Manchester History: The Jubilee of Baxendale & Co. Ltd: A Short History of the Firm* (1913).

Blue Circle Industries plc

Davis, Sir A. C., *A Hundred Years of Portland Cement, 1824–1924* (1924). 281 pp.

Lancaster, Michael, *Britain in View* (Blue Circle Santex, 1985). 100 pp.

Perks, R. H., *George Bargebrick Esquire: The Story of George Smeed the Brick and Cement King* (Messborough Books, 1981). 64 pp.

Prizeman, John, *Your House: The Outside View* (Blue Circle Sandtex, 1976). 100 pp.

Pugh, P., *The History of Blue Circle* (Cambridge Business Publications, 1988). viii 277 pp.

Bovis

A history of Bovis is in preparation.

Bradley (E. H.) & Sons Ltd

—— *Bradley – Building on a Name: The History of Edwin H. Bradley & Sons Ltd* (1983). 75 pp.

British Plaster Board Industries

Jenkins, D., *The History of BPB Industries* (The Firm, 1973). xvii 147 pp.

Routley, J., *A Saga of British Industry: The Story of the British Plasterboard Group* (1959). xvi 172 pp.

British Portland Cement Manufacturers Ltd: *see* Blue Circle Industries plc

Cape Industries plc

Barty-King, H. and Newton, M., *The Story of Cape Asbestos Company Limited 1893–1953* (The Company, 1953). 85 pp.

Champion (A. W.)

Champion, A., *It's Champion* (The Firm, 1966). 125 pp.

Charlton, Matthew & Sons

—— *The House of Charlton, Established 1842* (The Firm, 1981). 56 pp.

Cubitts London

Hobhouse, Mary H., *Thomas Cubitt, Master Builder* (Macmillan, 1971).

—— *This is Cubitts* (The Firm, 1975). 85 pp.

Dent & Hellyer

—— *Under Eight Reigns George I to George V 1720–1930 Bicentenary* (The Firm, 1930). 136 pp.

Dove Bros Ltd

Braithewaite, David, *Building in the Blood: The Story of the Dove Brothers of Islington, 1781–1981* (Geoffrey Cave Associates and Dove Bros, 1981). 160 pp.

Durtnell (Richard) & Sons Ltd

Barty-King, H., *A Country Builder, 1591–1991: The Story of Richard Durtnell & Sons of Brasted* (Melland, 1991). 50 pp.

Durtnell, C. S., *From an Acorn to an Oak Tree: A Study in Continuity* (The Firm, 1975). 64 pp.

Eastwoods Ltd

Willmott, F. G., *Bricks and 'Brickies'* (Messborough Books, 1977). x 78 pp.

Ford & Weston Ltd

—— *Craftsmen in Building since 1874* (The Firm, 1966). 66 pp.

—— *The Story of Ford & Weston* (The Firm, 1966). 63 pp.

Fosters

—— *The Story of Fosters: The Historic Building Firm* (1965). 57 pp.

Gerrard (J.) & Sons Ltd

—— *Building for Victory, 1935–1945* (1946?).

—— *Gerrards of Swinton* (1959).

Hall (Alexander) & Son Ltd

Mackie, W., *A Century of Craftsmanship: Alexander Hall & Son (Builders) Ltd, 1880–1980* (Mearns & Gill, 1980). 100 pp.

Haywards Ltd

—— *Years of Reflection 1783–1953: The Story of Haywards of the Borough* (Harley Publishing Co., 1953). 106 pp.

Holloway Brothers Ltd

Rolt, L. T. C., *Holloways of Millbank: The First Seventy-Five Years* (Newman Neame, 1958). 56 pp.

Howard Farrow

—— *A Story of Fifty Years 1908–1958* (Harley Publishing Co., 1958). 72 pp. (Commemorative Booklet.)

Hunting Gate Group Ltd

Reader, W. J., *To Have and to Hold: An Account of Frederick Bandet's Life in Business* (Hunting Gate Group Ltd, 1983). 277 pp.

Jones (J. M.) & Sons

—— *Built by Jones 1918–1968* (Newman Neame, 1968). 56 pp.

Laing (John) & Son Ltd

—— *Serving a Nation at War, 1939–1945* (Laing, 1946). 124 pp.

—— *Teamwork: The Story of John Laing & Son Ltd* (Laing, 1950). 108 pp.

Coad, Roy Frederick, *Laing, The Biography of Sir John W. Laing CBE, 1879–1978* (Hodder & Stoughton, 1979). 238 pp.

Harrison, G., *Life and Belief in the Experience of John W. Laing, CBE* (Hodder & Stoughton, 1954). 119 pp.

Lawrence (Walter) & Son

—— *A History of Walter Lawrence & Son 1871–1971* (The Firm, 1971). 108 pp.

Lind (Peter) & Co. Ltd

Symes, Gordon, *Concrete Achievements: A Survey of Work Completed … By Peter Lind & Co. Ltd to Commemorate Their Fortieth Anniversary, 1955* (Newman Neame, 1955). 56 pp.

London Brick Co. Ltd

Hillier, Richard, *Clay that Burns: A History of the Fletton Brick Industry* (The Company, 1981). 100 pp.

Woodforde, J., *Bricks to Build a House* (1976). 221 pp.

Longley (James) & Co.

Smith, Rhoda, *Longleys of Crawley* (Metra Print Ltd, 1983). 95 pp.

McAlpine (Alfred)

—— *Sir Alfred McAlpine and Son Ltd* (The Firm, n.d.). 126 pp.

Gray, A., *The Road to Success* (Park Lane Press, 1987). 208 pp.

McAlpine (Robert)

Childers, J. S., *Robert McAlpine: A Biography* (privately printed by Oxford University Press, 1925). 189 pp.

—— *Sir Robert McAlpine & Sons: Civil Engineering and Building Contractors* (Civil Engineering Publications, 1952). 173 pp.

—— *Sir Robert McAlpine & Sons Ltd 1869–1969: Souvenir Brochure and Brief History* (The Firm, 1969). 174 pp.

Russell, I., *Sir Robert McAlpine and Sons: The Early Years* (Parthenon Publishing, 1988). 270 pp.

Macadam

Reader, W. J., *The Macadam Family and the Turnpike Roads, 1798–1861* (Heinemann, 1980). 242 pp.

Martyn (H. H.) & Co.

Whitaker, J., *The Best: A History of H. H. Martyn and Co.* (Cheltenham: The Author, 1985). 360 pp.

Mitchell Construction Kinnear Moodie Group

—— *The Mitchell Construction Kinnear Moodie Group* (The Firm, 196?). 162 pp.

Monk (A.) & Co. Ltd

—— *A. Monk & Co. Ltd: Civil Engineering & Building Contractors* (The Firm, 1957). 95 pp.

Mowlem (John) & Co. plc

—— 'The Principal Engineering Building and Road Works Executed by John Mowlem & Co. Ltd 1874–1968'. [Typescript, no date, kept in company papers.]

Neal (Harry) Ltd

Gaskell, Martin, *A Family of Builders* (Granta Editions, 1989). xii 176 pp.

Portland Cement: *see* **Blue Circle plc** *above*

Ready Mix: *see* **RMC Group** *below*

Rendell (F.) & Sons

A Good Job Well Done: The Story of Rendell, A West Country Builder (Stocker & Hocknell, 1983). iii 175 pp.

Rennie (John)

Reyburn, W., *Bridge Across the Atlantic: The Story of John Rennie* (1972). 160 pp.

RMC Group

Cassell, M., *The Readymixers* (Pencorp Books, 1986). 154 pp.

Simons Group Ltd

Chatburn, A., *Master Builder: The Story of Peter Hodgkinson and the Simons Group* (James & James, 1990). 64 pp.

Stein of Bonnybridge

Sanderson, K. W., *Stein of Bonnybridge* (Edinburgh: The Author, 1985). 78 pp.

Tarmac plc

—— *Fifty Years of Progress, 1903–1953* (Tarmac, 1953). 57 pp.

Earle, J. B. F., *A Century of Road Materials: The History of The Roadstone Division* (Blackwells, 1971). 182 pp.

Taylor Woodrow Group

—— *Taylor Woodrow Group* (1960). 76 pp.

Jenkins, A., *On Site 1921–1971* (Heinemann, 1971). xiv 226 pp.

Jenkins, A., *Built on Teamwork* (Heinemann, 1980). xvi 245 pp.

Trentham (P. G.) Ltd

Bruce, G. L., *The Trentham Story* (Trentham, 1978). xii 192 pp.

Trollope & Colls Ltd

—— *City Press, Trollope & Colls Ltd* (1963).

—— *Trollope & Colls Ltd, City Builders for 200 Years 1778–1978: The History of Trollope & Colls* (Precision Press, 1978).

Twaddle (Hugh) & Sons Ltd

House, J., *The Plumber in Glasgow: The History of the Firm of Hugh Twaddle & Son Ltd ... from 1848 to 1948* (The Firm, 1948). 63 pp.

Wimpey (George)

—— *George Wimpey & Co. Ltd* (The Firm, 1963). 120 pp.

Wright (Wm) & Son

Wright, J. H., *Wm Wright & Son, 1836–1969: Builder's Handbook* (Burrow, 1969). 64 pp.

Building Societies

General

Ashworth, W., *The Building Society Story* (Franey, 1980). 252 pp.

Barnes. P., *Building Societies: The Myth of Mutuality* (1984). 186 pp.

Cleary, E. J., *The Building Society Movement* (Elek Books, 1965).

Price, Seymour J., *Building Societies; Their Origins and History* (Franey, 1958).

Abbey National

Bellman, Sir Charles H., *The Thrifty Three Millions: A Study of the Building Society Movement and the Story of Abbey Road Society* (1935). xii 357 pp.

Bellman, Sir Charles H., *Bricks and Mortals. A Study of the Building Society Movement and the Abbey National Building Society, 1849–1949* (Hutchinson, 1949). ix 228 pp.

Reid, M., *Abbey National: Conversion to PLC* (Pencorp Books, 1991). 193 pp.

Ritchie, B., *A Key to the Door: The Abbey National Story* (The Firm, 1990). 176 pp.

Bradford Equitable Building Society

Lumb, R. E., *Second Thoughts: A History of the Bradford Equitable Building Society, Formerly known as the Bradford Equitable Benefit Building Society* (1951). 60 pp. [Issued to commemorate its centenary on 18 August 1951.]

Bristol & West Building Society

Lowe, C. J., *The Building Society Movement: A Half-Century Record ...* (Crofton Hemmings, 1901). 158 pp.

Britannia Building Society

Redden, R., *A History of the Britannia Building Society 1856–1985* (Franey, 1985). 168 pp.

Cheltenham & Gloucester Building Society

Mantle, J., *The Story of the Cheltenham & Gloucester Building Society* (James & James, 1991). 95 pp.

Co-operative Permanent Building Society

Mansbridge, A., *Brick upon Brick: Fifty Years of the Co-operative Permanent Building Society* (Dent, 1934). xxii 236 pp.

Coventry Building Society

Davis, Martin, *Every Man His Own Landlord: A History of Coventry Building Society* (Warwick Printing Co. Ltd, 1985). 160 pp.

Cumberland Building Society

Middleton, J. C., *Through Two Half-Centuries 1850–1950* (Cumberland Building Society, 1950).

Halifax Building Society

—— *History of the Halifax Permanent Building Society: Being A Jubilee Memorial of This Society* (Reed & Co., 1903). 200 pp.

Alderson, J. W. and Ogden, A. E., *Halifax Equitable Benefit Building Society Jubilee 1871–1921* (1921). 148 pp.

—— *The Faith of 'Fifty-Three': A Brief History of the Halifax Permanent Benefit Building Society 1853–1921* (The Firm, 1921). 95 pp.

Bacon, R. K., *The Life of Sir Enoch Hill: The Romance of the Modern Building Society* (Nicholson & Watson, 1934). 159 pp.

—— *Halifax Building Society, Eighty Years of Home Building – The Halifax Plan* (William Clowes & Sons Ltd, 1937). x 124 pp.

Hobson, Sir O. R., *A Hundred Years of the Halifax: The History of the Halifax Building Society 1853–1953* (Batsford, 1953). x 190 pp.

Heart of England Building Society

Martin, P. W., *History of Heart of England Building Society* (The Firm, 1981). 216 pp.

Lambeth Building Society

—— *Lambeth Building Society, 1852–1952* (1952).

National Building Society

Elkington, G., *The National Building Society, 1849–1934* (Heffer, 1935). x 79 pp.

Nationwide Building Society

Cassell, Michael, *Inside Nationwide: One Hundred Years of Co-operation* (Lund Humphries, 1982). 151 pp.

Ramsbury Building Society

Phillips, R. J., *History of Ramsbury Building Society* (The Firm, 1982). 116 pp.

Scottish Amicable Building Society

—— *The Scottish Amicable Jubilees 1892–1942 and 1842–1952* (The Firm, 1942/52). Two volumes.

Staffordshire Building Society

Hunter, J., *The First £100 million: A History of the Staffordshire Building Society* (privately published, 1977). vii 93 pp.

Temperance Permanent Building Society

Hughes, F., *Into the Future: The Continuing Society of the Temperance Building Society* (The Firm, 1972). 99 pp.

Price, S. J., *From Queen to Queen: The Centenary Story of The Temperance Permanent Building Society 1854–1954* (Franey, 1954). xiii 133 pp.

Woolwich Equitable Building Society

Brooks, W. C., *The First Hundred Years of the Woolwich Equitable Building Society* (privately printed, 1947). 208 pp.

Brooks, W. C., *The First 100 Million* (The Firm, 1954). 62 pp.

York Equitable Industrial Society

Briggs, G., *Jubilee History of the York Equitable Society Ltd* (CWS, 1909) 280 pp.

Chemical Industries

[Including Industrial Chemicals, Detergents, etc].

General

Haber, L. F., *The Chemical Industry of the Nineteenth Century* (Oxford, 1958). x 292 pp.

Hardie, D. W. F. and Pratt, J. Davidson, *A History of the Modern British Chemical Industry* (Pergamon Press, 1966). 391 pp.

Morris, P. J. and Russell, C. A., *Archives of the British Chemical Industry 1750–1914: a Handlist* (Faringdon, British Society for the History of Science, 1988). 273 pp.

Struchis, J. H. (ed.), *Corporate History and the Chemical Industry: A Resource Guide* (1985).

Albright & Wilson Ltd

Threlfall, R. E., *The Story of 100 Years of Phosphorus Making 1851–1951* (Oldbury: The Firm, 1951). viii 400 pp.

—— *Albright & Wilson Ltd, Survey of Chemical Group* (1961). 73 pp.

Anodising & Platings Ltd

—— *21st Anniversary: 7th February 1938–1959* (1959).

Bakelite Ltd

Fielding, T. J., *History of Bakelite Limited* (The Firm, 1948). 80 pp.

Blundell, Spence & Co.

—— *The Blundell Book 1811–1951: A Short History* (The Firm, 1951). 76 pp.

Borax (Holdings) Ltd: *see* **Rio Tinto Zinc Borax Ltd** *below*

British Cellophane

Ward-Jackson, C. H., *The 'Cellophane' Story: Origins of a British Industrial Group* (The Firm, 1977). 144 pp.

British Industrial Plastics

Dingley, C. S., *The Story of B.I.P. 1894–1962* (The Firm, 1962). 64 pp.

British Xylonite Co. *see* **Xylonite Group** *below*

Brunner Mond & Co. *see under* **ICI plc Alkali Division** *below and* **Mond Nickel Co. Ltd** in 'Mining' (p. 200)

Bush (W. J.) & Co.

—— *A Pictorial Record of Bush World-Wide Development, Establishments and Personalities During One Hundred Years of Progress 1851–1951* (1951). 70 pp.

Butler (W.) & Co. (Bristol) Ltd

Butler, T. H., *W. Butler & Co. (Bristol) Ltd 1843–1959* (Bristol, 1954). 92 pp.

Canning (W.) plc

Thomas, D. A., *The Canning Story 1785–1985* (Springwood, 1985). xi 195 pp.

Castner-Kellner Alkali Co.

—— *Fifty Years of Progress: The Story of the Castner-Kellner Alkali Company 1895–1945* (The Firm, 1947). 65 pp.

Chemical Society

Moore, T. S. and Philip, J. C., *Chemical Society 1841–1941* (Chemical Society, 1947). 236 pp.

CIBA Ltd

—— *The Development of CIBA; Activities; Organisation and Social Services* (CIBA, 1963).

Clayton Aniline Co. Ltd

Abrahart, E. N., *The Clayton Aniline Company Limited 1876–1976* (The Firm, 1976). 95 pp.

Croda

Wood, F. A. S. and Cressey, S., *Croda – The Fastest Growing Name: A History of the First Fifty Years of a Chemical Company 1925–1975* (The Firm, 1975?).

Crosfield (Joseph) & Sons Ltd

Musson, A. E., *Enterprise in Soap and Chemicals: Joseph Crosfield & Sons Limited 1851–1965* (Manchester University Press, 1965). 395 pp.

Distillers Co. Ltd

—— *The Industrial Activities of the Distillers Co. Ltd* (1957). 56 pp.

Fisons plc

—— *This is Our Concern: Imperial Chemical Industries Limited* (The Firm, 1955). 91 pp. (3rd edition.)

Glaxo Holdings Ltd: *see* 'Pharmaceuticals' (p. 228)

Hedley (Thomas) & Co. Ltd

Dickinson, *P., Hedley in Trafford Park 1934–1959* (1959).

Imperial Chemical Industries plc

Hardie, D. W. F., *History of the Chemical Industry in Widnes, Cheshire* (ICI, 1950). xi 250 pp.

Kennedy, C., *ICI: The Company that Changed our Lives* (Hutchinson, 1986). 286 pp.

Parke, V. E., *Billingham – The First Ten Years* (Billingham, 1957).

Pettigrew, A. M., *The Awakening Giant: Continuity and Change in Imperial Chemical Industries* (Blackwell's, 1985). 543 pp.

—— *This is our Concern* (ICI, 1955). (3rd edition.)

—— *Pharmaceutical Research in ICI 1936–1957* (Alderley Park: The Firm, 1957). 78 pp.

—— *Landmarks of the Plastic Industry 1862–1962* (The Firm, 1962). 126 pp.

Reader, W. J., *ICI: A History* (1970). Volume I: *The Forerunners 1870–1926* (Oxford University Press, 1970); volume II: *The First Quarter-Century 1926–1952* (Oxford University Press, 1975).

Sherwood, Martin (ed.), *ICI at Fifty* (1976). 569 pp.

Supple, B., (ed.), *Essays in British Business History* (Oxford: Clarendon Press, 1977). (W. J. Reader, 'Imperial Chemical Industries and the State 1926–1945').

Details of books on ICI can be obtained from their Library at Millbank.

Imperial Chemical Industries plc Alkali Division: *see also* **Mond Nickel Co.** in 'Mining'.

—— *Brunner Mond & Co. 1873–1925* (The Company, 1925). xi 106 pp.

Cohen, J. M., *The Life of Ludwig Mond* (Methuen, 1956). xiv 295 pp.

Dick, W. F. L., *A Hundred Years of Alkali in Cheshire* (The Firm, 1973). 126 pp.

Goodman, J., *The Mond Legacy: A Family Saga* (Weidenfeld & Nicolson, 1982). xv 272 pp.

Watts, John. I., *The First 50 Years of Brunner Mond & Co.* (Derby: Brunner Mond & Co., 1923). xi 106 pp.

Imperial Chemical Industries plc Dyestuffs Division

—— *Chapters on the Development of Industrial Organic Chemistry* (1938).

Imperial Chemical Industries plc: *see in* **'Arms for War and Peace'** (p. 12) *for* **Nobel's Explosives Company Ltd**

Kestner Evaporator & Engineering Co. Ltd

—— *The Kestner Golden Jubilee Book 1908–1958. Fifty Years of Chemical Engineering Endeavour* (Davis-Poynter, 1958). 104 pp.

Laporte Chemicals Ltd

—— *An Account of the Development and Activities of the House of Laporte, 1888 to 1947* (Luton: The Firm, 1947). 92 pp.

—— *An Account of the Development of the House of Laporte, 1888 to 1951* (revised, 1951).

—— *The Raw Materials of Progress* (1959). 72 pp.

Levinstein Ltd

—— *Four Years Work: The Progress of the Coal Tar Chemical Industry in England during the War* (1918).

Marley plc

Porter, J., Marley plc 1924–1984: *60 Years of Achievement* (The Firm, 1984). 56 pp.

MTM plc

Rassam, C., *A Chemistry for Success: The Growth of MTM plc* (James & James, 1989). 136 pp.

Norton Chambers

Gringer, P. H. and Spender, J. C., *Turnaround: . . . The Fall and Rise of Norton Chambers Group* (Associated Business Press, 1979). xii 211 pp.

Perkin Dyeworks

—— *Perkin Centenary London: 100 Years of Synthetic Dyestuffs* (Pergamon Press, 1958). xii 136 pp.

Rentokil

—— *Fifty Years of Service 1927–1977* (Rentokil, 1977). 156 pp.

Rio Tinto Zinc Borax Ltd

—— *The Borax Story 1899–1953* (1953). 286 pp.

Gerstley, J. M., *Borax Years, Some Recollections 1933–1961* (1979).

Travis, N. J., and Cocks, E. J., *The Tincal Trial. A History of Borax* (Harrap, 1984). 311 pp. [Borax (Holdings) Ltd merged with RTZ in 1968.]

Scott Bader & Co.

Blum, F. H., *Work and Community: The Scott Bader Commonwealth and the Quest for a New Social Order* (Routledge & Kegan Paul, 1968). 392 pp.

—— *A Kind of Alchemy* (1973). 70 pp.

Stories

Christies, G., *Stories of Lancaster 1848–1964* (Collins, 1964). 256 pp.

Tennant Group of Companies

—— *A Short Account of the Tennant Companies 1792–1922* (1922). 53 pp.

—— *One Hundred and Forty Years of the Tennant Companies, 1797–1937* (1937). iv 65 pp.

—— *Enterprise: An Account of the Activities and Aims of the Tennant Group of Companies* (1945). 168 pp.

Blow, S., *Broken Blood: The Rise and Fall of the Tennant Family* (Faber, 1987). 224 pp.

Thetford Moulded Products

—— *100 Years, Thetford Moulded Products Limited 1879–1979* (The Firm, 1979).

Turner & Newall Ltd

—— *Turner & Newall Ltd: The First 50 Years 1920–1970* (The Company, 1970). 87 pp.

Dingley, Cyril S. *The Story of British Industrial Plastics 1894–1962* (1962). 65 pp.

Unilever Ltd: *See also* Unilever Ltd *in* 'Food' (p. 135)*; for brand names owned by* Unilever *see index under brand, e.g.* SPD Ltd *etc.*

—— *Unilever in a Changing Europe* (1963).

—— *The Story of Port Sunlight* (Port Sunlight: The Firm, 1953). 96 pp.

CIS, *Unilever's World: CIS Anti Report* (CIS, 1980). 103 pp.

Edwards, H. R., *Competition and Monopoly in the British Soap Industry* (Clarendon Press, 1962). 270 pp.

Fieldhouse, D. K., *Unilever Overseas: The Anatamy of a Multinational 1895–1965* (Croom Helm, 1978). 620 pp.

Jolly, W. P., *Lord Leverhulme: A Biography* (Constable, 1976). 246 pp.

Knox, Andrew M., *Coming Clean* (Heinemann, 1976). 252 pp.

Leverhulme, 2nd Lord [son], *Viscount Leverhulme* (Allen & Unwin, 1927). 325 pp.

Nicolson, *Nigel, Lord of the Isles* (Weidenfeld & Nicolson, 1960). 264 pp.

Reader, W. J., *Unilever: A Short History* (The Firm, 1960). 63 pp.

Reader, W. J., *Fifty Years of Unilever, 1930–1980* (Heinemann, 1980). vii 148 pp.

Supple, B. (ed.), *Essays in British Business History* (Clarendon Press, 1977). Chapter 7: 'Management and Policy in Large-Scale Enterprise: Lever Brothers and Unilever 1918–1939', by Charles Wilson.

Williams, E., *Port Sunlight: The First Hundred years, 1888–1988. The Short History of a Famous Factory* (The Firm, 1984). 51 pp.

Wilson, Charles, *The History of Unilever: A Study in Economic Growth and Social Change* (Cassell, 1954). [Reprinted in 1968 by Cassell with a third volume. A paperback edition was published in 1970.]

John Townsend has a vast collection of Unilever publications.

United Alkali Co. Ltd

—— *The Struggle for Supremacy: Chapters in the History of the Leblanc Alkali Industry in Great Britain* (The Firm, 1907). 77 pp.

—— *Centenary of the Alkali Industry 1823–1923: One Hundred Years of Scientific and Industrial Progress* (Widnes, 1923).

Wade (Malcolm) & Co.

Wade, M., *Malcolm Wade, Ink Makers 1800–1955* (Williams Sessions, 1955).

Wiggin (Henry) & Co. Ltd

—— *History of Henry Wiggin and Co. Ltd 1835–1935: Centenary Publication* (The Firm, 1935). 67 pp.

Williamson (James) & Son

—— *Williamson of Lancaster: A Centenary Memoir* (The Firm, 1944).

Xylonite Group

—— *Fifty Years 1877–1927* (The Firm, 1927).

China, Cutlery, Porcelain and Pottery

General

Jenkins, Clare and McClarence, Stephen (eds), *On the Knife Edge: The Inside Story of the Sheffield Cutlery Industry* (SCH, 1989). xiii 180 pp.

Pybus, S. M. and others (comps), *Cutlery: A Bibliography* (Sheffield City Libraries, 1982). 69 pp. (Typewritten script.)

Weatherill, Lorna, *The Pottery Trade of North Staffordshire 1660–1760* (Manchester University Press, 1971).

Adams (William)

Furnell, D., *An Account of William Adams, Potters 1779–1979* (1980).

Bow Porcelain Manufactory

Adams, B. E. and Redstone, D., *Bow Porcelain* (Faber & Faber, 1981). 251 pp.

Hurlbutt, F., *Bow Porcelain* (Bell, 1926). xviii 165 pp.

Brannam (C. H.) Ltd

Brannam, P., *A Family Business: The Story of a Pottery* (Brannam 1982). 137 pp.

Coalport

Mackenzie, Compton, *The House of Coalport 1756–1950* (Crescent Works, 1951). 128 pp.

Copeland (W. T.) & Sons Ltd

—— *W. T. Copeland & Sons Ltd* (Spode Works, Stoke-on-Trent, 1950).
76 pp.

Dudson

Dudson, A. M., *Dudson: A Family of Potters since 1800* (The Firm,
1985). 284 pp.

English China Clays Ltd

Hudson, K., *The History of English China Clays: Fifty Years of
Pioneering and Growth* (David & Charles, 1969). 189 pp.

Goss (W. H.)

Pine, L. and Pine, N., *William Henry Goss: The Story of the Staffordshire
Family of Potters who Invented Heraldic Porcelain* (Milestone
Publications, 1987). 256 pp.

Martin (R. W.) & Bros

Beard, C. R., *A Catalogue of the Collection of Martinware of F. J.
Nettlefold together with a Short History of the Firm* (1936).

Haslam, M., *The Martin Brothers, Potters* (Richard Dennis, 1078).
174 pp.

New Hall Porcelain

Stringer, G. E., *New Hall Porcelain* (1949). x 136 pp.

Royal Crown Derby

Twitchett, J. and Bailey, E., *Royal Crown Derby* (Barrie & Jenkins,
1980). 224 pp.

Royal Doulton (UK) Ltd

—— *Royal Doulton Potteries, A Brief Account of Their History* (The Firm, 1959). 55 pp.

Atterbury, Paul, *The Story of Minton from 1793 to the Present Day* (Royal Doulton Tableware Ltd, 1978).

Eyles, Desmond, *Royal Doulton 1815–1965: The Rise and Expansion of the Royal Doulton Potteries* (Hutchinson, 1965). viii 208 pp.

Eyles, Desmond, *The Doulton Burslem Wares* (Barrie & Jenkins for Royal Doulton Tableware Ltd, 1980). 190 pp.

Gosse, Edmund W. (Desmond Eyles, ed.), *Sir Henry Doulton: The Man of Business as a Man of Imagination* (Hutchinson, 1970). 218 pp.

Shelley Potteries

Watkins, C., *Shelley Potteries: The History and Production of a Staffordshire Family of Potters* (Barrie & Jenkins, 1986). 176 pp.

Stevens & Williams

Williams-Thomas, R. S., *The Crystal Years: A Tribute to the Skills and Artistry of Stevens and Williams, Royal Brierly Crystal* (The Firm, 1983). 80 pp.

Wedgwood (Josiah) & Sons Ltd

—— *The Story of Wedgwood: A Living Tradition* (The Firm, 1959). 62 pp. (4th edition.)

Kelly, A., *The Story of Wedgwood* (1963). 80 pp.

Kelly, A., *The Story of Wedgwood* (Faber, 1975). 91 pp.

Reilly, R., *Wedgwood* (1989).

Warrillow, E. J. D., *History of Etruria, Staffordshire, England 1760–1951* (Etruscan, 1953). 408 pp.

Clothing

[Includes Hatters, Shoemakers, Hosiers.]

See also Department Stores.

Amies (Hardy)

Amies, Edwin Hardy, *Still Here: An Autobiography* (Weidenfeld & Nicolson, 1984). xii 195 pp.

Aristoc

Williams, M. E., *Many a Lifetime of Aristoc Ltd, Langley Mill* (1954).

Atkins of Hinckley

—— *Atkins of Hinckley, 1722–1972* (The Firm, 1972). 52 pp.

Austin Reed Group

Ritchie, B., *A Touch of Class: The Story of Austin Reed* (James & James, 1993). 144 pp.

Balmain

Balmain, P., *My Years and Seasons* (Cassell, 1964). 182 pp.

Barran (John)

Ryott, D., *John Barran's of Leeds 1851–1951* (The Firm, 1951). 60 pp.

Biba

Hulanicki, B., *From A to Biba* (Hutchinson, 1983). 168 pp.

British Industrial Shoe Machinery Co.

—— *The Works and Products of the British Industrial Shoe Machinery Co.* (The Firm, 1937). 84 pp.

Broadbent & Turner

—— *Broadbent & Turner Ltd: The First Fifty Years: A Mass Observation Report* (Mass Observation, 1953).

Browns of Chester

Mass Observation, *Browns of Chester: Portrait of a Shop 1780–1946* (Lindsay Drummond, 1947). 225 pp.

Burton (Montague) Ltd

Fraser, Sir J. F., *Goodwill in Industry: Being the Semi-Jubilee Souvenir of Montague Burton Ltd 1900–1925* (1925). 88 pp.

Redmayne, R., (ed.), *Ideals in Industry: Being the Story of Montague Burton Ltd 1900–1950. Golden Jubilee* (Montague Burton, 1951). xxvii 481 pp.

Sigsworth, Eric M., *Montague Burton: The Tailor of Taste* (Manchester University Press, 1990). x 190 pp.

Christy & Co. Ltd

Sadler, A., *175 Years of The House of Christy* (1951).

Clark (C. & J.) Ltd

Clark, R., *Clark's of Street 1825–1950* (1950). 177 pp.

Hudson, K., *Towards Precision Shoemaking: C. & J. Clark Limited and the Development of the British Shoe Industry* (David & Charles, 1968). 109 pp.

Leharre, Brendon, *C. & J. Clark 1825–1975* (1975). 52 pp.

Sutton, G. B., *History of Shoemaking in Street, Somerset: C. & J. Clark 1833–1903* (William Sessions, 1979). viii 208 pp.

Clarkson (W.)

Jenkin, R., *The Wig-making Clarksons: In Search of their Life and Times* (Stockwell, 1982). 208 pp.

Coats Patons Ltd

—— *History of Coats Bros* (no date). [Registered in 1884 as J. & P. Coats Ltd.]

Blair, M., *The Paisley Thread Industry and the Men Who Created and Developed It* (Gardner, 1907). 206 pp.

Corah: *see in* 'Textiles' (p. 282)

Fakenham Enterprises

Wajcman, J., *Women in Control: Dilemma of a Workers' Co-operative* (Open University Press, 1983). 209 pp.

Foster (W. & J.) Ltd

Millington, J. T., *The Foster Story: 100 Years of Progress 1861–1961* (1961).

Gieves & Hawkes Ltd

Gieve, D. W., *Gieves & Hawkes 1785–1985: The Story of a Tradition* (Gieves & Hawkes, 1985). 128 pp.

Harris Tweed

Thompson, F. G., *Harris Tweed: The Story of a Hebridean Industry* (David & Charles, 1969). 191 pp.

Jenkinson (Joseph)

Jevon, K. M. B. (ed.), *The Diary of Joseph Jenkinson of Ironfield, 1833–1843* (Derbyshire Record Office, 1987). 95 pp.

Jewsbury & Wilson Ltd

—— *Centenary Celebrations: 1865–1965* (1965).

K Shoes

Crookenden, S., *K Shoes: The First 150 Years 1842–1992* (The Firm, 1992). 280 pp.

Somervell, J., *After 90 Years: The Evolution of K Shoes* (The Firm, c. 1932). 52 pp.

Kettering 'Union' Boot & Shoe

Stanton, G., *The Story of an Industrial Democracy 1896–1917* (Co-operative Printing Society, 1918). 52 pp.

Ladybird: *see in* 'Textiles' (p. 282)

Lobb (John) Bootmaker

Dobbs, Brian, *The Last Shall be The First: The Colourful Story of John Lobb the St James's Street Bootmakers* (Hamish Hamilton, 1972). 147 pp.

Lock (James) & Co.

Whitbourn, F., *Mr Lock of St James's Street – His Continuing Life and Changing Times* (Heinemann, 1971). xii 204 pp.

Maden (J.) & Son Ltd

Stock, Leslie A., *The History of John Maden & Son Ltd 1837–1977* (1978). 54 pp.

Mandleberg (J.) & Co. Ltd

—— *Milestones in the History of J. Mandleberg & Co. Ltd 1856–1946* (1946).

Marks and Spencer

—— *Fashion and Fabric, Marks and Spencer: The Story of a Retail Phenomenon* (1953).

Bookbinder, P., *Marks and Spencer: The War Years 1939–1945* (Century Benham, 1989). 144 pp.

Briggs, Asa, *Marks and Spencer 1884–1984* (Octopus Books, 1984). 128 pp.

Jopp, Keith, *Corah of Leicester 1815–1965* (Newman Neame, 1965). Chapter on Marks and Spencer.

Rees, M. G., *St Michael: A History of Marks and Spencer* (Weidenfeld & Nicolson, 1969). 261 pp. (Revised edition, 1983). 302 pp.

Sieff, Israel, *Memoirs of Israel Sieff* (Weidenfeld & Nicolson, 1970). 214 pp.

Sieff, M., *Don't Ask the Price: The Memoirs of the President of Marks and Spencer* (Weidenfeld & Nicolson, 1986). 260 pp.

Solomon, Flora and Litvinoff, Barnet, *Baku to Baker Street: Memoirs of Flora Solomon* (Collins, 1984). 240 pp. [Flora Solomon was a former employee of Marks and Spencer.]

Tse, K., *Marks and Spencer: Anatomy of Britain's Most efficiently Managed Company* (Pergamon Press, 1985). 240 pp.

Milwards of Reading

—— *Centenary 1857–1956* (Pelican Press, 1956). 177 pp.

Morlands

Russell, M., *Sheep into Shoes. The Development of Morlands Warm-lined Footwear* (The Firm, 1962). 64 pp.

Moss Bros Ltd

Tute, W. S., *The Grey Top Hat: The Story of Moss Bros of Covent Garden* (Cassell, 1961). 163 pp.

Norvic Shoe Co.

——— *A Wheldon Century: And the Men Who Made it 1846–1946* (Jarrold, 1946). 160 pp.

Sparks, W. L., *Story of Shoemaking in Norwich* (Norwich: Institute of Boot Industries, 1948). 119 pp.

Payne (Harry H.) Ltd

Richards, E. R., *Shoemakers. A Study of Goodwill in Industry* (1953). 91 pp.

Phipps-Faire

Garnett, R. S., *Phipps-Faire: A History 1822–1988* (The Firm, 1988). 51 pp.

Pocock Bros

——— *Shoe and Leather News, Pocock 1815–1962: A History of Pocock Bros, Shoe Trade Suppliers* (1962). 55 pp.

Start-rite Shoes Ltd

Holmes, K., *Two Centuries of Shoemaking: Start-rite 1792–1992* (The Firm, 1992). 112 pp.

Stead & Simpson Ltd

——— *Stead & Simpson Centenary 1834–1934: 100 Years in the Boot and Shoe Trade* (privately printed, 1934).

Timpson (William) Ltd

Timpson, D. J., *William Timpson Ltd: A Century of Service 1865–1965* (The Company, 1965). 67 pp.

Timpson, W. H. F., *My Father: Stages in the Life of William Timpson* (1936). (3rd edition, 1952).

Timpson, W. H. F., *Seventy Years Agrowing: Or an Early History of Timpsons* (Gloucester, 1938).

United Drapery Stores

Lyons, B., *The Thread is Strong: The Memoirs and Reflections of Bernard Lyons* (private circulation, 1981). 248 pp.

Vyella International: *see* Hollins & Vyella *in* 'Textiles' (p. 286)

Walker (Richard)

Walker, Richard, *The Savile Row Story: An Illustrated History* (Prion, 1988). 192 pp.

Wilkinson & Riddell Ltd

Wills, J., *Wilkinson & Riddell Limited 1851–1951* (The Firm, 1951). 64 pp.

Woolfenden (J.) & Co.

—— *One Hundred Years of Hat Making: A Story of Industrial Progress* (1930).

Confectionery

General

Strong, L. A. G., *The Story of Sugar* (Weidenfeld & Nicolson, 1954). [Commissioned by Tate & Lyle.]

Wagner, G., *The Chocolate Conscience* (Chatto & Windus, 1987). 178 pp.

Cadbury

Cadbury, Edward, *Experiments in Industrial Organisation* (Longmans, 1912).

Finch, R., *A World-wide Business* (Bourneville: The Firm, 1948). 64 pp.

Gardiner, A. G., *Life of George Cadbury* (Cassell & Co., 1923). 308 pp.

Rogers, T. B., *A Century of Progress 1831–1931* (Bourneville: Cadbury Brothers, 1931). 89 pp.

—— *Industrial Record, 1919–1939: A Review of the Interwar Years* (Bournville: The Firm, 1945). 84 pp.

Smith, C. and others, *Reshaping Work: The Cadbury Experience* (Cambridge University Press, 1990). 410 pp.

Williams, I. A., *The Firm of Cadbury 1831–1931* (Constable & Co, 1931). 295 pp.

—— *Cadbury Brothers, Education in Industry* (Bourneville: 1938).

—— *Cadbury Brothers Ltd, Industrial Record 1919–1939* (Bourneville: Cadbury Brothers, 1947). (3rd impression.)

—— *Industrial Challenge: The Experience of Cadburys of Bourneville in the Post-War Years* (Pitman, 1964). 92 pp.

Cadbury has now merged with Schweppes to become Cadbury Schweppes plc.

Caley (A. J.) & Son

Mackintosh, E. D., *Norwich Adventure . . . 1932–1942* (The Firm, 1947). 96 pp.

Fry (J. S.) & Sons Ltd

—— *Bi-centenary Number Fry's Works Magazine 1728–1928* (1928). 86 pp.

Fry, Joseph, *History of the Fry Family* (privately printed, 1926).

Nestlé: *see* 'Beverages'

Rowntree Mackintosh plc

Crutchley, G. W., *John Mackintosh: A Biography* (Hodder & Stoughton, 1921). 231 pp.

—— *One Man's Vision: The Story of the Joseph Rowntree Village Trust* (Allen & Unwin, 1954). 149 pp.

Mackintosh, H. V. (1st Viscount Mackintosh), *By Faith and Work: autobiography* (Hutchinson, 1966). 290 pp. (Edited and arranged by A. A. Thompsom.)

Vernon, Anne, *Three Generations: The Fortunes of a Yorkshire Family* (Jarrold, 1966). 191 pp.

Vernon, Anne, *A Quaker Businessman: The Life of Joseph Rowntree 1836–1925* (William Sessions, 1982). 207 pp.

Wallace, W., *Prescription for Partnership* (1959). 228 pp.

Willoughby's

—— *Willoughby's: A Century of Good Service 1850–1950* (The Firm, n.d.).

Decorating Materials

General

Sugden, A. V., *A History of English Wallpaper 1509–1914* (Batsford, 1925).

Berger (Lewis) & Sons Ltd

Berger, T. B., *A Century and a Half of the House of Berger: Being a Brief History* (Waterlow, 1910), xi 108 pp.

Farnol, J., *Portrait of a Gentleman in Colours: The Romance of Mr Lewis Berger* (Lowe Marston & Co., 1935). 85 pp.

Berger, Jenson & Nicholson

—— *Berger, Jenson & Nicholson: Records 1773–1986* (Hackney Archives Department, 1990). 54 pp.

Blundell, Spence & Co. Ltd

—— *The Blundell Book 1811–1951: A Short History of Blundell, Spence & Co. Ltd* (The Company, 1951). 76 pp.

Dobie & Son Ltd

Parker, W. M., *Dobie and Son Ltd 1849–1949* (The Firm, 1949). 79 pp.

International Paints

—— *International Paints 1881–1956: Seventy Five Years of Paint-Makers* (The Firm, 1958). 72 pp.

Manders (Holdings) plc

—— *The History of Mander Brothers 1773–1955* (Whitehead Brothers, 1953). 260 pp.

Nicholson (Wilfred)

Kimber, H. E., *Wilfred Nicholson 1821 to 1921: A Brief Record of His Life and Work* (1960). 91 pp.

Oil and Colour Chemists' Association

Copping, George, *A Fascinating Story: The History of OCCA, 1918–1968* (OCCA, 1968). xvi 89 pp.

—— *Fiftieth Anniversary Celebration 9th–10th May 1968* (1968).

Parsons (Thomas) & Sons Ltd

—— *150 Years of Paint and Varnish Manufacturing* (The Company, 1952). 63 pp.

Potter (C.) & (J. G.)

Sugden, A. V. and Entwistle, E. A., *Potters of Darwen 1839–1939* (The Firm, 1939). 120 pp.

Reeves & Sons

Goodwin, M., *Artist and Colourman* (Reeves, 1966). 51 pp.

Sanderson (Arthur) & Sons Ltd

—— *A History of the House of Sanderson* (1932).

Woods, C., *Sanderson 1860–1985* (The Company, 1985). 56 pp.

Thornley & Knight Ltd

—— *Proud Occasion: Some Notes Written in Reminiscent Mood on the Occasion of Our 150th Anniversary* (The Firm, 1947). 84 pp.

The Wall Paper Manufacturers Ltd

—— *W. P. M: The Pattern of a Great Organisation 1899–1949* (1950). 209 pp.

Walpamur Co. Ltd.

—— *Booklet Describing the Firm and its Activities: Published for the Firm's Golden Jubilee* (1956).

Watts & Co.

—— *Watts & Co. Ltd.* (The Firm, 197?). 60 pp.

Department Stores

General

Adburgham, Alison, *Shopping Style: London from the Restoration to Edwardian Elegance* (Thames & Hudson, 1979). 192 pp.

Adburgham, Alison, *Shops and Shopping 1800–1914: Where and in What Manner the Well-dressed Englishwoman Bought her Clothes* (Allen & Unwin, 1981). 304 pp. (2nd revised edition).

Barkers

Peel, D. W., *A Garden in the Sky: The Story of Barkers of Kensington 1870–1957* (Allen, 1960). 175 pp. [Includes Pontings and Derry & Toms.]

Bentalls plc

Bentall, R., *My Store of Memories* (Allen, 1974). 298 pp.

Herbert, C., *A Merchant Adventurer. Being the Biography of Leonard Hugh Bentall . . .* (Waterlow, 1936). 163 pp.

Bon Marché

Miller, M., *The Bon Marché: Bourgeois Culture and the Department Store, 1859–1920* (Allen & Unwin, 1981). 278 pp.

Browns of Chester

—— *Portrait of a Shop 1780–1946* (Lindsay Drummond, 1947). vii 225 pp.

Debenhams

Corina, Maurice, *Fine Silks and Oak Counters: Debenhams 1778–1978* (Hutchinson Benham, 1978). 200 pp.

Fenwick Ltd

Pound, Reginald, *The Fenwick Story* (Fenwick Ltd, 1972). 126 pp.

Fortnum & Mason plc

—— *Fortnum & Mason 275th Anniversary, 1982* (The Firm, 1983). 58 pp. [Christmas catalogue with celebratory history of the firm.]

Gamages

—— *Gamages Christmas Bazaar*, 1913 (David & Charles, 1974). 470 pp. [Introduction by Alison Adburgham.]

—— *Mr Gamage's Great Toy Bazaar 1902–1906* (Denys Ingram Publishers, 1982). [Introduction by Charlotte Parry-Crooke.]

Great Universal Stores Ltd

—— *Great Universal Stores: 25 Years of Progress 1932–1957* (1957). 55 pp.

Harrods Ltd (including House of Fraser)

—— *The House that Every Woman Knows: Harrods Limited* (1909). [For their Diamond Jubilee.]

—— *A Story of British Achievement 1849–1949* (1949). 58 pp.

—— *Victorian Shopping: Harrods' Catalogue 1895* (David & Charles, 1972). 1510 pp. [Introduction by Alison Adburgham.]

Callery, S. *Harrods, Knightsbridge: The Story of Society's Favourite Store* (Ebury Press, 1991). 176 pp.

Dale, Tim, *Harrods: The Store and the Legend* (Pan Books, 1981). 149 pp.

Frankau, Gilbert, 'Great Store' (no date). [Unpublished history of Harrods, Archive 1/44, Harrods, Knightsbridge, London.]

Moss, M. and Turton, A., *House of Fraser: A Legend of Retailing* (Weidenfeld & Nicolson, 1989). 384 pp.

Pottinger, G., *The Winning Counter: Hugh Fraser and Harrods* (Hutchinson, 1971). 192 pp.

Rowland, T., *A Hero from Zero: The Story of Kleinwort Benson and Mohamed Fayed* (Lonrho, 1988). 185 pp.

Lewis (John) Partnership plc

Briggs, A., *Friends of the People: The Centenary History of Lewis's* (1956) 242 pp.

Flanders, A. D. and others, *Experiment in Industrial Democracy: A Study of the John Lewis Partnership* (Faber, 1968). 261 pp.

Lewis, John Spedan, *Partnership For All* (John Lewis Partnership, 1952). xx 536 pp. [A reprint of 1948 edition.]

Lewis, John Spedan, *Fairer Shares: A Possible Advance in Civilisation and Perhaps the Only Alternative to Communism* (Staples, 1954). ix 244 pp.

MacPherson, H. (ed.), *John Spedan Lewis 1885–1963 Remembered by Some of his Contemporaries in the Centenary Year of his Birth* (The Firm, 1985). 222 pp.

―― *John Spedan Lewis 1885–1963* (John Lewis, 1985). 222 pp.

Liberty's plc

Adburgham, A., *Liberty's: A Biography of a Shop* (Allen & Unwin. 1975). 160 pp.

Lowe (James) (Wigan) Ltd

―― *Fifty Years of Progress 1887–1937: Victoria House Then and Now* (The Company, 1937).

―― *Lowe's Anniversary Observer, 1887–1962: 75 Years of Progress* (The Company, 1962).

Marks and Spencer plc: *see in* 'Clothing' (p. 83)

Marshall & Snelgrove Ltd

Settle, A., *A Family of Shops* (1951). 36 pp. [History of Marshall & Snelgrove.]

Owen Owen plc

Davies, D. Wyn, *Owen Owen, Victorian Draper* (The Firm, 1983). 156 pp.

Hargreaves, Ian, *They Always Come Back* (The Firm, 1968). 50 pp.

Paulden's Ltd

—— *The Growth of a Company 1866–1966* (1966).

Pendlebury & Co. Ltd

—— *Brief History of the Firm* (The Company, 1930).

Sainsbury (J.) plc: *see in* 'Food' (p. 133)

Schofields Ltd

—— *The Romance of Schofields 1901–1922: The History of A Progressive House* (1922). 13 pp.

—— *1901–1951: Schofields' Golden Jubilee* (1951). 32 pp.

—— *Schofields – The Rebuilding of a Department Store* (1962). 26 pp.

Selfridges Ltd

Honeycombe, R. G., *Selfridges, Seventy-Five Years: The Story of the Store 1909–1984* (Park Lane Press, 1984). 240 pp.

Pound, R., *Selfridge: A Biography* (Heinemann, 1960). 268 pp.

Williams, A. H., *No Name on the Door: A Memoir of Gordon Selfridge* (Allen, 1956). 255 pp.

Whiteleys

Lambert, R. S., *The Universal Provider: A Study of William Whiteley and the Rise of the London Department Store* (Harrap, 1938). 276 pp.

Woolworth

—— *Fifty Years of Progress 1909–1959* (The Firm, 1959). 202 pp.

—— *Woolworth's First 75 Years: The Story of Everybody's Store* (The Firm, 1954). 62 pp.

Winkler, J. K., *Five and Ten: The Fabulous Life of F. W. Woolworth* (The Firm, 1941). 247 pp.

Electricity, Electrical Firms and Communications

[*Including Electrical Engineering, Telecommunications and Cables etc.*]

General

Electricity Council, *Electricity Supply in Great Britain: A Chronology from the Beginnings of the Industry to 31st December 1982* (The Council, 1987).

Bowers, Brian, *A History of Electric Light and Power* (IEE History of Technology, 3, 1982). vii 278 pp.

Cooper, G., *Electrical Heritage: A Guide and Reference Sources* (Elm Publications, 1986). 192 pp.

Hannah, Leslie, *Electricity Before Nationalisation* (Macmillan, 1979). 467 pp.

Hannah, Leslie, *Engineers, Managers and Politicians. The First Fifteen Years of Nationalised Electricity in Britain* (Macmillan, 1982). 350 pp.

Young, Peter, *Person to Person* (Granta Editions, 1991). viii 285 pp.

Aberdare Cables

Richardson, W. A. (ed.), *Aberdare Cables Coming of Age 1958* (Aberdare: Beacon, 1959). 64 pp.

Aerialite

—— *Aerialite Story 1932–1957: Twenty Five Years of Progress* (The Firm, 1957). 60 pp.

Anderson Boyes & Co. Ltd

Carvel, J., *Fifty Years of Machine Mining and Progress 1899–1949* (Motherwell: Flemington Electrical Works, 1949). 113 pp.

ASEA Ltd

—— *A History of ASEA Electric Limited and Fuller Electrical Manufacturing Company Limited During Fifty Years Development* (The Firm, 1949). 118 pp.

Associated Electrical Industries

Jones, R. and Marriott, O., *Anatomy of a Merger: A History of GEC, AEI and English Electric* (Cape, 1970). 346 pp.

Babcock & Wilcox Ltd: *see in* 'Engineering' (p. 107)

Belling & Co. Ltd

Jukes, G. (ed.), *The Story of Belling 1912–1962* (The Firm, 1963). 95 pp.

Birmingham Battery & Metal Co.

Rowntree, A. (ed.), *The Birmingham Battery and Metal Company: One Hundred Years 1836–1936* (The Firm, 1936). 109 pp.

Boilermakers Society

Mortimer, J. E., *History of the Boilermakers Society* (George Allen & Unwin, 1973 and 1982). Two volumes.

Bowthorpe Holdings

Bowthorpe, J., *The Sky's the Limit* (The Firm, 1966). 68 pp.

British Electrical & Applied Manufacturers

—— *The BEAMA Book: A History and Survey* (The Firm, 1926).

British Insulated Callenders Cables Construction Ltd

—— *The Story of Callenders 1882–1932, Callenders Cable and Construction Company Ltd* (privately printed, 1932). 106 pp.

Morgan, R. M., *Callenders': 1882–1945* (Prescott, Merseyside: BICC plc, 1982). ix 256 pp.

—— *The BIIC Group of Companies* (The Firm, 1962). 108 pp.

British Telecom

Earl, R. A. J., *The Development of the Telephone in Oxford, 1877–1977* (The Company, 1983).

Newman, K., *The Selling of British Telecom* (Holt, Rinehart & Winston, 1986). 176 pp.

British Thomson-Houston Co. Ltd

Price-Hughes, H. A., *B. T. H. Reminiscences: Sixty Years of Progress* (The Firm, 1946). 176 pp.

Brown, Boveri & Co. Ltd

—— *75 Years of Brown Boveri: 1891–1966* (Baden, 1966). 289 pp.

Cable & Wireless plc

Baglehole, K. C., *A Century of Service 1868–1968* (Bournehall Press Ltd, 1969). 54 pp.

Barty-King, H., *Girdle Round the Earth, The Story of Cable & Wireless* (Heinemann, 1979). 413 pp.

Graves, C., *The Thin Red Lines* (1946). 183 pp.

Stray, J. F., *Inside an International: Forty Years with 'Cable and Wireless'* (Regency, 1982). 332 pp.

Chloride Batteries Ltd

—— *Batteries Are Our Business* (The Firm, 1955). 56 pp.

Currys

Lerner, H., *Currys: The First 100 Years* (Woodhead-Faulkner, 1984). 112 pp.

Cussins & Light

—— *The CandL Golden Book: Cussins & Light Ltd* (The Firm, 1971). 204 pp.

Dale Electric Group

Barty-King, H., *Light Up the World: The Story of Leonard Drake and Dale Electric Group 1935–1985* (The Firm, 1985). 144 pp.

Dorman Smith

Lee, N. and Stubbs, P. C., *The History of Dorman Smith 1878–1972* (Neame, 1972). 176 pp.

Eastern Associated Telegraph Co. Ltd

—— *Fifty Years of 'Via Eastern'* (1922). 203 pp.

Eastern Electricity

Melling, C., *Light in the East* (Eastern Electricity, 1987). x 166 pp.

Edison Swan Electric Co. Ltd

—— *The Pageant of the Lamp: The Story of the Electric Lamp* (1948). 72 pp.

Josephson, M., *Edison: A Biography* (Eyre & Spottiswoode, 1961). xiii
512 pp.

Parsons, R. H., T*he Early Days of the Power Station Industry* (Babcock
& Wilcox, 1939). 217 pp.

Electric Telegraph Co.

Kieve, J. L., *Electric Telegraph: A Social and Economic History*
(David & Charles, 1973). 310 pp.

English Electric Co. Ltd

—— *War Diary of the English Electric Company Ltd, March
1938–August 1945* (1949). 253 pp.

Andrews, H. H., *Electricity in Transport Over 60 Years Experience:
English Electric Co. 1882–1950* (The Firm, 1951). 183 pp. *See also*
Siemens Brothers *below.*

Jones, R. and Marriott O., *Anatomy of a Merger: a History of GEC, AEI
and English Electric* (Cape, 1970). 346 pp.

White, A. G., 'A History of the English Electric Co.' (A typescript copy
of this work is available in the Library of GEC's Preston Works.)

Faraday Electrical Manufacturing Co.

Lipscomb, F. W., *The Wise Men of the Wires: The History of Faraday
House* (Hutchinson, 1973). xix 203 pp.

Fenner (J. H.) & Co. Ltd

Davis, R., *Twenty-One and A Half Bishop Lane: A History of J. H.
Fenner & Co. Ltd 1861–1961* (Neame, for private circulation, 1961).
110 pp.

Ferranti plc

Bailey, F., *The Life and Work of S. Z. de Ferranti* (1931).

Ferranti, G. Z. de and Ince, R., *The Life and Letters of Sebastian Ziani de Ferranti* (Williams & Norgate, 1934; reprinted 1956). 240 pp.

Lunt, T. J., *Sir Vincent de Ferranti* (privately printed, 1980). (Address at memorial service.)

Randell, Wilfred L., *S. Z. de Ferranti and his Influence upon Electrical Development* (Longmans: Green & Co., 1946).

Wilson, John F., 'The Ferrantis and the Growth of the Electrical Industry 1882–1952' (Manchester University PhD, 1980).

Wilson, John F., *Ferranti and the British Electrical Industry, 1864–1930* (Manchester University Press, 1988). 165 pp.

—— *Ferranti: Selling Technology* (The Firm, 1985). 57 pp.

Fuller Electric Ltd: *see entry for* **ASEA LTD** *above*

GEC-Marconi Electronics Ltd

—— *Jubilee Year of the Marconi Company* (1947). 57 pp.

Baker, W. J., *A History of the Marconi Co.* (Methuen, 1970). 414 pp.

Donaldson, F., *The Marconi Scandal* (Hart-Davis, 1962). 304 pp.

Goodwin, G., *Marconi: 1939–1943: A War Record* (1946). 127 pp.

Hancock, H. E., *Wireless at Sea: The First 50 Years: A History . . . of Maritime Wireless Communications written to commemorate the Jubilee of the Marconi International Marine Communications Co. Ltd, Chelmsford* (1950). 252 pp.

General Electric Co. plc

—— *The General Electric Company Limited: Britain's Largest Electrical and Electronics Company* (The Firm, 1973). 104 pp.

Jones, R. and Marriott, O., *Anatomy of a Merger; A History of GEC, AEI and English Electric* (Cape, 1970). 346 pp.

Latham, Sir Joseph, *Take-Over: The Facts and the Myths of the GEC/AEI Battle* (Iliffe Books, 1969). 128 pp.

Whyte, A. G., *Forty Years of Electrical Progress: The Story of GEC* (Benn, 1930). 166 pp.

Henley's Telegraph Works

Slater, E., *One Hundred Years 1837–1937: The History of Henley's* (The Firm, 1937). 77 pp.

IERE

Graham, D. C. and Sharp, F. W., *A Twentieth Century Professional Institution: The Story of the IERE 1925–1988* (IEE, 1989).

Institution of Electrical Engineers

Appleyard, Rollo, *The History of the Institution of Electrical Engineers 1871–1931* (The Institution, 1939).

Reader, W. J., *A History of the Institution of Electrical Engineers 1871–1971* (IEE, 1987).

ITT

—— *The Breath of Invention. The Story of Frederick G. Creed* (ITT Creed Ltd, 1976). [Creed & Co. was acquired by ITT IN 1927.]

Sampson, Anthony, *The Sovereign State: The Secret History of ITT* (Hodder & Stoughton, 1973).

Jersey Electricity Company Ltd

Hawkley, L. J., *The Story of the Jersey Electricity Company Ltd* (The Company, 1983). 306 pp.

Johnson & Phillips Ltd

Brooks, W. C., *The History of Johnson and Phillips: A Romance of Seventy-Five Years of Cable Laying* (Collin Brooks, 1950). xi 211 pp.

Lucas: *see* 'Engineering' (p. 118) *and* 'Motor Industry and Bicycles' (p. 209)

Merz & Mclellan

Rowland, J., *Progress in Power: The Contribution of Charles Merz and his Associates to 60 Years of Electrical Development 1899–1959* (Newman Neame, 1960). 130 pp.

Metropolitan Vickers Electrical Co. Ltd: *see also* GEC *above*

Dummelow, J., *Metropolitan Vickers Jubilee Book 1899–1949* (The Company, 1949). x 250 pp. (Includes British Westinghouse.)

Rowlinson, Frank (ed.), *Contribution to Victory: An Account of Some of the Special Work of Metropolitan Vickers Electrical Co. Ltd in the Second World War* (The Company, 1947). 199 pp.

North Western Electricity Board

—— *A Record of Ten Years' Progress 1948–1958*. (The Board, 1959).

Swale, W. E., *Forerunners of the North Western Electricity Board* (1963). 118 pp.

Peebles (Bruce) & Co.

—— *The Story of Bruce Peebles 1866–1954* (The Firm, 1955). 51 pp.

Philips

Jansen, C. F. M., *Philips Company Archives* (1987).

Philips, Frederick, *45 Years with Philips* (Blandford, 1976).

Plessey Co. Ltd

—— *The Electronics and Equipment Group of the Plessey Company Ltd* (Plessey, 1962).

Ritchie, B., *Into the Sunrise: A History of Plessey* (James & James, 1989). 59 pp.

Protector Lighting

Heyes, P., *The Protector Lamp and Lighting Company Limited 1873–1973: The First Hundred Years* (The Firm, 1973). 54 pp.

Reyrolle (A.) & Co. Ltd

—— *Fifty Years on Tyneside 1901–1951* (The Company, 1951).

Robertson Electric Lamps

Loring, H., *From the Beginning* (Jarrold, 1905?). 114 pp.

Rolls Razor

Bloom, J., *It's No Sin to Make a Profit* (W. H. Allen, 1971). 251 pp.

Royal Mail

Daunton, M. J., *Royal Mail: Britain's Post Office Since 1840* (Athlone Press, 1985).

Scholes (George H.) & Co. Ltd

—— *Half-Century: Souvenir in Celebration of the Jubilee of George H. Scholes & Co. Ltd 1897–1947* (1947).

Siemens Bros & Co. Ltd

Scott, J. D., *Siemens Brothers, 1858–1958: An Essay in the History of Industry* (Weidenfeld & Nicolson, 1958). 279 pp.

Simms Motor & Electronics Co.: *see also in* 'Motor Industry' (p. 212)

—— *Simms Motor & Electronics Corporation Limited: 40 Years of Simms Expansion* (The Firm, 1959). 54 pp.

Morgan, B. S. *Acceleration: The Simms Story from 1891–1964* (Newman Neame, 1965). ix 61 pp.

South Eastern Electricity Board

Gordon, R., *One Hundred Years of Electricity Supply 1881–1981* (The Board, 1981). 83 pp.

Robinson, Sidney, *Seeboard: The First Twenty-Five Years* (The Board, 1974). 115 pp.

Standard Telephones & Cables Ltd

—— *The Story of STC 1883–1958* (The Firm, 1958). 105 pp.

Reekie, D., *These and Other Things Were Done: The War Story of Standard Telephones and Cables Limited* (n.d). 96 pp.

Young, Peter, *Power of Speech: A History of Standard Telephones and Cables 1883–1983* (George Allen & Unwin, 1983). 224 pp.

Telegraph Construction & Maintenance Co. Ltd

Lawford, G. L. and Nicholson, L. R., *The Telcon Story 1850–1950* (1950). 173 pp.

Ward & Goldstone Group

—— *75 Years: Established 1892* (1967).

West (Allen) & Co. Ltd

—— *The Allen West Story 1910–1960: Fifty Years of Electric Control Gear Development* (The Firm, 1960). 60 pp.

Engineering

General

Floud, R. C., *The British Machine Tool Industry 1850–1914* (Cambridge University Press, 1976). xiv 217 pp.

Saul, S. B., 'The Market and the Development of the Mechanical Engineering Industries in Britain, 1860–1914', in *Economic History Review*, second series, volume xx, no. 1, April 1967. [As a rule articles have not been included: this is an exception.]

Skempton, A. W., *British Civil Engineering 1640–1840 (A Bibliography)* (Mansell Publishing, 1987).

Aiton & Co. Ltd

—— *Water Distillation Plant, Chemical Plant and Evaporation PWV Mixers* (The Firm, n.d.). 90 pp.

Alden (Fred G.)

Mann, C., *The Alden Heating Story: A History of Fred G. Alden (Heating) Ltd, Oxford* (Alden Press, 1981). 66 pp.

APV Company Ltd

Dummett, G. A., *From Little Acorns: A History of the APV Company Ltd* (Hutchinson Benham, 1981). xiv 247 pp.

Archdale (James) & Co. Ltd

—— *Archdale Machine Tools 1868–1948* (The Firm, 1948). 100 pp.

Armstrong (Sir W. G.) Whitworth & Co. Ltd: *see also in* 'Arms for War and Peace' (p. 12) *and in* 'Shipping and General Merchants' (p. 274) *and as* **Vickers** *below*

—— *A Short Account of the Openshaw Works of Sir W. G. Armstrong, Whitworth & Co. Ltd* (1906).

Cochrane, A., *The Early History of Elswick* (Mawson Swan, 1909). 90 pp.

—— *Sir W. G. Armstrong, Whitworth & Co. Ltd 1810–1910: A Short History* (1910).

—— *The War Work of Sir W. G. Armstrong, Whitworth & Co. Ltd* (1920).

Ashworth & Parker Ltd

—— *Fifty Years of Progress: The Story of Ashworth & Parker Ltd 1901–1951* (1951).

Associated Equipment Co.

—— *AEC: The First Fifty Years* (The Firm, 1962).

Avery (W. & T.) & Co. Ltd

Broadbent, J. H., *The Avery Business 1730–1918* (Birmingham, 1949). 86 pp.

Leigh-Bennett, E. P., *Weighing the World . . . 200 Years of the Past History of an English House of Business . . .* (The Firm, 1930). 90 pp.

Avimo Ltd

—— *The Story of Avimo 'Progress of Quality: A Short Account of a Development of the Firm of Avimo Ltd, Taunton, Somerset* (The Company, 1946). 104 pp.

Babcock & Wilcox

—— 'Babcock: History of Babcock & Wilcox Ltd' (The Firm, 1950). 162 pp. Typescript.

Baker Perkins Holdings plc

Gilpin, E. H., 'Memories of Fifty Four Years' (1945). [Unpublished typescript, 1945, at Baker Perkins Holdings plc.]

Muir, C. A., *The History of Baker Perkins* (Heffer, 1968). x 214 pp.

Beardmore

Hume, John R. and Moss, Michael S., *Beardmore. The History of a Scottish Industrial Giant* (Heinemann, 1979). xx 364 pp.

Begg, Cousland & Co. Ltd

—— *Note it in a Book: The Story of Begg, Cousland & Company Ltd of Glasgow 1854–1954* (Harley Publishing, 1955). 56 pp.

Benham & Sons Ltd

Benham, S. J., *Under Five Generations: The Story of Benham & Sons Ltd* (The Firm, 1937). 51 pp.

Boulton & Paul

—— *The Leaf and the Tree 1797–1947* (Riverside Works, Norwich, 1947). 88 pp.

Boulton & Watt

Roll, Sir Eric, *An Early Experiment in Industrial Organisation: Being A History of the Firm of Boulton & Watt 1775–1805* (Cass, 1930). xvi 320 pp. (1st edition; reprinted by Cass, 1968.)

Tann, J. (ed.), *The Selected Papers of Boulton & Watt: vol. I: The Engine Partnership 1775–1825* (Mechanical Engineering Diploma, 1981). 425 pp.

Bradley & Craven

Craven, W. A., *The First Hundred Years: The Early History of Bradley Craven Limited, Wakefield* (The Firm, 1963). 140 pp.

Brightside Foundry & Engineering Co. Ltd

—— *Fifty Years of Progress 1899–1949* (1949).

—— *The Brightside Group of Companies* (n.d.) 114 pp.

British Electric Traction: *see also* 'Transport and Road Haulage' (p. 301)

Mingay, G. E., *Fifteen Years On: The BET Group 1856–1971* (The Company, 1973). xi 118 pp. [Concerned with BET's expansion into engineering.]

Brocklebank & Co. Ltd

Gibson, J. G., *Brocklebank & Co. Ltd 1770–1950* (Liverpool, 1953). Two volumes.

Brotherhoods

Leleux, S. A., *Brotherhoods, Engineers* (David & Charles, 1965). 85 pp.

Brown (David) Corporation Ltd

Donnelly, Desmond, *David Brown's: The Story of a Family Business 1860–1960* (Collins, 1960). 128 pp.

Brown (John) (Engineering) Ltd: *see also in* 'Iron and Steel' (p. 169) *and* 'Shipping and General Merchants' (p. 255)

—— *John Brown Atlas Works, Sheffield, Shipyard and Engineering Works, Clydebanks* (The Firm, 1903). 118 pp.

Grant, Sir A., *Steel and Ships: The History of John Brown's* (Michael Joseph, 1950). 97 pp.

Mensforth, Sir E., *Family Engineers* (Ward Lock, 1981). 168 pp.

Bruntons

Adam, A. T., *Bruntons 1876–1962* (The Firm, 1962). vi 77 pp.

Bryan Donkin Co. Ltd

Cross, E. K. (ed.), *A Brief Account of Bryan Donkin . . . and the Company he Founded 150 Years Ago, 1803–1953* (1953). 70 pp.

Burrell (Charles) & Sons

Clark, R. H., *Chronicles of a Country Works: A History of Messrs Charles Burrell & Sons Ltd of Thetford, Traction Engine Builders* (Percival Marshall, 1952). xv 305 pp.

Caird & Raynor

Palfrey, K., *Water Under the Bridge: The First Hundred Years of Caird & Raynor* (The Firm, 1989). 191 pp.

Campbell, Smith & Co.

—— *Campbell, Smith & Company 1873–1973: A Century of Decoration Craftsmanship* (The Firm, 1973). ix 77 pp.

Carlaw (David) & Sons Ltd

House, J., *A Family Affair: The Story of David Carlaw & Sons Ltd of Glasgow* (The Firm, 1960). 70 pp.

Cary (William E.) Ltd

Phillips, Gordon, *A Century of Springs: A Record of Williams E. Cary Ltd, Red Bank, Manchester from 1848–1948* (1948).

Churchill (Charles) & Co.

Rolt, L. T. C., *Charles Churchill 1865–1965* (The Firm, 1965). 72 pp.

Clapham Brothers Ltd

Field, M. and Field, R., *The History of Clapham Brothers Ltd, Keighly 1837–1962* (Tring: The Authors, 1983). 220 pp.

Clayton Goodfellow & Co. Ltd

—— *Souvenir of Centenary Celebrations 1857–1957* (1957).

Coles Cranes Ltd

Wilson, Martyn and Spink, K., *Coles 100 Years: The Growth Story of Europe's Leading Crane Manufacturers 1879–1979* (The Company, 1979). 64 pp.

Crapper (Thomas) & Co.

Reyburn, W., *Flushed with Pride: The Story of Thomas Crapper* (Futura, 1980). vi 95 pp.

Curran (Edward)

—— *The Edward Curran Companies: A Review of Half a Century, 1903–1953* (The Firm, 1953). 88 pp.

Dean Smith & Grace Ltd

—— *Centenary Brochure 1865–1965* (1965). 60 pp.

Grierson, E., *A Little Farm Well Tilled* (1965). 83 pp.

Dowty Group Ltd

Edwards, R. S. and Townsend, H. (eds), *Studies in Business Organisation* (Macmillan, 1961). [Chapter entitled 'Development and Organisation of the Dowty Group Ltd'.]

Rolt, L. T. C., *The Dowty Story* (Newman Neame, for private circulation, 1962–73). Two volumes.

Ensor & Co.

Pipes, E., *Ensor* (The Firm, 197?). 75 pp.

E. P. E. A.

Slinn, Judy, A., *Engineers in Power: 75 Years of the EPEA* (1989).

Erskine, Heap & Co. Ltd

—— *Switchgear: Motor Control Gear: General Description of Works and Products* (Salford, 1953). [Includes historical and descriptive notes.]

Fawcett Preston & Co. Ltd

White, Horace, *Fossets: A Record of Two Centuries of Engineering 1758–1958* (The Company, 1958). 96 pp.

Foseco Minsep plc

Atterton, D., *Foseco Minsep plc: Fifty Years of Development in Materials Technology* (The Firm, 1982). 64 pp.

Fowlers (Leeds)

Lane, M. R., *The Story of Steam Plough Works: Fowlers of Leeds* (Northgate, 1980). 410 pp.

Fullwood & Bland

Mytton-Davies, C., *Their First Two Centuries: The History of Fullwood and Bland of Ellesmere* (The Firm, 1977). 70 pp.

Gardner (L.) & Sons Ltd

Whitehead, David, *Gardners of Patricroft 1868–1968* (Neame, 1968). 51 pp.

Gibbs (Sir Alexander) & Partners

Harrison, G., *Alexander Gibbs: The Story of an Engineer* (1950). 222 pp.

Gillette Industries Ltd

Coster, I., *The Sharpest Edge in the World: The Story of a Great Industry* (The Firm, 1948). 82 pp.

Glenfield & Kennedy Ltd

Morris, J. A., *A Romance of Industrial Engineering* (Kilmarnock, 1939). vii 141 pp.

Goodwin Barsby & Co.

Pechin, R. E., *Over My Shoulder and Beyond* (The Firm, 1954). 87 pp.

Green (E.) & Sons Ltd

—— *Waste Not: The Story of Green's Economiser* (Harley, 1956). 166 pp.

Greening (N.) & Sons Ltd

Mais, S. P. B., *A History of N. Greening & Sons Ltd, Warrington, England, from 1799 to 1949* (The Company, 1949). 61 pp.

Greenwood & Batley

Floud, Roderick C., *The British Machine Tool Industry 1850–1914* (Cambridge University Press, 1976). xiv 217 pp.

Guest Keen & Nettlefold: *see in* 'Iron & Steel' (p. 173).

Haden (G. N.) & Son Ltd

—— *Haden 150 Years* (Newman Neame, 1966). 56 pp.

Hall & Co. Ltd

Dobson, C. G., *A Century and a Quarter. The Story of Hall & Co. Ltd from 1824* (The Company, 1951). x 228 pp.

Hall (J. & E.) Ltd

Hesketh, E., *Hall Ltd 1785–1935* (Glasgow University Press, 1935). viii 58 pp.

Miller, H., *Halls of Dartford 1785–1985 . . . Pioneer of Refrigeration* (Hutchinson Benham, 1985). 232 pp.

Hall-Thermotank Ltd

Miller, H., *Halls of Dartford 1785–1985: Founded in the Industrial Revolution, Halls of Dartford Celebrate 200 Years of Progress* (Hutchinson Benham, 1985). 231 pp.

Harveys of Hale

Vale, H. E. T., *Harveys of Hale: Engine Builder, Shipwrights and Merchants of Commerce* (Gradford Barton, 1966). 356 pp.

R. & W. Hawthorn Leslie

Browne, Sir Benjamin Chapman, *History of R. & W. Hawthorn's from 1870 to 1885* (1914).

Clarke, J. F., *Power on Land and Sea: 160 years of Industrial Enterprise on Tyneside: A History of R. & W. Hawthorn Leslie & Co. Ltd (Clark Hawthorn Ltd*, 1979). 117 pp.

Heap & Partners

Miller, J., *William Heap and his Company* (The Firm, 1976). 246 pp.

Holden & Brooke Ltd

—— *75: The Story of Holden & Brooke Ltd 1883–1958* (1958).

Holman Bros

Hollowood, A. B., *Cornish Engineers* (Samson Clark, 1951). 96 pp.

Howden (James) & Co.

—— *A Hundred Years of Howden Engineering: A Brief History 1854–1954* (The Firm, 1954). 56 pp.

Humphreys & Glasgow

Edwards, F., *Humphreys & Glasgow: A Century of Achievement 1892–1992* (Melland, 1992). 209 pp.

Institution of Mechanical Engineers

Parsons, Robert Hodson, *A History of the Institution of Mechanical Engineers 1847–1947* (The Institution, 1947). xi 299 pp.

Rolt, L. T. C., *The Mechanicals: Progress of a Profession* (Heinemann, 1967). xii 163 pp.

Jackson (P. R.) & Co. Ltd

—— *The Works and Products of P. R. Jackson & Co. Ltd, Salford Works, Hampson St, Manchester* (The Company, 1954).

Jenkins (Robert) & Co. Ltd

Simons, E. N., *Jenkins of Rotherham 1856–1956. A Chapter of Industrial History* (The Company, 1956). 87 pp.

Simons, E. N. and Sessions, E. M., *Jenkins of Rotherham 1856–1981: 125 Years* (William Sessions, 1981). 120 pp.

Johnson (C. H.) & Sons Ltd

Timaeus, C. E., *A Century and a Half of Wire Weaving. The Story of C. H. Johnson & Sons Ltd* (The Company, 1952). 56 pp.

Johnson (Richard) & Nephew

—— *The Part We Play* (The Firm, 1947). x 62 pp.

Jones (A. A.) & Shipman Ltd

Miller, H., *Tools that Built a Business: The Story of A. A. Jones & Shipman Ltd* (Hutchinson Benham, 1972). 128 pp.

Keir & Cawder

—— *From Project to Practice* (The Firm, 1949). 64 pp.

Kent (George) Ltd

—— *George Kent Limited 1838–1938* . . . (The Firm, 1938). 100 pp.

Kenyon (William) & Sons

—— *A Century's Work 1866–1966* (The Firm, 1966). 83 pp.

Kestner Evaporator & Engineering Co.

—— *The Kestner Golden Jubilee Book, 1908–1958. Fifty Years of Chemical Engineering* (Davis-Poynter, 1958). 104 pp. [Commemorative booklet.]

Kynoch-Arklow Ltd

—— *Under Five Flags: Story of Kynoch Works 1862–1962* (1962). 100 pp. [Presentation edition.]

Murphy, H., *The Kynoch Era in Arklow* (1977). 77 pp.

Laing (John) & Son Ltd: *see in* 'Building and Construction' (p. 58)

Lilleshall Engineering Ltd

Gale, W. K. V., *The Lilleshall Company Limited: A History 1764–1964* (Moorland Publishing Co. for Lilleshall Co. Ltd, 1979). 134 pp.

Lister (R. A.)

Evans, David Ewart, *Lister's: The First Hundred Years* (Alan Sutton Publishing Ltd, 1979). 256 pp.

Lockwood & Carlisle Ltd

Merrill, J., *A Hundred Years of History: Lockwood & Carlisle Ltd 1876–1976* (The Firm, 1976).

Simons, E. N., *Lockwood & Carlilse Ltd of Sheffield: A Chapter of Marine History* (The Firm, 1962). 67 pp.

Lucas Industries Ltd

Nockolds, Harold, *Lucas: The First 100 Years* (David & Charles, 1976 and 1978). Two volumes.

Luke and Spencer Ltd: *see* Unicorn Industries, *below*

Massey (B. & S.)

Janes, H., *Sons of the Forge: The Story of B. & S. Massey Limited, 1861–1961* (Harley Publishing, 1961). 106 pp.

McAlpine (Robert) & Sons Ltd: *see in* 'Building and Construction' (p. 60)

McLellan & Partners

—— *McLellan & Partners: Consulting Engineers to Industry* (The Firm, 1961; revised 1962). 103 pp.

Massey–Ferguson Ltd

Neufeld, E. P., *A Global Corporation. A History of the International Development of Massey–Ferguson Limited* (Toronto: University of Toronto Press, 1969). ix 427 pp.

Matthews Wrightson Group of Companies

—— *Irons in the Fire: A Record of the Group of Companies 1901–1951* (1952). 83 pp.

Meakin (J. & G.)

Hollowood, A. B., *The Story of J. & G. Meakin* (The Firm, n.d.). 64 pp.

Mirrlees, Bickerton & Day Ltd

—— *A British Engineering Shop During the War of 1914–1918* (The Company, 1918).

—— *50 Years of Diesel Progress* (The Company, 1957).

Molins Ltd

Hall, R., *The Making of Molins: The Growth and Transformation of a Family Business 1874–1977* (The Firm, 1978). 102 pp.

Morgan Crucible Co. Ltd

Bennett, R., *Battersea Works: 1856–1956* (The Company, 1956). 67 pp.

Husin, Sir A., *The Brothers Morgan* (privately printed, 1953). 65 pp.

Morgan, Sir K. P. V., *Morgans At War: Achievement under Fire 1939–46* (The Company, 1946). 76 pp.

—— *In the Melting Pot* (The Company, 1957).

Morris (Herbert) Ltd

Wainwright, D., *Cranes and Craftsmen: The Story of Herbert Morris Limited* (Hutchinson Benham, 1974). 88 pp.

Morris Singer Foundry

James, D. S., *A Century of Status: A History of the Morris Singer Foundry* (1984). 61 pp.

Mott, Hay & Anderson

—— *Mott, Hay & Anderson: Consulting Civil Engineers* (Newman Neame, 1965). 88 pp.

Napier (D.) & Sons, Engineers Ltd

Wilson, C. H. and Reader, W. J., *Men and Machines: A History of D. Napier & Son, Engineers Ltd 1808–1958* (Weidenfeld & Nicolson, 1958). 187 pp.

Needle Industries Group

Lee, B. T., *The Personal Reminiscences of a Needlemaker* (Merlin Books, 1986). 163 pp.

Newey Group

Hunt, J., *Pinmakers to the World: An Illustrated History of the Newey Group* (James & James, 1989). 64 pp.

Norton (Sir James Farmer) & Co. Ltd

—— *One Hundred Years Advance: The Story of a Century's Progress in Engineering* (The Company, 1952).

Oldham & Son Ltd

—— *1865–1948: The Story of an Enterprise* (1949). 52 pp.

Owen Organisation

—— *An Industrial Commonwealth: The Owen Organisation of Great Britain* (The Firm, 1951). 104 pp.

Pegler–Hattersley Group

Nicholson, H., *Pegler–Hattersley Group: An Historical Review, 1871–1971* (The Firm, 1974). 73 pp.

Pollock, Walter

Pollock, W., *The Pollocks as Engineers* (The Firm, 1939). 228 pp.

Preece Cardew & Rider

Baker, E. C., *Preece and Those Who Followed: Consulting Engineers in the Twentieth Century* (Reprographic Centre, 1980). xiv 288 pp.

Rabone Chesterman Ltd

Hallam, D. J., *The First 200 Years: A Short History of Rabone Chesterman Ltd* (The Firm, 1984). 136 pp.

Ransomes Sims & Jefferies Ltd

—— *Ransomes' 'Royal' Records: A Century and a Half in the Service of Agriculture* (The Firm, 1937). 96 pp.

Grace, D. R. and Phillips, D. C., *Ransomes of Ipswich: A History of the Firm and Guide to its Records* (The Company, 1975). 66 pp.

Lewis, R. Stanley, *Eighty Years of Enterprise 1869–1949* (The Company, 1949). 112 pp.

Weaver, Carol and Michael, *Ransomes 1789–1989: 200 Years of Excellence* (The Firm, 1989). 130 pp.

Rendel Palmer & Tritton

—— *Rendel, Palmer & Tritton* (The Firm, 1966). 126 pp.

Lane, M. R., *The Rendel Connection: A Dynasty of Engineers* (Quiller Press, 1989). 224 pp.

Renold Ltd

Renold, C. G., *Joint Contribution Over Thirty Years: A Case Study* (The Firm, 1950). 195 pp.

Tripp, B. H., *Renold Chains: A History of the Company and the Rise of the Precision Chain Industry 1879–1955* (Allen & Unwin, 1956). 191 pp.

Tripp, B. H., *Renold Ltd 1956–1967* (Allen & Unwin, 1969). 188 pp.

—— *The Story of Hans Renold Ltd, Chairmakers, 1879–1929* (The Company, 1929).

Roe (A. V.) & Co. Ltd

—— *Fifty Years Nearer the Sky 1908–1953* (The Company, 1958).

Rolls-Royce: *see in* 'Motor Industry and Bicycles' (p. 211)

Ruston & Hornsby Ltd

Newman, B., *One Hundred Years of Good Company – The Occasion of the Ruston Centenary 1837–1957* (Ruston & Hornsby Ltd, 1957). vii 272 pp.

Ryland Brothers Ltd

Janes, Hurford, *Rylands of Warrington 1805–1955: The Story of Ryland Brothers Ltd* (1956). 141 pp.

—— *'Live Wire': 150th Anniversary Number* (Spring 1985).

Salter (Geo.) & Co. Ltd

Bache, M., *Salter: The Story of a Family Firm. 1760–1960* (The Firm, 1960). 95 pp.

Savages

Braithewaite, D., *Savage of King's Lynn: Inventor of Machines and Merry-Go Rounds* (Patrick Stephens, 1975). 136 pp.

Serck plc

Harley, B., *A History of the Serck Group* (The Firm, 1982). 85 pp.

Simon Engineering Group

Simon, Lord Anthony, *The Simon Engineering Group* (1947). 175 pp. (2nd edition, 1953.)

Singer

—— *Singer in World War Two, 1939–1945* (The Firm, 1946?) 95 pp.

Eastley, C. M., *The Singer Saga* (Merlin Books, 1983). 51 pp.

The 600 Group plc

Cohen, G., *The 125 Year Book of 600: 1834–1959* (The Firm, 1959). 172 pp.

Nye, C. E. G. (comp.) and others, *George Cohen: One Hundred Years 1834–1934* (1934). 244 pp.

—— *The 600 Group of Companies* (The Firm, 194?). 134 pp.

Skefko Bale Bearing

—— *Skefko, The First Fifty Years: Skefko 50 Jubilee 1910–1960* (Newman Neame, 1960). 76 pp.

Snow (Sir Frederick) & Partners

—— *Sir Frederick Snow and Partners: Consulting Engineers* (The Firm, 1968). 128 pp.

Standard Engineering

—— *The First Fifty Years* (The Firm, n.d.). 80 pp.

Stephenson Blake & Co. Ltd

Pollard, S., *Stephenson Blake & Co. Ltd, Sheffield: Typefounders* (privately printed, 1960). 277 pp.

Stewarts & Lloyds Ltd

—— *Stewarts & Lloyds 1903–1953* (The Company, 1954). xlviii 160 pp.

Scopes, F., *The Development of Corby Works* (The Firm, 1968). xiv 283 pp.

Stothert & Pitt

Torrens, H., *The Evolution of a Family Firm: Stothert and Pitt of Bath* (Stothert & Pitt, 1978). 86 pp.

Tangyes Ltd

Waterhouse, R. E., *A Hundred Years of Engineering Craftsmanship 1857–1957* (1957). 109 pp.

Thermal Syndicate Ltd

Hetherington, G., *Portrait of a Company: Thermal Syndicate Limited 1906–1981* (The Firm, 1981). xv 253 pp.

Unicorn Industries – UK Ltd

—— *Luke and Spencer Ltd 1877–1977 Centenary Year, 100 Years of Grinding Wheel Manufacture* (privately printed, 1977).

United Wire Works

Phillips, J., *A History of the United Wire Works* (Granton, 1947). 63 pp.

Vickers plc: *see also in* 'Arms for War and Peace' (p. 13) and 'Aviation' (p. 20); *see also* **Armstrong/Whitworth.**

—— *125 Years* (The Firm, 1954). 162 pp.

Beynon, H., and Wainwright, H., *The Workers' Report on Vickers* (Pluto, 1979). 208 pp.

Davenport-Hines, R., *Dudley Docker: The Life and Times of a Trade Warrior* (Cambridge University Press, 1984). 295 pp.

Evans, Harold, *Vickers against the Odds 1956–1977* (Hodder & Stoughton, 1978). 287 pp.

Sanson, L., *Camera in the Works: A Miscellany of Pictures from the Vickers* (Heinemann, 1970). 148 pp.

Scott, J. D., *Vickers: A History* (Weidenfeld & Nicolson, 1963). xxiii 416 pp.

Trebilcock, C., *The Vickers Brothers, Armaments and Enterprise 1884–1914* (Europa Publications, 1977). 181 pp.

Victor Products

—— *Victor: The First Fifty Years 1929–1979* (The Firm, 1979).

Vulcan Boiler & General Engineering Co. Ltd: *see also in* 'Iron and Steel' (p. 177)

Chaloner, W. H., *Vulcan: The History of One Hundred Years of Engineering and Insurance 1859–1959* (1959).

Ward (T. W.) Ltd

—— *Fifty Years of Progress 1878–1928* (The Company, 1928). 52 pp.

—— *Sixty Years' Service 1878–1938* (The Company, 1938). 76 pp.

—— *End of A Chapter: A Brief Record of Thomas W. Ward Ltd and its Subsidiary Companies During the War Years 1939–45* (The Company, 1946). 80 pp.

—— *Outline of Progress 1873–1953* (privately printed, 1953). 212 pp.

—— *The Ward Group of Companies: Products and Services* (The Company, 1959). 67 pp.

—— *Wards at Work 1962: A Pictorial Survey of Recent Activities of the Ward Group of Companies* (The Company, 1962). 162 pp.

—— *Round Britain With Wards* (The Company, 1967). 134 pp.

—— *Ward's World: Centenary Year 1978* (The Firm, 1978). Two booklets.

The Weir Group: *see in* 'Shipping and General Merchants' (p. 274)

Wellworthy

Pearce, D. and Hodges, D. I., *Wellworthy: The First Fifty Years* (The Firm, 1969). 191 pp.

Whessoe

Anderson, R., *The History of Whessoe* (The Firm, 1955).

Wickman Ltd

—— *This is Wickman: What We Are and What We Do* (The Firm, 1963). 96 pp.

Williams (Samuel) & Sons Ltd

—— *A Company's Story in its Setting: Samuel Williams & Sons Ltd, 1855–1955* (The Company, 1955). 85 pp.

Williamson (G. H.) & Sons

Walker, D., *G. H. Williamson & Sons, Providence Works, Worcester* (The Firm, 1976). 91 pp.

Woodall–Duckham

—— *Woodall–Duckham 1903–1978* (The Firm, 1978).

Food

[See separately Beverages, Confectionery]

Allied–Lyons

—— *This is Allied–Lyons* (The Firm, 1984). 72 pp.

Allied Suppliers Group

Mathias, Peter, *The Retailing Revolution: A History of Multiple Retailing in the Food Trades based upon the Allied Suppliers Group of Companies* (Longmans, 1967). xix 425 pp.

Batchelors Foods

——*Just the Job* (Newman Neame, 1963). 51 pp.

Berwick Salmon Fisheries Co. Ltd

——*A Salmon Saga: The Story of the Berwick Salmon Fisheries Company Ltd 1856–1956* (privately printed, 1956).

Bibby (J.) & Sons Ltd

Bibby, J. B. and Bibby, C. L., *A Miller's Tale: A History of J. Bibby & Sons Ltd Liverpool* (The Company, 1978). xi. 218 pp.

Bibby, J., *The Bibby's of Condor Mill and their Descendants* (The Author, 1979). 163 pp.

Bird (Alfred) & Sons

Foley, J., *The Food Makers: A History of General Foods Ltd* (The Firm, 1972). 65 pp.

Booth (E. E.) & Co. Ltd

—— *A Century of Progress 1848–1947* (Derby, 1947).

Borthwick (Thomas) & Sons Ltd

Harrison, Godfrey, *Borthwick's: A Century in the Meat Trade 1863–1963* (1963). 212 pp.

Bovril Ltd

Hadley, Peter (ed.), *A History of Bovril Advertising* (Ambassador Publishing Services Ltd, 1970). 111 pp.

British Vinegars

Sarson, H., 'Family Tradition: the Biography of a Business 1841–1941' (The Firm, 1943: reprinted 1960). Typescript, 89 pp.

Brooke Bond Oxo

Vinchezi, Penny, *Taking Stock* (Collins, 1985). 128 pp.

Carr's Biscuits

—— *The Story of Carr's Biscuits* (The Firm, no date).

Colman Ltd

Colman, Helen Co., *Jeremiah James Colman: A Memoir* (Norwich, 1905). xviii 464 pp.

——*Yellow, White & Blue: The Advertising Art of J. & J. Colman Ltd* (The Company, 1977). 84 pp.

Czarnikow Ltd

Janes, H. and Sayers, H., *The Story of Czarnikow* (Harley Publishing, 1963). 176 pp.

Dalgety

Vaughan-Thomas, W., *Dalgety: The Romance of a Business* (Melland, 1984). 96 pp.

Danish Bacon Co.

Spinks, R., *DBC: The Story of the Danish Bacon Company 1902–1977* (DBC, 1977). 96 pp.

Express Dairy Co. Ltd.

—— *Express Story (1864–1964)* (The Company, 1964). 55 pp.

Morgan, Bryan Stanford, *Express Journey 1864–1964* (Newman Neame, 1964). 139 pp.

Fitch Lovell plc

Keevil, Sir Ambrose, *The Story of Fitch Lovell 1784–1970* (Phillimore, 1972). xvi 304 pp.

Fletchers

Hill, H., *Secret Ingredient: The Story of Fletchers' Seven Bakeries* (E. P. Publishing, 1978). 94 pp.

Food Brokers Ltd

—— *Food Brokers Ltd, Europe's Leading Food Brokers: Silver Jubilee 1961–1986 (The Grocer*, 1986). 58 pp.

Fortnum & Mason Ltd: *see* in 'Department Stores' (p. 92)

Fyffes Group Ltd

Beaver, Patrick, *Yes! We Have Some: The Story of Fyffes* (Publications for Companies, 1976). 124 pp.

Davies, P. N., *Fyffes and the Banana: A Centenary History 1888–1988* (Athlone Press, 1990). xviii 301 pp.

Geest

Stemman, R., *Geest: 1935–1955* (The Firm, 1986). 252 pp.

Hanson (Samuel) & Son Ltd

Godwin, G. S., *Hansons of Cheapside, 1747–1947* (1947). 99 pp.

Hartleys

Peake, A. S., *The Life of Sir William Hartley* (1926). 224 pp.

Heinz (H. J.) Co. Ltd

Alberts, R. C., *The Good Provider: H. J. Heinz and his 57 Varieties* (Barker, 1974). 297 pp.

Cutliffe, N., *100 Years of Progress* (The Firm, 1986). 59 pp.

Potter, S., *The Magic Number: The Story of '57' Varieties* (Max Reindhardt, 1959). 182 pp.

Holbrooke Pure Malt Vinegar Brewery Ltd

Wren, H. F. T., *Trouble Brewing under Eight Reigns* (The Firm, 1948). 75 pp.

Hovis Ltd: *see* **Rank Hovis McDougall** *below*

Huntley and Palmers Food plc

Corley, T. A. B., *Quaker Enterprise in Biscuits: Huntley and Palmers of Reading 1822–1972* (Hutchinson, 1972). xii 320 pp.

Irwin (John) Sons & Co. Ltd

—— *Irwins of Liverpool 1874–1950* (no date).

Lipton: *see also in* 'Beverages and Soft Drinks' (p. 41)

Waugh, A., *The Lipton Story* (Cassell, 1961).

There is a section on Lipton in P. Mathias, *The Retailing Revolution* (Longmans, 1967).

Lyons (J.) & Co. Ltd: *see* **Allied–Lyons** *above*

McDonald's

Love, J. F., *McDonald's: Behind the Arches* (Bantam, 1987). 470 pp.

Manbré & Garton Ltd

Stoddart, J., *Manbré: A Hundred Years of Sugar Refining in Hammersmith 1874–1974* (Fulham and Hammersmith Historical Society, 1974). 54 pp.

Marks and Spencer: *see in* 'Clothing' (p. 83)

Marriage (E.) & Son

Strong, L. A. G., *The Annals of One Hundred Years of Flour Milling* (The Firm, 1940).

Nelstrop (William) & Co. Ltd

Bramwell, A. G., *The Nelstrop Family in History: 1661–1900* (typescript). 195 pp.

—— *150 Years: 1820–1970* (The Firm, 1970).

Rank Hovis McDougall plc

Burnett, R. G., *Through The Mill: The Life of Joseph Rank* (Epworth Press, 1945). 226 pp.

—— *War Record of Hovis Ltd, 1939–45* (1947).

Janes, Hurford, *The Master Millers: The Story of the House of Rank 1875–1955* (Harley Publishing, 1955). 98 pp.

—— *The World of Rank Hovis McDougall* (The Company, 1973).

Reckitt & Colman plc: *see in* 'Pharmaceuticals' (p. 229) *for* Reckitt & Sons Ltd; *see above for* Colman Ltd

Robinson (Thomas) & Son Ltd

—— *Robinson of Rochdale 1838–1938* (The Firm, 1938).

Povey, D. W. and Clayton, H., *A History of Thomas Robinson Ltd* (The Company, 1962).

Sainsbury (J.) plc

—— *JS 100: The Story of Sainbury's* (The Company, 1969). 96 pp.

Williams, B., *The First 120 Years of Sainsbury* (1989).

Simon (Henry) Ltd

—— *Simon in the Service of Milling* (The Company, 1951).

Skilbeck Bros Ltd

Dawe, D. A., *Skilbecks: Drysalters 1650–1950* (1950). 116 pp.

Smedley – HP

Wright, Louise, *The Road from Aston Cross: An Industrial History 1875–1975* (1975). xx 80 pp.

Tate & Lyle Ltd

Andrews, Allen, *Tate & Lyle: A Record of the Activities of the Tate & Lyle Group* (1965). 88 pp.

Chalmin, P., *The Making of a Sugar Giant: Tate & Lyle 1859–1989* (Harwood Academic Publications, 1990) 782 pp.

Hugill, J. A. C., *Sugar* (1949). 64 pp. [2nd edition with special reference to Tate & Lyle.]

Hugill, J. A. C., *Sugar and All That: A History of Tate & Lyle* (Gentry Books, 1978). 320 pp.

Lyle, O., *The Plaistow Story* (The Firm, 1960).

Lyle of Westbourne, Lord, *Mr Cube's Fight Against Nationalisation* (Hollins & Carter, 1954). 306 pp.

Watson, J. A., *100 Years of Sugar Refining* (1973). 155 pp.

Watson, J. A., *The End of a Liverpool Landmark: The Last Years of Love Lane Refinery* (The Firm, 1985). 93 pp.

Tesco Stores (Holdings) Ltd

Corina, Maurice, *Pile it High, Sell it Cheap: The Authorised Biography of Sir John Cohen* (Weidenfeld & Nicolson, 1978). 204 pp.

Greater London Council, *The Impact of a Superstore: Tesco, Finchley Central* (The Council, 1981). 63 pp.

Powell, D., *Counter Revolution: The Tesco Papers 1975–1982* (Hallam & Mellen, 1983). x 125 pp.

Powell, D., *Counter Revolution: The Tesco Story* (Grafton Books, 1991). ix 237 pp.

Travers (Joseph) & Sons Ltd

—— *Past and Present in an Old Firm* (1907). 55 pp.

—— *A Few Records of An Old Firm* (1924). 74 pp.

Travers, F., *Chronicles of Cannon Street: A Few Records of An Old Firm* (1957). 64 pp.

Tuke & Co.

Sessions, W. K. and Sessions, E., *The Tukes of York* (William Sessions, 1971). x 117 pp.

Unilever Ltd: *see also* **Unilever** *in* 'Chemicals' (p. 74); *for brand names owned by* **Unilever** *see index under brand, e.g.* **Birds Eye**, **SPD Ltd** *etc.*

Fieldhouse, D. K., *Unilever Overseas: The Anatomy of a Multinational 1895–1965* (Croom Helm, 1979). 620 pp.

Jolly, W. P., *Lord Leverhulme: A Biography* (Constable, 1976). 246 pp.

Leverhulme, 2nd Lord (son), *Viscount Leverhulme* (Allen & Unwin, 1927). 325 pp.

Nicolson, Nigel, *Lord of the Isles* (Weidenfeld & Nicolson, 1960). 264 pp.

Reader, W. J., *Unilever: A Short History* (The Firm, 1960). 63 pp.

Reader, W. J., *Fifty Years of Unilever, 1930–1980* (Heinemann, 1980). vii 148 pp.

Supple, B. (ed.), *Essays in British Business History* (Clarendon Press, 1977). [Chapter 7: 'Management and Policy in Large-Scale Enterprise: Lever Brothers and Unilever 1918–1939', by Charles Wilson.]

Wilson, Charles, *The History of Unilever: A Study in Economic Growth and Social Change* (Cassell, 1954). [Reprinted in 1968 by Cassell with a third volume. A paperback edition was published in 1970.]

United Biscuits Group

Adam, James S., *A Fell Fine Baker: The Story of United Biscuits* (Hutchinson Benham, 1974). xi 164 pp.

Laing, Sir Hector, *A Parting Shot* (The Firm, 1990). 200 pp.

Pugh, P., *A Clear and Simple Vision* (Cambridge Business Publishing, 1991). x 193 pp.

United Dairies

Enoch, A. G., *This Milk Business: A Study from 1895–1943* (H. K. Lewis, 1943). lii 243 pp.

United Molasses Co.

Meneight, W. A., *A History of the United Molasses Co. Ltd* (1977). xi 212 pp.

Vestey

Knightley, P., *The Vestey Affair* (Macdonald Futura, 1981). 159 pp.

Vickers (Benjamin R.) & Sons

—— *This Family Business, Vickers* (The Firm, 1954). 60 pp.

Warburtons Ltd

—— *Warburton's Bakeries* (1966).

Wilkin & Sons

Benham, M., *The Story of Tiptree Jam: The First Hundred Years 1885–1985* (The Firm, 1985). 56 pp.

Woodhouse, Drake & Carey

Woodhouse, C. H., *The Woodhouses, Drakes and Careys of Mincing Lane* (Burrup Matthieson, 1977). 54 pp.

Furniture and Fittings

General

Beard, G. and Beard, G. C., *Dictionary of English Furniture Makers 1660–1840* (Leeds: Furniture History Society, 1986). 1046 pp.

Evans A. (ed.), *Dictionary of English Furniture Makers 1660–1840: Index* (Leeds: Furniture History Society, 1990). 166 pp.

Heal, Sir A., *The London Furniture Makers from the Restoration to the Victorian Era 1660–1840* (Postman Books, 1953; reprinted 1988). 276 pp.

Oliver, J. L., *The Development and Structure of the Furniture Industry* (Pergamon, 1966). xviii 187 pp.

Barnsley (Edward)

—— *Edward Barnsley: Sixty Years of Furniture Design and Cabinet Making* (Edward Barnsley Educational Trust, 1982). 75 pp.

Ercolani (L. R.)

Ercolani, L. R., *A Furniture Maker: His Life, His Work and His Observations: An Autobiography* (Ernest Benn, 1975). 182 pp.

Habitat

Phillips, Barty, *Conran and the Habitat Story* (Weidenfeld & Nicolson, 1984). 150 pp.

Heal & Son Ltd

Gooden, Susanna, *At the Sign of the Four Poster: A History of Heal's* (Heal's, 1984). 137 pp.

Heal, Sir Ambrose and others, *The Records of the Heal Family* (1932). xxix 167 pp.

Maples

Barty-King, H., *Maples: Fine Furnishers, A Household Name for 150 Years* (Quiller, 1992). 208 pp.

Myer & Co. Ltd

Myer, E., *Myer's First Century 1876–1976: The Story of Myer's Comfortable Beds* (The Company, 1976). 52 pp.

Vaughan Family

—— *The Vaughans: East End Cabinet Makers: Three Hundred Years of a London Family* (Inner London Education Authority, 1984). 95 pp.

Waring & Gillow Ltd

—— *Gillow's: A Record of a Furnishing Firm During Two Centuries* (1901). 84 pp. (2nd edition)

Furs and Skins

Avalon Leatherboard Co.

McGarrie, M., *Bowlingreen Mill: A Century History* (Street: The Firm, 1979). 154 pp.

Barrow Hepburn & Gale Ltd

Bardens, D., *Everything in Leather: The Story of Barrow Hepburn & Gale Ltd* (1948). 89 pp.

Eastern Counties Leather Co. Ltd

Davies, B., *Eastern Counties Leather Company Ltd: One Hundred Years* (Crampton & Sons, 1979). 100 pp.

Forestal Land Timber & Railway

Hicks, A. H., *The Story of the Forestal* (The Firm, 1956). 102 pp. [Leather Tanning.]

Martin (C. W.) & Sons Ltd

——— *Under Eight Monarchs 1823–1953: The History of a London Fur Dressing Firm* (The Company, 1953). 69 pp.

Pittard (C. W.) & Co.

——— *Pittard's 1826–1976: A Commemorative History* (The Firm, 1976). 80 pp.

Gas

General

Bird, A. and Nabb H., *Stoking up the past ... History of the Gas Industry.* ... (Bristol: British Gas, 1989). 65 pp.

British Gas Corporation, *The Development of the British Gas Industry* (The Corporation, 1983). [A chronology.]

Chandler, D. and Lacey, A. D., *The Rise of the Gas Industry in Britain* (British Gas Council, 1949). vii 156 pp.

Williams, T. I., *A History of the British Gas Industry* (Oxford University Press, 1981). 304 pp.

British Gas Corporation

Williams, T. I., *A History of the British Gas Industry* (Oxford University Press, 1981). xvii 304 pp.

British Gas Light Co. Ltd

—— *British Gas Light Co. Ltd 1824–1924* (1924), 53 pp.

Gas Light & Coke Co.

—— *An Account of the Progress of The Company 1812 to the Present Time* (1912). 91 pp.

—— *A Record of Progress* (The Firm, 1930–31). 2 parts.

Everard, S., *The History of the Gas Light & Coke Company 1812–1949* (Benn, 1949). 428 pp.

Holmes (W. C.) & Co. Ltd

—— *The Story of One Hundred Years of Endeavour in the Service of the Gas Industry 1850–1950* (1950). 64 pp.

Imperial Continental Gas Association

—— *Imperial Continental Gas Association 1824–1974* (privately printed, 1974). 66 pp.

Leicester Gas Undertaking

Roberts, David E., *The Leicester Gas Undertaking, 1821–1921* (East Midlands Gas, 1978). 51 pp.

Manchester Corporation Gas Department

—— *Inauguration of the Partington Gas Works, 8th May 1929* (1929).

—— *One Hundred and Forty Three Years of Gas in Manchester* (1949).

North Thames Gas

Falkus, M. E., Always Under Pressure: A History of North Thames Gas since 1949 (Macmillan, 1988). ii 21 pp.

North Western Gas Board

Harris, Stanley A., *The Development of Gas Supply on Merseyside* (North-Western Gas Board, 1956).

Nottingham Gas-Light & Coke Co.

Roberts, D.E., *The Nottingham Gas Undertaking, 1818–1949* (East Midlands Gas, 1980). 55 pp.

West's Gas Improvement Co. Ltd

West, Sir Frederick F., *Reflections and Reminiscences* (1948). 96 pp.

Glass

General

Barry, B., *Glass: Sources of Information on the History, Science, Technology and Art of the Remarkable Material* (BBC, 1985). 87 pp.

Alloa Glass Work Co.

Carvel, J. L., *The Alloa Glass Work: An Account of its Development since 1750* (The Firm, 1953). viii 102 pp.

Beatson Clark & Co. Ltd

—— *Glass Bottle Manufacturers, 1751–1951* (The Firm, 1951). 52 pp.

Clark, A. W., *Through a Glass Clearly* (Golden Eagle, 1980). 159 pp.

Greene, D., *The Glass Works 1751–1951* (The Firm, 1952). 52 pp.

Schofield, J. A., *The Story of Rotherham Glassworks* (1978). 10 pp.

Chance Bros & Co.

Chance, James F., *A History of the Firm of Chance Bros & Co.* (privately printed, 1919). iv 302 pp.

—— *Mirror for Chance* (The Firm, 1951). 72 pp.

Edinburgh Crystal

Woodward, H. W., *The Story of Edinburgh Crystal* (The Firm, 1984). v 92 pp.

Lax & Shaw Ltd

Watson, Nigel, *The Celestial Glass Bottle Company: A Short Centenary History of Lax & Shaw Ltd 1891–1991* (Granta Editions, 1991). 54 pp.

Pilkington Brothers Ltd

—— *Now Thus, Now Thus: 1826–1926* (1926). 93 pp.

—— *Pilkington Brothers Limited, St. Helen's Lancs* (The Firm, 1951).

—— *The Pilkington Organisation: The Story of the Manufacture and Distribution of Glass Throughout the World* (The Firm, 1959). 56 pp.

Barker, T. C., *Pilkington Brothers and the Glass Industry* (Allen & Unwin, 1960). 296 pp.

Barker, T. C., *The Glassmakers: The Rise of An International Company 1826–1976* (Weidenfeld & Nicolson, 1977). xxi 557 pp.

Supple, Barry (ed.), *Essays in British Business History* (Clarendon Press, 1977). (T. C. Barker, 'Business Implications of Technical Development in the Glass Industry 1945–1965: A Case Study'.)

A shorter and updated history of Pilkingtons, 1826–1992, is due for publication shortly.

Webb (Thomas) & Sons Ltd

Woodward, H. W., *Art, Feat and Mystery: The Story of Thomas Webb & Sons, Glassmakers* (Mark & Moody Ltd, 1978). 61 pp.

Goldsmiths, Jewellers, Silversmiths and Watchmakers

Armstrong (Thomas) & Brother Ltd

—— *A Hundred Years of Progress, 1825–1925* (1925).

Aspreys

Hillier, B., *Aspreys of Bond Street 1781–1981* (1981). 144 pp.

Barraud Clockmakers

Barraud, Enid M., *Barraud: The Story of a Family* (Research Publishing Co., 1967). 190 pp.

Jagger, C., *Paul Philip Barraud: The Family Business 1750–1929* (1968).

Cartier

Gautier, G., *Cartier The Legend* (Arlington Books, 1983).

Nadelhoffer, Hans, *Cartier:Jewellers Extraordinary* (Thames & Hudson, 1984). 312 pp.

Dennison Watch Case Co.

Tramayne, Arthur, *One Hundred Years After, Being a Little History of a Great Achievement* (Dennison Watch Case Co., 1912).

Garrard & Co. Ltd

Broadley, A. M., *Garrard's 1721–1911, Crown Jewellers and Goldsmiths During Six Reigns* (Stanley Paul, 1912). 182 pp.

Mappin & Webb Ltd

—— *Mappin and Webb Limited: Notes on the History of the Firm* (1957)
[Typescript in the Guildhall Reference Library.]

Smith (S.) & Sons Ltd

—— *Word of Meaning ... A Panorama of the Great Organisations of
Smiths* (n. d.) 98 pp.

Storr (Paul)

Penzer, N. M., *Paul Storr: The Last of the Goldsmiths* (1954). 292 pp.

Whiley (George M.) Ltd

—— *Leaves of Gold (A History of Goldbeating)* (1951). 70 pp.

Hardware and Household

Addis

Beaver, P., *Addis 1780–1980: All About the Home* (Publications for Companies, 1980). v 55 pp.

Dayer, R. A., *Finance and Empire: Sir Charles Addis 1861–1945* (Macmillan, 1988). 456 pp.

British Ropes Ltd

Rees, D. M., *Warmsworth Hall: Head Office of the British Ropes Group of Companies: A Short History* (1964). 64 pp.

Bryant & May Ltd

—— *Making Matches 1861–1961* (1961).

—— *Match-Making* (1965).

—— *We Started With a Match* (1966?).

Beaver, P., *The Match Makers: The Story of Bryant & May* (Melland, 1985). 128 pp.

Miller, Christy, *The Bryant and May Museum of Fire-Making Appliances*. [Catalogue, with supplement, of the exhibits 1926–1928, two vols.]

Chubb & Son plc

Briggs, A. N. C., *Contemporary Observations on Security from the Chubb Collecteanea 1918–1968* (The Company, 1968). 57 pp

Briggs, A. N. C., *Security Attitudes and Techniques for Management* (Hutchinson, 1968). 154 pp.

Chubb, Sir George H. and Churcher, Walter G., *The House of Chubb 1818–1918* (Jenkins, 1919). x 111 pp.

Hamilton & Co. (London) Ltd

Girtin, T. H., *In Love and Unity: A Book about Brushmaking* (Hutchinson, 1961). 112 pp.

Jarrett, Rainsford & Laughton Ltd: *see* **Laughton & Sons Ltd** *below*

Jeyes Group Ltd

Palfreyman, David, *John Jeyes: The Making of a Household Name* (Jeyes, 1977). 127 pp.

Kenricks (Archibald) & Sons

Church, R. A., *Kenricks in Hardware: A Family Business 1791–1966* (David & Charles, 1969). 340 pp.

Supple, B. (ed.), *Essays in British Business History* (Clarendon Press, 1977). [Chapter 6: 'Family and Failure: Archibald Kenrick & Sons Ltd 1900–1950' by Roy Church.]

Kent (G. B.) & Sons Ltd

Woodall, Doris, *A Short History of The House of G. B. Kent & Sons Ltd* (The Firm, 1959). 50 pp.

Laughton & Sons Ltd

—— *A Century of Achievement: The Story of Laughton & Sons Ltd, formerly known as Jarrett, Rainsford & Laughton Ltd 1860–1960* (William Sessions, 1960). 185 pp.

Reckitt & Sons Ltd: *see in* 'Pharmaceuticals' (p. 229)

Hotels and Catering

Arden & Cobden Hotels Ltd

—— *Enfield 90 Years Young: A Brief History of Arden & Cobden Hotels Ltd* (privately printed, 1977).

The Dorchester

Stanley, L., *Sixty Years of Luxury: The Dorchester* (Pearl & Dean, 1991). 194 pp.

Goring Hotel

Goring, O. G., *50 Years of Service* (1960). 164 pp.

Grand Hotel (Eastbourne)

Pugh, P., *Grand Hotel* (The Hotel, 1987), 215 pp.

Grand Metropolitan plc

—— *Facts and Figures: 25 Dynamic and Successful Years* (1988). 75 pp.

Slinn, Judy A. (with Reader, W. J.), A history of Grand Metropolitan is to be published shortly.

Hatchett's Restaurant

—— *Old Coaching Days and the White Horse Seller, Piccadilly, Established 1720* (1920?). 60 pp. [Advertising booklet.]

Imperial Hotel (Torquay)

Denes, G., *The Story of the Imperial: The Life and Times of Torquay's Great Hotel* (David & Charles, 1982). 158 pp.

Parker & Sons Ltd

—— *Parker's 'Book of Words': Being a Few Words by a Few Customers* (1931).

Prunier

Prunier, Mdme S. G. B., *La Maison. The History of Pruniers* (Longmans, 1957). x 298 pp.

The Ritz

Watts, Stephen, *The Ritz* (Bodley Head, 1963).

Romano's

Deghy, G., *Paradise in the Strand: The Story of Romano's* (Richards, 1958). 256 pp.

The Savoy

—— *The Savoyard* (The Hotel, 1911). 92 pp.

Mackenzie, Sir Compton, *The Savoy* (Harrap, 1953). [A short monograph.]

Jackson, Stanley, *The Savoy, The Romance of a Great Hotel* (Muller, 1964). 320 pp.

Trust House

Vale, Edmond, *The Trust House Story* (Trust House, 1949).

Insurance

General

Cockerell, H. A. L. and Green, E., *The British Insurance Business 1547–1970: An Introduction and Guide to Historical Records in the United Kingdom* (Heinemann, 1976). xiii 142 pp.

Haines, F. H., *Chapters of Insurance History: The Origins and Development of Insurance in England* (1926). 387 pp.

Hannah, L., *Inventing Retirement: The Development of Occupational Pensions in Britain* (Cambridge University Press, 1986).

Morrah, D., *A History of Industrial Life Assurance* (Allen & Unwin, 1955). 243 pp.

Raynes, H. E., *A History of British Insurance* (1948). 387 pp.

Westell, O. M., *The Historian and the Business of Insurance: Aspects of the History of Insurance* (Manchester University Press, 1984). 208 pp.

Withers, H., *Pioneers of British Life Assurance* (Staples Press, 1951). 112 pp.

The Actuaries Club

Recknell, G. H., *The Actuaries Club 1848–1948* (The Club, 1948). vii 75 pp.

Alliance Assurance Co. Ltd

Schooling, Sir W., *Alliance Assurance 1824–1924* (Alliance Assurance Co., 1924). 119 pp.

Atlas Assurance Co. Ltd

Levien, J. W. J., *Atlas at War 1939–1945* (1947). 214 pp. (2nd edition.)

Yeo, A. W., *Atlas Reminiscent* (Dent, 1908). 83 pp.

Bain (A. W.) & Sons

Bain, P., *A History of A. W. Bain & Sons* (The Firm, 1976).

Bevington, Vaizey and Foster

—— *B. V. and F. (An Account of a Firm of Insurance Brokers* (Harrap, 1954). 83 pp. (Privately printed).

Bolton Group

Hennessy, E., *The Bolton Group, 1874–1982* (Publications for Companies, 1983). 91 pp.

Bowring (C. T.) & Co. Ltd

Keir, David, *The Bowring Story* (Bodley Head, 1962). 448 pp.

Wardle, A. C., *Benjamin Bowring and his Descendants* (Hodder, 1940). 229 pp.

Britannic Assurance

—— *The Britannic Magazine Jubilee Edition, Spring 1980* (The Firm, 1980). 61 pp.

British & Foreign Marine Insurance Co. Ltd

—— *1863–1963: A Centenary Account of the Firm* (1963). 104 pp.

—— *The British and Foreign Marine Insurance Company Limited 1863–1963* (The Firm, 1963). 104 pp.

British Engine Insurance

—— *A Century's Program, 1878–1978: 100 Years of Service to Industry* (The Firm, 1978). 127 pp.

Edwards, N., *100 Years of British Engine* (The Firm, 1978). 72 pp.

Chartered Insurance Institute

Cockerell, H. L., *Sixty Years of the Chartered Insurance Institute 1897–1957* (The Institute, 1957). 92 pp.

Clerical, Medical & General Life Assurance Society

Besant, A. D., *1824 to 1924. Our Centenary, Being the History of the First Hundred Years of the Clerical, Medical and General Life Assurance Society* (1924). v 342 pp.

Commercial Union Assurance Co. plc

Liveing, E. G. D., *A Centenary of Insurance: The Commercial Union Group of Insurance Companies, 1861–1961* (Witherby, 1961). 320 pp.

Co-operative Insurance Society Ltd

Garnett, R. G., *A Century of Co-operative Insurance: The Co-operative Insurance Society 1867–1967* (Allen & Unwin, 1968). 324 pp.

County Fire Office Ltd

Noakes, A., *The County Fire Office 1807–1957: A Commemorative History* (Witherby, 1957). xv 189 pp.

Eagle Star Insurance Group

Shepherd, A. F., *Links with the Past: A Brief Chronicle of the Eagle and British Dominions Insurance Co. Ltd* (1917). 297 pp.

Watkin, D. J. and others, *A House in Town: 22 Arlington Street, Its Owners and Builders* (Batsford, 1984). 201 pp.

Employers' Liability Assurance Corporation Ltd

Robinson, Sir H. P., *The Corporation 1880–1930* (1930) 177 pp.

The Equitable Life Assurance Society

Anderson, J. G., *The Birthplace and Genesis of Life Assurance* (Muller, 1937). 93 pp.

Ogborn, M. E., *The Story of Life Assurance in the Experience of the Equitable Life Assurance Society 1762–1962: Equitable Assurance* (Allen & Unwin, 1962). 271 pp.

Essex & Suffolk Equitable Insurance Society Ltd

Drew, B., *'The Fire Office': Being a History of the Essex and Suffolk Equitable Insurance Society Ltd, 1802–1952* (1952). ix 166 pp.

Friends' Provident Life Office

Tregoning, David and Cockerell, Hugh, *Friends for Life: Friends' Provident Life Office 1832–1982* (Melland, 1982) 196 pp.

General Accident, Fire & Life Assurance Corporation plc

Gray, I. E., *A Business Epic 1885–1935* (1935). 72 pp.

General Life Assurance Co.

Champness, A., *A Century of Progress* (1937). 62 pp.

Guardian Assurance Co. Ltd

Tam, A. W. and Byles, C. E. (compilers), *A Record of the Guardian Assurance Co. Ltd 1821–1921* (Blades, 1921). 153 pp. (Privately printed.)

Hadley (Joseph) Holdings Ltd

Janes, H. H., *A Wonderful Heritage: The Hadley Story* (Melland, 1977). 104 pp.

Hearts of Oak Insurance Society

Newman, T. S., *History of the Hearts of Oak Benefit Society 1842–1942* (The Firm, 1942). 205 pp.

Indemnity Marine Assurance Co. Ltd

Mainland, J. F. and Howard, E. H., *A Century Retrospect 1824–1924* (1924). 65 pp.

—— *Indemnity Marine Insurance Co. Ltd* (Privately printed, 1975).

The Institute of Actuaries

Simmonds, R. C., *The Institute of Actuaries 1848–1948* (Institute of Actuaries, 1948). xi 317 pp.

Institute of London Underwriters

Hewer, C., *A Problem Shared. A History of the Institute of London Underwriters 1884–1984* (1984). xiii 136 pp.

Insurance and Actuarial Society of Glasgow

Ingram, C. A., *Four Score and Four: The Story of the Insurance and Actuarial Society of Glasgow* (The Society, 1967).

Insurance Institute of London

—— *The History and Development of Protecting and Indemnity Clubs* (The Firm, 1957). 55 pp.

Insurance Institute of Manchester

—— *Jubilee: A Short History of the Insurance Institute of Manchester* (1923).

—— *Diamond Jubilee Handbook* (1933).

Cockerell, H. A. L., *Sixty Years of The Chartered Insurance Institute 1897–1957* (1957). 92 pp.

Legal & General Assurance Society Ltd

Hannah, L., *Inventing Retirement* (Cambridge University Press, 1986).

Leigh-Bennett, E. P., *On This Evidence: A Study in 1936 of the Legal & General Assurance Society Since its Formation in 1836* (1937). 121 pp.

Leslie and Godwin

Head, V., *Two's Company: A History of Leslie and Godwin, 1885–1985* (The Firm, 1985). 121 pp.

Liverpool & London & Globe Insurance Co. Ltd

Simpson, J. D., *1936, Our Centenary Year: The Liverpool & London & Globe Insurance Co.* (1936). 160 pp.

Lloyd's

—— *Lloyd's: Being (a Section of) the Exchanges of London at the Beginning of the Twentieth Century* (1905). 119 pp.

Beeman, M. M., *Lloyd's London: An Outline* (1937). x 114 pp.

—— *Lloyd's Under Fire: A Tribute to the Civil Defence Services of Lloyd's 1938–1945* (1947). 126 pp.

Blake, G., *Lloyd's Register of Shipping* (Lloyd's 1960). 194 pp.

Brown, A., *Hazard Unlimited: The Story of Lloyd's of London* (Davies, 1973). xi 199 pp. (2nd edition 1979). xi, 226 pp.

Brown, A, *Cuthbert Heath: Maker of the Modern Lloyd's of London* (David & Charles, 1980). 220 pp.

Cameron, A. and Farndon, R., *Scenes from Sea and City: Lloyd's List 1734–1984* (Lloyd's 1984). 288 pp.

Cockerell, Hugh, *Lloyd's of London – A Portrait* (Woodhead Faulkner, 1984). 157 pp.

Dawson, W. R., *The Treasures of Lloyd's* (1930). 200 pp. (4th edition).

Emanuel, G. J., *Memories of Lloyd's 1890–1937* (1937). 118 pp.

Flower, R. C. and Wynn-Jones, E. M. S., *Lloyd's of London: An Illustrated History* (David & Charles, 1974). 192 pp. (3rd revised edition 1987.)

Gibb, D. E. W., *Lloyd's of London: A Study in Individualism* (Macmillan, 1957). 387 pp.

Golding, C. E., and Page, D. K., *Lloyd's* (New York: McGraw-Hill, 1952). vii 220 pp.

Grey, H. M., *Lloyd's Yesterday and Today* (1922). 115 pp.

Harding, V. and Metcalfe, P., *Lloyd's at Home: Part 1: The Background. Part 2: The Buildings* (Lloyd's, 1986). 168 pp.

Hodgson, G. M. T., *Lloyd's of London: A Reputation at Risk* (Allen Lane, 1984). 378 pp.

Mackie, J. M., *Lloyd's: The Gateway to Romance* (1937–9). 100 pp.

Straus, R., *Lloyd's: A Historical Sketch* (Hutchinson, 1937). 292 pp.

Worsley, F. A. and Griffith, G., *The Romance of Lloyd's from Coffee-House to Palace* (Hutchinson, 1932). 292 pp.

Wright, C. and Fayle, C. E., *A History of Lloyd's* (Macmillan, 1928). xxi 475 pp.

London & Lancashire Insurance Co. Ltd

—— *After Fifty Years (A Short History of the London & Lancashire Fire Insurance Company)* (1912). 61 pp.

Francis, E. V., *London and Lancashire History: The History of the London and Lancashire Insurance Company Limited* (Newman Neame, 1962). 171 pp.

London Assurance

Drew, B., *The London Assurance: A Chronicle* (1928). 155 pp.

Drew, B., *The London Assurance: A Second Chronicle* (1949). xv 334 pp.

Street, G. S., *The London Assurance, 1720–1920* (1920). 51 pp.

London Life Association Ltd

Condor, W. S., *The Story of the London Life Association Ltd* (The Firm, 1979). 304 pp.

McLarens

A history is currently being prepared.

Marine Insurance Co. Ltd

—— *The Marine Insurance Company Ltd 1836–1936* (Hazell, Watson & Viney, 1936). 81 pp.

Matthews Wrightson Group of Companies

—— *Irons in the Fire 1901–1951* (1952). 83 pp.

Medical Sickness Annuity & Life Assurance Society Ltd

Knapman, G. J., *Care for the Caring: Medical Sickness Annuity & Life Assurance Society Limited, 1884–1984* (Melland, 1984). 240 pp.

Municipal Mutual Insurance Ltd

McDonald, C. R., *Covering Seventy-Five Years: The Continuing Story of Municipal Mutual Insurance Ltd 1903–1978* (The Firm, 1978). xxiv 211 pp.

Watson, A. J. G., *The First Fifty Years: Being The Story of Municipal Insurance Ltd 1903–1953* (1953) 161 pp.

National Boiler & General Insurance Co.

Chaloner, W. H., *National Boiler 1864–1964: A Century of Progress in Industrial Safety* (The Firm, 1964). 68 pp.

National Farmers Union Mutual Insurance Society Ltd

Head, V., *A Triumph of Hope: The Story of the National Farmers Union Mutual Insurance Society Limited* (The Firm, 1985). 125 pp.

National Mutual Life Assurance Society

Finch, R. and Roberts, A., *The History of the National Mutual Life Assurance Society 1830–1930* (1930). 93 pp.

Recknell, G. H., *National Mutual Life Society* (1936). 53 pp. [Foreword by J. M. Keynes.)

Street, E. E. G., and Glenn, R., *The History of the National Mutual Life Assurance Society 1830–1980* (The Society, 1980). v 122 pp.

National Provident Institution for Mutual Life Assurance

Hazell, S., *A Record of The First Hundred Years of the National Provident Institution 1835–1935* (Cambridge University Press, 1935). 96 pp.

Toulson, Norman, *The Squirrel and the Clock: The National Provident Institute 1835–1985* (Melland, 1985).

National Vulcan Engineering Insurance Group Ltd

Chaloner, W. H., *Vulcan, The History of One Hundred Years of Engineering and Insurance 1859–1959* (privately printed, 1959). viii 65 pp.

Chaloner, W. H., *National Boiler 1864–1964: A Century of Progress in Industrial Safety* (privately printed, 1964). 68 pp.

Navigation & General Insurance Co.

Villiers, A., *'The Navigators' and the Merchant Navy* (Brown, Son & Ferguson, 1954). 58 pp.

North British & Mercantile Insurance Co. Ltd

—— *Centenary, 1809–1909* (The Firm, 1909). 75 pp.

Norwich Union Insurance Group

Bignold, Sir C. R., *Five Generations of the Bignold Family, 1760–1947, and Their Connection With the Norwich Union* (Batsford, 1948). 319 pp.

Blake, R. N. W., *Esto Perpetua: The Norwich Union Life Insurance Society* (Newman Neame, 1958). 117 pp.

Clark, G., *Peeps into the Past: Bicentenary of the Old Amicable Society and Centenary of the Norwich Union Life Office 1705–1908* (Jarrold, 1908). 81 pp.

Ryan, Roger J., 'A History of the Norwich Union Fire and Life Insurance Societies from 1797 to 1914' (University of East Anglia PhD, 1984).

Pearl Assurance plc

—— *Centenary Year* (1964). 112 pp.

—— *Pearl Assurance. An Illustrated History* (The Firm, 1990). 192 pp.

Phoenix Assurance plc

—— *History of the London Offices of the Company, 1782–1915* (1916). 103 pp.

—— *Phoenix in War Time* (1945).

—— *Phoenix Family Story* (1953). 156 pp.

Ashmead, J., *The Wings of the Phoenix* (The Firm, 1954). 142 pp.

Crocker, K. B., *Things Phoenix 1782–1982* (Phoenix Assurance Co. 1982). 80 pp.

Hurren, G., *Phoenix Renascent: A History of the Phoenix Assurance Company Limited 1782–1968 and of the Pelican Life Assurance Company* (The Company, 1973). xviii 173 pp.

Trebilock, C., *Phoenix Assurance and the Development of British Insurance: Volume One 1782–1870* (Cambridge University Press, 1986). 792 pp.

Poland (John) & Co.

Bruce, G., *Poland's at Lloyd's* (Melland, 1979). 160 pp.

Price, Forbes & Co. Ltd

—— *And at Lloyd's: The Story of Price, Forbes & Co. Ltd* (Harley Publishing Co. 1954). 71 pp.

Provident Mutual Life Assurance Association

Sherriff, F. H., *From then Till Now: A Short History of the Provident Mutual Life Assurance Association 1840–1940* (Nissen & Arnold, 1940). 122 pp.

Provincial Insurance Co. Ltd

—— *Cover – Jubilee Issue 1953* (1953).

Westall, Oliver M., *The Provincial Insurance Company 1903–1938: Family, Markets and Competitive Growth* (Manchester University Press, 1993). 480 pp.

Prudential Assurance Company Ltd

Barnard, R. W., *A Century of Service: The Story of the Prudential 1848–1948* (The Firm, 1948). viii, 139 pp.

Boisseau, H. E., *The Prudential Staff and the Great War* (The Firm, 1938).

Hosking, G. L., *Salute to Service: The Prudential in the Second World War* (1947). xii 146 pp.

Plaisted, H., *Prudential Past and Present: Story of the Rise and Progress of the Prudential Assurance Company* (C. & E. Layton, 1917). vii 262 pp.

Railway Passengers' Assurance Co.

Cox, F. H., (compiler), *The Oldest Accident Office in the World 1849–1949* (1950). 67 pp.

Refuge Assurance plc

Clegg, C., *Friend in Deed: The History of a Life Assurance Office from 1858 as the Refuge Friend in Deed Life Assurance and Sick Fund Friendly Society to 1958 as the Refuge Assurance Co. Ltd* (Stone & Cox, 1958). xvii 160 pp.

Robins Davies & Little

Carter, E. F. Cato, *The Real Business* (Clowes, 1972). xii 264 pp.

Rock Life Assurance Co.

—— *Life Assurance in the 19th Century, As Illustrated by the Rock Life Assurance Co., Established 1806* (1901). viii 105 pp.

—— *Centenary 1806 (to) 1906* (The Company, 1906). 140 pp.

Royal Exchange Assurance

Mason, A. E. W., *The Royal Exchange: A Note on the Occasion of the Bicentenary of the Royal Exchange Assurance* (1920). 103 pp.

Supple, B. E., *The Royal Exchange Assurance: A History of British Insurance 1720–1970* (Cambridge University Press, 1970). xx 584 pp.

Royal Insurance (UK) Ltd

—— *Fire Insurance and the City of Liverpool* (1903).

—— *Old Lombard Street: Some Notes by the Company on the Occasion of the Opening of Their New Building* (1912). 55 pp.

Royal London Mutual Insurance Society Ltd

Allen, W. G., *We the Undersigned: A History of the Royal London Mutual Insurance Society and Its Times, 1861–1961* (Newman Neame, 1961). 80 pp.

Royal United Kingdom Beneficent Association

Mande, E. J. (ed.) *The Story of the Royal United Kingdom Beneficent Association 1863–1963* (The Firm, 1963). v 86 pp.

Salvation Army Assurance Society

Watson, B., *A Unique Society: A History of the Salvation Army Assurance Society Ltd* (Salvationist Publishing, 1968). 135 pp.

Scottish Amicable Life Assurance Society

Worland, H. S. and Patterson, M. D., *A History of Scottish Amicable Life Assurance Society 1826–1976: SALAS 150* (Glasgow, 1976). 128 pp.

Scottish Equitable Life Assurance Society

McInroy, C. C., *Scottish Equitable Life Assurance Society 1831–1980*
(The Firm, 1981). 92 pp.

Scottish Life Assurance Co.

Denholm, J. M., *One Hundred Years of Scottish Life: A History of the
Scottish Life Assurance Company 1881–1981* (Chambers, 1981).
155 pp.

Scottish Mutual Assurance Society

Magnusson, Mamie, *A Length of Days: The Scottish Mutual Assurance
Society 1883–1983* (Melland, 1983). 154 pp.

Scottish Provident Institution

Lindsay, M., *Count All Men Mortal: A History of Scottish Provident
1837–1987* (Edinburgh, 1987). 224 pp.

Stenart, M. D., *The Scottish Provident Institution 1837–1937*
(The Firm, 1937). 56 pp.

Scottish Union & National Insurance Co.

Gray, W. F., *A Brief Chronicle of the Scottish Union & National
Insurance Company 1824–1924* (The Firm, 1924). 192 pp.

Scottish Widows' Fund

—— *Life Assurance . . . the Origins, Constitution and Early History of
the Scottish Widows' Fund and Life Assurance Society* (The Firm,
1901). 160 pp.

Maxwell, Sir H., *Annals of the Scottish Widows' Fund Life Assurance
Society During One Hundred Years 1815–1914* (The Firm, 1914).
139 pp.

Shipowners' Mutual Protection Society

—— *The History and Development of Protecting and Indemnity Clubs: Report* (Insurance Institute of London, 1951?). 55 pp.

Standard Life Assurance Co.

Schooling, Sir W., *The Standard Life Assurance Company 1825–1925* (Blackwoods, 1925). 122 pp.

Sterling Offices Ltd

—— *A History of Reinsurance with Sidelights on Insurance* (1927).

Sun Life Assurance Group

Baumer, E., *The Early Days of the Sun Fire Office* (Causton, 1910). 71 pp.

Dickson, P. G. M., *The Sun Insurance Office 1710–1960* (Oxford University Press, 1960). 324 pp.

Minnitt, J., *The Sun Life Story* (The Firm, 1985). 111 pp.

Schull, J., *The First Hundred Years of Sun Life Assurance Company of Canada* (The Firm, 1971). 158 pp.

Sunderland Marine Mutual Insurance Co. Ltd

Beaver, P., *Sunderland Marine Mutual Insurance: The First Hundred Years 1882–1982* (Publications for Companies, 1982). 56 pp.

Tatham Bromage & Co. Ltd

—— *Tatham's Log 1858–1958* (1958). 100 pp.

Thames & Mersey Marine Insurance Co. Ltd

—— *Thames & Mersey Marine Insurance Co. Ltd 1860–1960* (1960). 79 pp. (A centenary account.)

Union Marine & General Insurance Co. Ltd

—— *Centennial Story 1863–1963* (1963). 99 pp.

United Kingdom Provident Institution

Withers, H. and Nicholas, C. (eds), *Pioneers of British Life Assurance* (Staples, 1951). 112 pp. [pp. 84–100 refer to the Institution.]

Vulcan Boiler and General Insurance Co. Ltd

Chaloner, W. H., *Vulcan: The History of One Hundred Years of Engineering and Insurance 1859–1959* (The Firm, 1959). 70 pp.

Westminster Fire Office

Davies, E. A., *An Account of the Formation and Early Years of Westminster Fire Office* (Country Life Ltd, 1952). 90 pp.

The Widows' Fund Association

McLachlan, H., *The Widows' Fund Association (Established 1764): An Historical Sketch 1764–1937* (1938).

Yorkshire Insurance Co. Ltd: *now part of* General Accident

Raine, A., *100 Years: The Centenary of the Yorkshire Insurance Company Limited 1824–1924* (The Firm, 1924). 51 pp.

Iron and Steel

General

Ashton, T. S., *Iron and Steel in the Industrial Revolution* (Manchester University Press, 1963). (3rd edition.)

Barraclough, K. C., *Steelmaking 1850–1900* (Institute of Metals, 1990). viii 320 pp.

Birch, Alan, *The Economic History of the British Iron and Steel Industry 1784–1879* (Cass, 1967).

Boswell, Jonathan S., *Business Policies in the Making. Three Steel Companies Compared* (Allen & Unwin, 1983). 241 pp.

Burn, D., *The Economic History of Steel-Making 1867–1939: A Study in Competition* (Cambridge University Press, 1940). x 548 pp.

Burn, D., *The Steel Industry 1939–1959: A Study in Competition and Planning* (Cambridge University Press, 1966). xvi 728 pp.

Carr, J. C. and Taplin, W., *History of the British Steel Industry* (Blackwell, 1962). xii 632 pp.

Cottrell, Elizabeth, *The Giant with Feet of Clay: The British Steel Industry 1945–1981* (Centre for Policy Studies, 1981). vi 222 pp.

Flinn, M. W., *Men of Iron: The Crowleys in the Early Iron Industry* (Edinburgh University Press, 1962). xii 270 pp.

Payne, Peter L., *Colvilles and the Scottish Steel Industry* (Clarendon Press, 1979). xxi 458 pp.

Accles & Pollock

Accles & Pollock, *Accles & Pollock 1899–1974: The First Seventy-Five Years of Achievement* (The Firm, 1974). 222 pp.

Accles & Pollock, *Have you a Transport Handy? Jubilee Brochure 1899–1949* (The Firm, 1949). 90 pp.

Allied Cromfounders Ltd

Tripp, B. H., *Grand Alliance: A Chapter of Industrial History* (Chantry Publications, 1951). 56 pp.

Appleby–Frodingham Steel Co.

—— *Appleby–Frodingham Steel Company: A Technical Survey* (Industrial Newspapers, 1965). 378 pp.

Walshaw, G. R. and Behrendt, C. A. J., *The History of Appleby–Frodingham* (The Firm, 1950). x 172 pp.

Bain (William) & Co. Ltd

House, J., *Lochrin's Hundred Years: The Story of William Bain of Coatbridge* (The Firm, 1959). 91 pp.

Balfour (Arthur) & Co. Ltd

—— *Arthur Balfour & Co. Ltd: A Centenary 1865–1965* (The Firm, 1967). 80 pp.

Bennetts' Iron Foundry Co. Ltd

—— *Souvenir Programme: Dinner and Social Evening* (17 December 1937). [Includes a brief history of the firm.]

Black Dyke Mills

Sigsworth, E. M., *Black Dyke Mills: A History* (Liverpool University Press, 1958). xvii 385 pp.

Braby Group

Richardson, J. E., *Chronicles of Fitzroy Works and of Frederick Braby & Co. Ltd* (The Firm, 1925). 338 pp.

British Steel

Tolliday, S., *Business, Banking and Politics: The Case of British Steel 1918–1939* (Harvard University Press, 1987) 455 pp.

Vaizey, J., *The History of British Steel* (Weidenfeld & Nicolson, 1974). xviii 205 pp.

Briton Ferry Ironworks

Roberts, C. W., *A Legacy from Victorian Enterprise: The Briton Ferry Ironworks and the Daughter Companies* (Alan Sutton, 1983). x 277 pp.

Brockhouse, J. & Co.

Mackenzie, E. M. C., *Brockhouse: A Study in Evolution* (The Firm, 1945). 54 pp.

Bromford Iron & Steel Co.

Gale, W. K. V., *A History of Bromford 1780–1980* (Publicitywise, 1983). 66 pp.

Brown (John) & Co. Ltd: *see also* Brown (John) (Engineering) Ltd *in* 'Engineering' (p. 109) *and in* 'Shipping and General Merchants' (p. 255) *and* Firth & Brown *below*

Grant, Sir Allan J., *Steel and Ships: The History of John Brown's* (Michael Joseph, 1950). 97 pp.

—— *General Description of the Works and Products of John Brown and Company Ltd Atlas Works, Sheffield* (The Firm, 1924). 84 pp.

Brown & Tawse plc

Mantle, J., *Brown & Tawse: An Illustrated History* (James & James, 1989). 64 pp.

Bruntons

Adam, A. T., *Bruntons 1876–1962* (The Firm, 1962). 83 pp.

Butterley Co.

Mottram, R. H. and Coote, C. R., *Through Five Generations: The History of the Butterley Company* (Faber, 1950). 181 pp.

Riden, Philip J., *The Butterley Company 1790–1830: A Derbyshire Ironworks in the Industrial Revolution* (The Author, 1973). 63 pp.

Cammell & Co.: see **Wilson Cammell,** below

Carrick & Brockbank

—— *History of the Firm 1854–1927* (1928).

Carron Company

Campbell, Roy Hutcheson, *Carron Company* (Oliver & Boyd, 1961). xi 346 pp.

—— *Carron Company 1759–1959* (The Company, 1959). 63 pp.

Clay Cross Co.

—— *A Hundred Years of Enterprise: Centenary of the Clay Cross Company 1837–1937* (The Firm, 1937). 52 pp.

Coalbrookdale

Raistrick, A., *Dynasty of Ironfounders: The Darbys of Coalbrookdale* (Sessions Book Trust, in association with the Ironbridge Gorge Museum Trust, 1989; reprint of 1953 edn.). xvi 331 pp.

Trinder, B., *The Darbys of Coalbrookdale* (Phillimore, 1974). 79 pp.

Cohen (George) & Sons

—— *One Hundred Years 1834–1934* (The Firm, 1934). 244 pp.

Coltness Iron Co.

Carvel, J., *A Study in Private Enterprise* (Constable, 1948). viii 200 pp.

Macleod, W. H., and Houldsworth, H. H., *The Beginnings of the Houldsworth of Coltness* (Jackson, 1937). vx 164 pp.

Colvilles

Payne, Peter L., *Colvilles and the Scottish Steel Industry* (Clarendon Press, 1979). xxi 458 pp.

Consett Iron

—— *Leaves from Consett Iron Company Letter Books 1887–1893* (The Firm, 1962). 192 pp.

Hornsby, R. M., *History of the Consett Iron Company* (The Firm, 1958).

Warren, L., *Consett Iron, 1840 to 1980: A Study in Industrial Location* (Oxford University Press, 1990). 206 pp.

Crawleys of Stourbridge

Flinn, M. W., *Men of Iron: The Crowleys in the Early Iron Industry* (Edinburgh University Press, 1962). xiii 270 pp.

Crawshay Dynasty

Addis, J. P., *A Study in Industrial Organisation and Development, 1765–1867* (University of Wales Press, 1957). 184 pp.

Dallmellington Iron Co.

Smith, D. L., *The Dallmellington Iron Company: Its Engineers and Men* (David & Charles, 1967). 256 pp.

Dorman, Long & Co. Ltd

—— *Works on the North-East Coast of Dorman, Long & Company Limited* (The Firm, 1937). 74 pp.

Wilson, C., *A Man and His Times and – A Memoir of Sir Ellis Hunter* (1962). 54 pp.

Dowlais Iron Co.

Elsas, M. (ed.), *Iron in the Making: Dowlais Iron Company Letters 1782–1860* (Glamorgan County Records Office, 1960). 260 pp.

Owen, John A., *The History of the Dowlais Ironworks 1759–1970* (Starling Press, 1977). 161 pp. [Based on the author's earlier book, *The History of the Dowlais Ironworks 1759–1936*, 1972.]

Firth (Thomas) & Brown (John) Ltd: *see also* Brown (John) & Co. Ltd *above*

—— *100 Years in Steel: Being an Account of the History and Progress of the Firm of John Brown & Co. Ltd and Thomas Firth & Sons Ltd from Their Earliest Beginnings to the Celebration of the Centenary 1937* (T. Firth & J. Brown, 1937). 76 pp.

Marshall, A. C. and Newbould, H., *The History of Firth's 1834–1918* (1924). 112 pp.

—— *Firth Brown, Thomas Firth and John Brown Ltd* (Firth Brown, 1954). 68 pp.

Fisher & Ludlow

—— *F&L 100: The Story of a Hundred Purposeful Years* (S. D. Toon, 1950). 52 pp.

Fox (Samuel) & Co. Ltd

Moxon, S., *A Fox Centenary: Umbrella Frames 1848–1948* (1948). 56 pp.

Guest Keen & Nettlefold

—— *Guest Keen & Nettlefold: An Outline History of this Group of Companies* (The Company, c. 1925).

—— *Guest Keen Baldwins Iron & Steel Co. Ltd* (1937). 68 pp.

Jones, E., *A History of Guest Keen & Nettlefold. Volume 1: 1760–1918* (Macmillan, 1987). 442 pp.

Jones, E., *A History of Guest Keen & Nettlefold (GKN).* Volume 2: *The Growth of a Business, 1918–1945* (Macmillan, 1990). xxxvii 389 pp.

Johnson (Richard) & Nephew

Johnson, Michael, *The Part We Play: History of the Company* (The Company, 1947). 71 pp.

Seth-Smith, M., *Two Hundred Years of Richard Johnson and Nephew* (The Company, 1973). xiv 292 pp.

King & Co. Ltd

Spring, A. E., *The Bicentenary of the House of Kings* (privately printed, 1946).

Lucy (W.) & Co. Ltd

Andrews, P. W. S. and Brunner, E., *The Eagle Ironworks, Oxford: The Story of W. Lucy and Company Limited* (Mills & Boon, 1965). 64 pp.

Lysaght (John)

—— *The Lysaght Century 1857–1957* (The Firm, 1957). 64 pp.

McArthur Group

Torrens, H. S., *Men of Iron: The History of the McArthur Group* (The Firm, 1984). 76 pp.

Marsh Brothers & Co.

Pollard, S., *Three Centuries of Sheffield Steel: The Story of a Family Business* (Marsh Brothers, 1954). x 82 pp.

Marshall (William) Sons & Co.

Lane, M. R., *The Story of Britannia Iron Works: A History of William Marshall & Co., Gainsborough* (Quiller, 1993). 224 pp.

Nicholl's

Mclean, D., *Nichol's Ironmaking in the Forest of Dean* (1981). 82 pp.

Osborn (Samuel) & Co. Ltd

Osborn, F. M., *The Story of the Mushets* [Whitecliff Iron Works] (Nelson, 1952). xii, 195 pp.

Seed, T. A., *Pioneers for a Century 1852–1952: A History of the Growth and Achievement of Samuel Osborn & Co. Ltd* (Sheffield, 1952). 82 pp.

Park Gate Iron and Steel Co. Ltd

Royston, G. P., *A History of the Park Gate Iron and Steel Co. Ltd 1823–1923* (1924). 96 pp.

Pressed Steel Co. Ltd

—— *Pressed Steel Co. Ltd* (The Firm, 1960?). 69 pp.

Round Oak Steel Works Ltd

Knox, C., *Steel at Brierley Hill 1857–1957: Round Oak Steel Works Ltd* (Newman Neame, 1957). 73 pp.

Sheffield Smelting Co. Ltd

Wilson, R. E., *A History of the Sheffield Smelting Company Limited, 1760–1960* (Ernest Benn, 1960). 316 pp.

Shotts Iron Company Ltd

Muir, Augustus, *The Story of Shotts* (1954). vii 59 pp.

Skelton (C. J.) & Co.

—— *Announcing One Hundred Years of Progress 1855 and 1955* (The Firm, 1955).

Skinningrove Iron Company Ltd

Willis, W. G., *Skinningrove Iron Company Ltd: A History* (The Firm, 1968?) ix 54 pp.

Smith & Jackson Ltd

Jones, P. d'A. and Simons, E. N., *The Story of the Saw 1760–1960: Published to Mark the Second Centenary of the World's Oldest Sawmakers* (1961). 80 pp.

Smith & Wellstood Ltd

Borthwick, A., *Ironfounders 1854–1954* (The Firm, 1954). 89 pp.

Smith's Stamping Works

Muir, Augustus, *Smith–Clayton Forge, Lincoln: 75 Years. A Record of Progress* (1958). 104 pp.

Smiths of Chesterfield

Robinson, P. M., *The Smiths of Chesterfield: A History of the Griffin Foundry, Brampton 1775–1833* (The Firm, 1957). 104 pp.

The South Durham Steel and Iron Co. Ltd

Willis, W. G., *The South Durham Steel and Iron Co. Ltd* (Eyre & Spottiswoode, 1969). 54 pp.

Sterne (L.) & Co. Ltd

Beale, Sir Samuel, *The Crown Iron Works 1874–1949* (1951). 85 pp.

Stothert & Pitt: *see in* 'Engineering' (p. 124)

Stubs Wood & Co.

Ashton, T. S., *An Eighteenth-Century Industrialist: Peter Stubs of Warrington* (Manchester University Press, 1939). x 156 pp. (Reprinted 1961 and 1964.)

Taskers (Andover)

Rolt, L. T. C., *Waterloo Ironworks: A History of Taskers of Andover, 1809–1968* (David & Charles, 1969). 240 pp.

TI Metsec

—— *TI Metsec: 1931–1981: Steel Components for the World's Industries* (Melland, 1981). 56 pp.

Thomas (Richard)

Wainwright, D., *Men of Steel: A History of Richard Thomas and His Family* (Quiller, 1986). 150 pp.

Thomas (Richard) & Baldwins

—— *Into the Future* (The Firm, 1962). 57 pp.

United Steel Companies Ltd

Andrews, P. W. S. and Brunner, E., *Capital Development in Steel: A Study of the United Steel Companies Ltd* (1951). 374 pp.

—— *The Products of United Steel* (The Firm, 195?). 71 pp.

—— *This is United Steel: A General Review of the United Steel Companies Limited* (The Firm, 1960). 55 pp.

Peddie, R., *The United Steel Companies Ltd, 1918–1968: A History* (Nicholls & Co. Ltd, 1969). 70 pp.

Vaizey, J., *The History of British Steel* (Weidenfeld & Nicolson, 1974). xvii, 205 pp.

Vulcan; *see also* in 'Engineering' (p. 125)

—— *Built by Stephenson: The Early History of the Vulcan Foundry Ltd and Stephenson & Hawthorne Ltd* (1958). 214 pp.

Docherty, C., *Steel and Steelworks: The Sons of Vulcan* (Heinemann, 1983). x 247 pp.

Webster & Horsfall

Horsfall, John H. C., *The Iron Masters of Penns 1720–1970* (Roundwood Press, 1971). xii 311 pp.

Wilson Cammell: *see also* **Cammell Laird** in 'Shipping and General Merchants' (p. 256)

Austin, J. and Ford, M., *Steel Town: Dronfield and Wilson Cammell 1873–1983* (Scarsdale Publications, 1983). 118 pp.

—— *Charles Cammell & Co. Ltd* (Charles Cammell & Co. Ltd, 1900).

Workington Iron & Steel Co.

—— *Workington Iron & Steel Co.: Branch of the United Steel Companies Ltd* (The Firm, n.d.). 144 pp.

Law Firms

General

Kirk, H., *Portrait of a Profession: A History of the Solicitor's Profession, 1100 to the Present Day* (Oyez, 1976). ix 218 pp.

Robson, Robert, *The Attorney in 18th Century England* (1959).

Williams, Peter Howell, *A Gentleman's Calling – The Liverpool Attorney-at-Law* (Incorporated Law Society of Liverpool, 1980). [Includes Laces & Co., Brabner Holden, Woodcock & Sons.]

Birmingham Law Society

Butts, G.M., *A Short History of the Birmingham Law Society 1818–1968* (privately printed, 1968).

Boodle Hatfield & Co.

Belcher, V., *Boodle Hatfield & Co.: The History of a London Law Firm in Three Centuries* (privately printed, 1985). 175 pp.

Clifford Chance: *an amalgamation of Clifford-Turner and Coward Chance*

Scott, J., *Legibus: A History of Clifford-Turner 1900–1980* (King Thorne & Stace Ltd, 1980). 211 pp.

Slinn, Judy A., *Clifford Chance: Its Origins and Development* (Granta Editions, 1993).

Dundas & Wilson C.S.

Burns, D., *Dundas & Wilson, C. S.: The First Two Hundred Years* (The Firm, 1987). 71 pp.

Ellis, Wood, Bickersteth and Hazel

Read, J., *Ellis, Wood, Bickersteth and Hazel 1883–1983* (The Firm, 1983). 54 pp.

Frere Cholmeley & Nicholsons

—— *The Story of a Law Firm* (1950).

—— *Frere Cholmeley 1750–1980* (John Roberts Press, 1981). 55 pp.

Freshfields

Slinn, Judy A., *A History of Freshfields* (privately printed, 1984). 208 pp.

Grays of York

Cobb, W., *A History of Grays of York 1695–1988* … (William Sessions, 1989). 234 pp.

Gregory, Rowcliffe & Co.

Davis, Patrick, *Number One: A History of the Firm of Gregory, Rowcliffe & Co., 1784–1984* (The Firm, 1984). 80 pp.

Incorporated Law Society of Liverpool

Williams, Peter H., *A Gentleman's Calling. The Liverpool Attorney-at-Law* (privately printed, 1980).

Linklaters & Paines

Slinn, Judy A., *Linklaters & Paines: The First Hundred and Fifty Years* (Longman, 1988). 260 pp.

Manchester Law Society

Atkinson, Kenneth H., *A Short History of the Manchester Law Society 1838–1924* (privately printed, 1924).

Mills & Reeve

Jackson, C., *A Cambridge Bicentenary: The History of a Legal Practice 1789–1989* (Morrow & Co., 1990). xix 324 pp.

Norton Rose

Dr Andrew St George is currently preparing a history of Norton Rose. Publication with Granta Editions is planned for 1995.

Slaughter and May

Dennett, Laurie, *Slaughter and May. A Century in the City* (Granta Editions, 1989). xvii 282 pp.

Dennett, Laurie, *Slaughter and May. A Short History* (Granta Editions, 1989). xi 97 pp.

Taylor & Humbert

Drummond, D., *Taylor & Humbert, 1722–1982: A Short History* (The Firm, 1982). xiv 79 pp.

Wilde Sapte

Salman, A. G., *The History of Wilde Sapte* (privately printed, 1985). 189 pp.

Leisure and Media

[*Including Cinema, Music, Newspapers (selected histories only), Television, Radio. See also separate lists for Hotels, Printing and Publishing, Booksellers, Paper manufacturers*]

MISCELLANEOUS

Bassett–Lowke

Fuller, R., *The Bassett–Lowke Story* (New Cavendish, 1984). 352 pp. [Toys.]

Bishop (J. C.) & Son

Elvin, L., *Bishop and Son, Organ Builders: The Story of J. C. Bishop and His Successors* (The Author, 1984). 356 pp.

Broadwood (John) & Sons

Wainwright, David, *Broadwood by Appointment: A History* (Quiller Press, 1982). 360 pp.

Exchange Telegraph Co. Ltd

Scott, J. M., *Extel 100: The Centenary History of the Exchange Telegraph Company* (Ernest Benn, 1972). 239 pp.

Ilford Ltd

Hercock, R. J. and Jones, G. A., *Silver by the Ton: The History of Ilford Ltd 1879–1979* (McGraw-Hill, 1979). 170 pp.

Ladbrokes

Kaye, R. and Peskett, R., *The Ladbrokes Story* (1969). 304 pp.

Lehmann (E. P.)

Cieslik, J. and Cieslik, M., *Lehmann Toys: The History of E. P. Lehmann 1881–1981* (New Cavendish, 1982). 220 pp.

Lines Bros

Lines, W., *Looking Backwards and Forwards, Being a Short History* (The Firm, 1958). 76 pp. [Toys and Sports Goods.]

Littlewoods

—— *From This Pool a Sword* (Standard Art Book Co., 194?). 87 pp.

Nathan

—— *Costumes by Nathan* (Newnes, 1960). 207 pp.

Pineapple

Moore, D., *When a Woman Means Business* (Pavilion, 1989). 155 pp.

Willis (Henry) & Sons Ltd

Sumner, W. L., *Father Henry Willis* (privately printed, 1955). 64 pp.

CINEMA, RADIO, RECORDING AND TELEVISION

General

The Independent Television Commission (70 Brompton Road, London SW3 1EY) has compiled a bibliography of major reports by consulting research organisations, entitled 'The Broadcasting Industry in the United Kingdom, 1979–1992', including reports analysing future trends in the broadcasting industry.

Cable, J., *The Tuppeny Punch and Judy Show: 25 Years of TV Commercials* (Michael Joseph, 1980). 192 pp.

Geddes, K. and Bussey, G., *The Setmakers: A History of the Radio and Television Industry* (British Radio & Electronic Equipment Manufacturers' Association, 1991). 464 pp.

Hind, J. and Mosco, S., *Rebel Radio: The Full Story of British Pirate Radio* (Pluto, 1985). 60 pp.

Oliver, E., *Researchers' Guide to British Film and Television Collections* (British Universities Film & Video Council, 1985). 176 pp.

Pocock, R. F., *The Early British Radio Industry* (Manchester University Press, 1988). 224 pp.

Taplin, Walter, *The Origin of Television Advertising in the United Kingdom* (1961).

Abbey Road Studios

Southall, Brian, *Abbey Road: The Story of the World's Most Famous Recording Studios* (Stephens, 1982). 217 pp. [Foreward by Paul McCartney.]

Anglia Television

—— *About Anglia '75* (Boydell Press, 1974). 128 pp.

—— ... *The First Twenty-One Years* (The Firm, 1980). 128 pp.

Border Television

Brown, A., *Tyne Tees Television: The First 20 Years* (The Firm, 1978). 80 pp.

British Broadcasting Corporation

Block, P., *The Biggest Aspidistra in the World: A Pictorial Celebration of 50 Years of the BBC* (BBC, 1972). 243 pp.

Briggs, Asa, *The History of Broadcasting in the United Kingdom* (Oxford University Press, 1979). Four volumes.

Briggs, Asa, *The BBC: A Short History of the First Fifty Years* (Oxford University Press, 1985).

Rawley, E., *BBC Engineering 1922–1972* (1972).

British Phonograph Committee

—— *The British Records: The Gramophone Record Industry's Services to the Nation from 1898* (1959). 64 pp.

Channel 5

Blanchard, S. (ed.), *The Challenge to Channel 5* (British Film Industries, 1990). 68 pp.

Channel Four

Blanchard, S. and Morley, D., *What's This Channel Four? An Alternative Report* (1982). 186 pp.

Isaacs, J., *Storm Over 4: A Personal Account* (Weidenfeld & Nicolson, 1989). viii 215 pp.

Lambert, S., *Channel Four: Television with a Difference?* (British Film Institute, 1982). 178 pp.

Channel Television

—— *CT21: Channel Television, A Special (21st) Anniversary Publication* (Channel Islands Communications (Television), 1983). 62 pp.

Decca Record Co. Ltd

Lewis, E. R., *No C(apital) I(ssues) C(ommittee): A History of the Decca Record Company* (1956). 95 pp.

Ealing Studios

Perry, G., *Forever Ealing: A Celebration of the Great British Studio* (Pavilion Books, 1985). 208 pp.

EMI

Miller, R., *The Incredible Music Machine* (Quartet, 1982). 288 pp.

Goldcrest Films

Eberts, J and I. T., *My Indecision is Final: The Rise and Fall of Goldcrest Films* (Faber, 1990). 220 pp.

Granada Television

—— *Year One: An Account of the First Year of Operation of an Independent Television Company in England* (1958). 117 pp.

—— *Year Ten: Granada Television 3 May 1956 – 3 May 1966* (The Company, 1966). 132 pp.

—— *As Others See It* (The Company, 1981). 69 pp.

—— *Granada: The First 25 Years* (British Film Institute, 1981). 132 pp.

Independent Television

Briggs, A. and Spicer, J., *The Franchise Affair: Creating Fortunes and Failures in Independent Television* (Century Hutchinson, 1986). iv 226 pp.

—— *Twenty-one Years of Independent Television 1955–1976* (Broadcast, 1976). 139 pp.

Davidson, A., *Under the Hammer: Greed and Glory Inside the TV Business* (1992).

Potter, J., *Independent Television in Britain* (1990). Four volumes.

Sendall, Bernard, *Independent Television in Britain* (Macmillan, 1982). Two volumes.

London Weekend Television

Doherty, D., *Running the Dhow: 21 Years of London Weekend Television* (Boxtree, 1990). vi 218 pp.

Taylor, E. D., *The Great TV Book: 21 Years of LWT* (Sidgwick & Jackson, 1989). 96 pp.

Murphy Radio

Long, J., *A First Class Job: The Story of Frank Murphy, Radio Pioneer* ... (Norfolk: The Author, 1985).

Odeon

Bruce, Sir Michael W. S., *The History of Odeon* (Odeon Theatres, 1937).

Pinewood Studios

Perry, G., *Movies from the Mansion: A History of Pinewood Studios* (Pavilion, 1986). 192 pp.

Pye

Bussey, G., *The Story of Pye Wireless* (The Company, 1979).

Radio Luxembourg

—— *Radio Luxembourg 1979: The Story of Radio Luxembourg Past and Present* (1979).

Nicholls, R., *Radio Luxembourg: The Station of the Stars* (1983).

Radio Times

Briggs, S., *The Radio Times* (Weidenfeld & Nicolson, 1981). 232 pp.

Rank Organisation plc

Wood, Alan, *Mr Rank: A Study of J. Arthur Rank and British Films* (Hodder & Stoughton, 1952). 228 pp.

Sony

Lyons, N., *The Sony Vision* (Crown Publishers, 1976).

Thames Television

—— *Twenty-One Years* (The Company, 1989). 68 pp.

TV-am

Leapman, M., *Treasury? The Power Struggle at TV-am* (Allen & Unwin, 1984). x 211 pp.

Yorkshire Television

—— *Yorkshire Television: The First 10 Years* (The Company, 1978). 80 pp.

PRESS

There are an enormous number of histories of individual newspapers and I could not possibly do justice to them here; I have therefore referred readers to an excellent bibliography and included only selected, individual books, published in the last five years.

General

Bourne, R., *Lords of Fleet Street* (Unwin Hyman, 1990). xi 258 pp.

Griffiths, Dennis M., *Encyclopaedia of the British Press* (Macmillan, 1992).

Linton, David and Boston, Ray, *The Newspaper Press in Britain: An Annotated Bibliography* (Mansell Publishing, 1987).

Barrow's Worcester Journal

—— *Tercentenary 1690–1990* (Reed Midland Newspapers, 1990).

Daily Telegraph

Hart-Davis, D., *The House the Berrys Built: Inside the Telegraph 1928–1986* (Hodder & Stoughton, 1990). 368 pp.

Financial Times

Kynaston, David, *The Financial Times: A Centenary History* (Viking, 1988). 554 pp.

The Illustrated London News

—— *150th Anniversary Issue* (May 1992). 220 pp.

Punch

—— *150th Anniversary Edition* (17 July 1991).

Reuters

Read, Donald, *The Power of News: The History of Reuters* (Oxford
University Press, 1992). 450 pp.

TRAVEL

General

Ward, C. and Hardy, D., *Goodnight Campers! The History of the British Holiday Camp* (Mansell, 1986). 256 pp.

Butlin's Ltd

Butlin, Sir William H. E. C. and Dacre, Peter, *The Billy Butlin Story: 'A Showman to the End'* (Robson Books, 1982). 287 pp.

North, Rex, *The Butlin Story* (Jarrold, 1962). 150 pp.

Read, S. and Haynes, B., *Hello Campers!* (Bantam Press, 1986). 176 pp.

Club Méditerranée

Franco, V., *The Club Méditerranée* (Shepherd Walwyn, 1972). iv 173 pp.

Cook (Thomas) Ltd

Brendon, P., *Thomas Cook: 150 Years of Popular Tourism* (Secker & Warburg, 1991). 372 pp.

Pudney, John, *The Thomas Cook Story* (Michael Joseph, 1953). 264 pp.

Swinglehurst, E., *The Romantic Journey: The Story of Thomas Cook and Victorian Travel* (Pica, 1974). 208 pp.

Swinglehurst, E., *Cook's Tours: The Story of Popular Travel* (Blandford, 1982). 192 pp.

Cunningham's Holiday Camp

Drower, J., *Good Clean Fun: The Story of Britain's First Holiday Camp* (Arcadia Books, 1982). 63 pp.

Eccles (Birmingham) Ltd

Noble, D., *Eccles Has A Jubilee: A Review of the 25 Years Steady Growth of Eccles (Birmingham) Ltd* (The Company, 1947). 64 pp.

Frame's Tours

Frame, J., *My Life of Globe-trotting* (Camelot Press, 1931). 127 pp.

Mays (A. T.)

Webster, J., *'Tis Better to Travel: The Story of A. T. Mays and the Tourist Revolution* (Mainstream Publishing, 1989). 155 pp.

Premier Travel Services

Linson, M. M. E. (ed.), *Premier's Progress 1936–1986: The History of Premier Travel Limited* (The Firm, 1986). 159 pp.

Metals

General

Hamilton, Henry, *The English Brass and Copper Industries to 1800* (Cass, 1967). (2nd edition with new introduction by J. R. Harris.)

Harris, J. R., *The Copper King* (Liverpool University Press, 1964). xiii 194 pp.

Hatcher, J. and Barker, T. C., *A History of British Pewter* (Longman, 1974).

Rowe, D. J., *The British Lead Manufacturing Industry 1778–1982* (Croom Helm, 1983). xiv 427 pp.

Aluminium Corporation Ltd

—— *Aluminium Corporation Ltd: Company History* (The Firm, 1983).

—— *Golden Jubilee, 1909–1959* (The Firm, 1959).

Aluminium Plant & Vessal Co. (A.P.V.)

(Dummett, G. A., *From Little Acorns: A History of the A.P.V. Company Ltd* (Hutchinson Benham, 1981). xiv 247 pp.

Anodising & Platings Ltd

—— *21st Anniversary: 7th February 1938–1959* (1959).

Bedford (John) & Sons Ltd

—— *J. Bedford & Sons: 150th Anniversary* (1942). 56 pp.

Best (R. H.)

—— *Best of Birmingham, Brass Chandelier* (Allen & Unwin, 1940). 251 pp.

Hiley, E. N., *Brass Saga* (Benn, 1947). xi 166 pp.

Bolton (Thomas) & Sons Ltd

Morton, J., *Thomas Bolton & Sons Ltd 1783–1983: The Bicentenary History of a Major Copper and Brass Manufacturer* (Moorland Publishing, 1983). 154 pp.

Borax (Holdings) Ltd: *see* Rio Tinto-Zinc Borax Ltd *in* 'Chemical Industry' (p. 72) and 'Mining' (p. 201)

British Aluminium

—— *The History of the British Aluminium Company Limited 1894–1955* (The Firm, 1955). 75 pp.

British Metal Corporation

Schmitz, *British Metal Corporation – An Outline* (Budd, 1959).

Brown & Englefield

Englefield, E., *A Treatise on Pewter and its Manufacture, together with a Brief Account of the Firm of Brown & Englefield, the Last of the Great General Pewter Manufacturing Firms of London* (Priory Press, 1933). 85 pp.

Delta Metal Co. Ltd

—— *The Delta Metal Company Ltd, London and Birmingham* (The Firm, 1930). 124 pp.

Gillette Industries

Coster, I., *The Sharpest Edge in the World: The Story of the Rise of a Great Industry* (The Firm, 1948). 78 pp.

Glacier Metal Co.

Jaques, Elliott, *The Changing Culture of a Factory* (1951).

Harlow (Robert) & Son Ltd

Harlow, Irma S., *The 125th Anniversary of Robert Harlow and Son Ltd, Stockport, Cheshire* (1958).

Holland (W. L.) Ltd

—— *Centenary Souvenir 1847–March 1947* (1947).

Johnson, Matthey & Co. Ltd

McDonald, D., *A History of Platinum: Johnson Matthey & Co. Ltd* (1960). 254 pp.

McDonald, D., *Percival Norton Johnson* (1951). 224 pp.

—— *An Industry Within Industry: The Place and Purpose of Johnson Matthey* (no date).

—— *History of Johnson Matthey* (1951).

McDonald, D., *The Johnsons of Maiden Lane* (Martins, 1964). 180 pp.

McDonald, D. and Hunt, L. B., *A History of Platinum and its Allied Metals* (The Firm, 1983). 460 pp.

London Metal Exchange

Economist Intelligence Unit Ltd, *The London Metal Exchange* (The Exchange, 1958). ix 224 pp.

Gibson-Jarvie, J. R. T., *The London Metal Exchange: A Commodity Market* (Woodhead Faulkner, 1983). xi 203 pp.

London (Quaker) Lead Co.

Raistrick, A., *Two Centuries of Industrial Welfare, 1692–1905* (1938). 152 pp.

Massey (B. & S.) Ltd

Janes, Hurford, *Sons of the Forge: The Story of B. & S. Massey Ltd 1861–1961* (Harley Publishing, 1962). 106 pp.

Metal Box plc

Moses, H., *A Short History of the Hudson Scott Branch of the Metal Box Company Ltd* (privately printed, 1962).

Reader, W. J., *Metal Box. A History* (Heinemann, 1976). xii 256 pp.

Metal Market and Exchange Co. Ltd

Economist Intelligence Unit, *The London Metal Exchange* (1958). 224 pp.

Orr's Zinc White

—— *Orr's Zinc White: The First Fifty Years at the Vine Works, Widnes* (The Firm, 1948). 61 pp.

Sheffield Smelting Co. Ltd

Wilson, R. E., *Two Hundred Precious Metal Years: A History of the Sheffield Smelting Co. Ltd 1760–1960* (Benn, 1960). xxii 316 pp.

Spear & Jackson

Jones, P. A., and Simons, E. N., *Story of the Saw: Spear & Jackson Limited 1760–1960* (Newson Neame, 1961). 80 pp.

Spencer–Clerk

—— *Spencer–Clerk Bi-Centenary: 200 Years of Metal Craftsmanship* (The Firm, 1978).

Star Aluminium Co.

—— *The First Twenty-Five Years 1933/4–1958/9* (The Firm, 1960).

Vivian, Younger & Bond Ltd

Harrison, G. P., *VYB: A Century of Metal Broking, 1859–1959* (The Firm, 1959). 103 pp.

Ward (T. W.) Ltd

—— *Fifty Years of Progress 1878–1928* (The Company, 1928). 52 pp.

—— *Sixty Years Service 1878–1938* (The Company, 1938). 76 pp.

—— *End of a Chapter: A Brief Record of Thomas W. Ward Ltd and its Subsidiary Companies During the War Years 1939–1945* (The Company, 1946). 80 pp.

—— *Outline of Progress 1870–1953* (The Company, 1953).

—— *The Ward Group of Companies: Products and Services* (The Company, 1959). 67 pp.

—— *Ward at Work: Pictorial Survey of Recent Activities of the Ward Group of Companies* (The Company, 1962). 160 pp.

—— *Round Britain with Wards* (The Company, 1967). 134 pp.

Mining

[*Including Coal, Metals, Gems: see also Metals, Iron and Steel for manufacturing*]

General

Ashton, T. S. and Sykes, J., *The Coal Industry in the Eighteenth Century* (Manchester University Press, 1964).

Ashworth, W. and Pegg, W., *The History of the British Coal Industry, vol. 5: The Nationalised Industry, 1946–1982* (Clarendon Press, 1986). xix 710 pp.

Barry, A. (ed.), *Aluminium, 1886–1986* (Morgan Grampian, 1986). 98 pp.

Benson, J., Neville, R. G. and Thompson, C. H., *Bibliography of the British Coal Industry* (Oxford University Press, 1981). 760 pp.

Burt, Roger (ed.), *Cornish Mining: Essays on the Organisation of Cornish Mines and the Cornish Mining Economy* (David & Charles, 1969).

Church, R. A., *The History of the British Coal Industry, vol. 3: 1830–1913, Victorian Pre-Eminence* (Oxford University Press, 1986). 800 pp.

Flinn, Michael W. and Stoker, David, *The History of the British Coal Industry, vol. 2: 1700–1830, The Industrial Revolution* (Clarendon Press, 1984). [Volume 2 is the first volume to appear in an extensive history commissioned by the National Coal Board.]

Galloway, R. L., *A History of Coal Mining in Great Britain* (1882; reprint, David & Charles, 1969). 286 pp.

Kirby, M. W., *The British Coal Mining Industry 1870–1946. A Political and Economic History* (Macmillan, 1977). vii 278 pp.

Nef, J. U., *The Rise of the British Coal Industry* (Routledge, 1932).

Supple, B., *The History of the British Coal Industry, vol. 4: 1913–1946, Political Economy of Decline* (Clarendon Press, 1987). 733 pp.

Alloa Coal Co.

Carvel, J. L., *One Hundred Years in Coal: The History of the Alloa Coal Company* (privately printed, 1944). 208 pp.

Barber Walker & Co. Ltd

Whitelock, G. C. H., *250 Years in Coal. The History of Barber Walker and Company Limited 1680–1946* (1955).

Cannock Chase Colliery Co.

Francis, J. R., *A History of Cannock Chase Colliery Company* (Staffordshire Industrial Archaeological Society, 1980). 73 pp.

Charrington, Gardner, Locket & Co.

Fraser-Stephen, E., *Two Centuries in the London Coal Trade: The Story of Charringtons* (The Firm, 1952). viii 157 pp.

Consolidated Goldfields

Johnson, P., *Consolidated: A Centenary Portrait* (Weidenfeld & Nicolson, 1987). 256 pp.

Consolidated Goldfields of South Africa Ltd

—— *The Gold Fields, 1887–1937* (The Company, 1937). viii 185 pp.

Cartwright, Alan Patrick, *Gold Paved the Way: The Story of the Goldfields Group of Companies* (Macmillan, 1967). x 326 pp.

Cornish Copper Co.

Pasco, W. H., *CCC: The History of the Cornish Copper Company* (Dyllansow Truran, 1982). 222 pp.

The Diamond Trading Co. (Pty) Ltd

Chilvers, H. A., *The Story of De Beers* (Cassell, 1939). 344 pp.

Evans (Richard) & Co. Ltd.

—— *The Romance of Coal: Richard Evans & Co. Ltd, Haydock Collieries, St Helens, Lancs* (1928).

Fife Coal Co. Ltd

Muir, A., *Fife Coal Co. 1872–1946* (Fife, 1952). vii 133 pp.

Gunstonemaker

Teesdale, E., *Queen's Gunstonemaker* (Lindel, 1984). 125 pp.

Institution of Mining & Metallorgy

Wilson, R. A. J., *The Professionals* (The Institution, 1992) 348 pp.

Institution of Mining Engineers

Strong, G. R., *A History of the Institution of Mining Engineers 1889–1989* (The Institution, 1988) 124 pp.

Wilson, R. A. J., *The Professionals* (The Firm, 1992). 348 pp.

Leicestershire and South Derbyshire Coalfield

Owen, C. C., *The Leicestershire and South Derbyshire Coalfield, 1200–1900* (Moorland, 1984). 321 pp.

Lilleshall Co.

Gale, W. K. V. and Nicholls, C. R., *The Lilleshall Co. Ltd: A History 1764–1964* (The Firm, 1979). 134 pp.

London Coal Exchange

—— *Society of Coal Merchants. Historical Notes on the Exchange* (1950). 50 pp.

Smith, R., *Sea-Coal for London: History of the Coal Factors in the London Market* (1961). 388 pp.

Toovey, J. W., *The London Coal Exchange* (1957). 79 pp.

Lonrho plc

Cronje, Suzanne, Ling, Margaret and Cronje, Gillian, *Lonrho: Portrait of a Multinational* (Friedman in association with Penguin Books, 1976). 316 pp.

Hall, Richard, *My Life with Tiny: A Biography of Tiny Rowland* (Faber, 1987). 257 pp.

—— *The Bond Group of Companies: A Financial Analysis* (The Firm, 1988). 93 pp.

—— *Bond Group Statement of Affairs: A Valuation of Group Operations* (The Firm, 1989). 154 pp.

Mining Engineering Co.

Howse, R. M. and Harley, F. H., *History of the Mining Engineering Company 1909–1959* (The Firm, 1959). 123 pp.

Moira Colliery Co.

Beaumont, P., *History of the Moira Collieries* (Bemrose, 1919). 130 pp.

Mond Nickel Co. Ltd: *see also* Imperial Chemical Industries plc Alkali Division (formerly Brunner Mond & Co. Ltd) *in* 'Chemical Industries' (pp. 70–1)

Goodman, Jean, *The Mond Legacy: A Family Saga* (Weidenfeld & Nicolson, 1982). 272 pp.

Sturney, A. C., *The Story of Mond Nickel* (privately printed, 1951). 63 pp.

Murex

Bird, E. A., *Murex: The History of a Company and its People* (The Firm, 1980). 80 pp.

Parys & Mona Mines

Harris, J., *The Copper King: A Biography of Thomas Willow of Clanidan* (Liverpool University Press, 1964). xiii, 194 pp.

Pease (J. & J. W.)

Campbell, R. H., *Men of Politics and Business: A History of the Quaker Pease Dynasty of North East England 1750–1939* (Allen & Unwin, 1981).

Powell Duffryn

—— *The Powell Duffryn Steam Coal Company Limited 1864–1914* (The Firm, 1914). 95 pp.

Rio Tinto-Zinc Corporation plc

—— *The Borax Story 1899–1953* (1953). 286 pp.

Avery, D., *Not on Queen Victoria's Birthday: The Story of the Rio Tinto Mines* (Collins, 1974). 464 pp.

Harvey, C. E., *The Rio Tinto Company: An Economic History of a Leading International Mining Concern, 1873–1954* (Alison Hodge, 1981). 390 pp.

Travis, N. J. and Cocks, E. J., *The Tincal Trail: A History of Borax* (Harrap, 1984). 311 pp.

West, Richard, *River of Tears: The Rise of the Rio Tinto-Zinc Mining Corporation Ltd* (Earth Island Ltd, 1972). 201 pp.

Stanton & Staveley

Chapman, S. D., *Stanton and Stavely: A Business History* (Woodhead
Faulkner, 1981). 240 pp.

Sutcliffe (Richard) Ltd

Sutcliffe, R. J. and Sutcliffe, E. D., *Richard Sutcliffe: The Pioneer of
Underground Belt Conveying* (The Firm, 1955). 143 pp.

Motor Industry and Bicycles

[Including Automobile Engineering]

General

Hopwood, A., *Whatever Happened to the British Motorcycle Industry* (Haynes, 1981). 315 pp.

Lowe, J. (comp.), *Register of Business Records of Coventry and Related Areas* (Department of Politics and History, Lanchester (now Coventry) Polytechnic, 1977).

Lowe, J., *A Guide to Sources in the History of the Cycle and Motor Industries in Coventry 1880–1939* (Coventry Polytechnic, 1982). 108 pp.

Richardson, K., *The British Motor Industry 1896–1939* (Macmillan, 1977). xiii 258 pp.

Turner, G., *The Car Makers* (Eyre & Spottiswoode, 1963). 262 pp.

AFN Ltd

Jenkinson, Denis, *From Chain Drive to Turbocharger* (Stephens, 1984). 312 pp.

Alfa Romeo

Hill, P. and Slater, H. R., *Alfa Romeo: A History* (Cassell, 1965). 512 pp.

Alvis Ltd

Day, K., *Alvis – The Story of the Red Triangle* (Gentry Books, 1981). 335 pp.

Armstrong Siddeley

Cook, R., *Armstrong Siddeley: The Parkside Story, 1896–1939* (Rolls-Royce Heritage Trust, 1988). 139 pp.

Redman, M., *The Evening and the Morning* (Toon & Heath, 1957).
  103 pp.

Aston Martin Ltd

Courtney, Geoff, *The Power Behind Aston Martin* (Oxford Illustrated
  Press). x 134 pp.

Austin Motor Co. Ltd: Austin Rover

—— *1905–1955 Our First Fifty Years* (1955). 87 pp.

Church, R. A., *Herbert Austin: The British Motor Car Industry to 1941*
  (Europa Publications Ltd, 1979). iii 233 pp.

Williams, K. and others, *The Breakdown of Austin Rover: A Case-Study
  in the Failure of Business Strategy and Industrial Policy* (Leamington
  Spa: Berg, 1987). 150 pp.

Wyatt, Robert J., *The Austin 1905–1952* (David & Charles, 1981).
  298 pp.

Barker & Co.

—— *From Chariot to Car* (1930). 74 pp.

Bentley Motors Ltd

Bentley, Walter Owen, *An Illustrated History of the Bentley Car* (Allen &
  Unwin, 1964). 192 pp.

Frostick, M., *Bentley: From Cricklewood to Crewe* (Osprey Publishing,
  1980). 240 pp.

Birmingham Small Arms Co.

—— *BSA Group News: Centenary Issue, June 7 1961* (The Firm, 1961).
  78 pp.

—— 'The History of the Birmingham Small Arms Company 1861–1973'
  (typescript at Solihull Central Library). Three volumes.

Davenport-Hines, Richard P. T., *Dudley Docker: The Life and Times of a Trade Warrier* (Cambridge University Press, 1984). 295 pp.

Frost, G. H., *Munitions of War: A Record of the BSA and Daimler Companies During the World War 1914–1918* (The Firm, 1921). 222 pp.

Holliday, R. R., *The Story of BSA Motor Cycles* (Patrick Stephens, 1978). 128 pp.

Ryerson, Barry, *The Giants of Small Heath: The History of Birmingham Small Arms* (Foulks, 1980). 190 pp.

Ward, D. M., *The Other Battle: Being a History of the Birmingham Small Arms Co. Ltd.* (The Firm, 1946). 180 pp.

British Leyland

—— *And Then – Tanks, And Still More Tanks: Being a Brief Record of the War Effort of Leyland Motors Ltd and its Foundries* (Leyland, 1945).

—— *The First Fifty Years* (Leyland, 1948).

—— *Leyland Motor Corporation: Growth – Constitution – Factories – Products* (1965). 78 pp.

—— *Leyland: Seventy Years of Progress* (1967). 55 pp.

Daniels, J., *British Leyland: The Truth About the Cars* (Osprey, 1980). 192 pp.

Edwardes, Sir Michael, *Back from the Brink: An Apocalyptic Experience* (Collins, 1983). 301 pp.

Ryder, Sir D., *British Leyland: The Next Decade: an Abridged Version of a Report . . . by a Team of Inquiry led by Sir Don Ryder* (HMSO, 1975). 75 pp.

Turner, Graham, *The Leyland Papers* (Eyre & Spottiswoode, 1971). 216 pp.

Burman & Sons Ltd

Burman, Thomas, *Short History of Burman & Sons Ltd* (privately printed, 1944).

Chrysler Corporation

Iacocca, L., *Iacocca: An Autobiography* (Sidgwick & Jackson, 1985). xv 352 pp.

Jeffreys, S., *Management and Managed: Fifty Years of Crisis at Chrysler* (Cambridge University Press, 1986). 290 pp.

Wyden, P., *The Unknown Iacocca* (Sidgwick & Jackson, 1988). v 346 pp.

Young, S. and Hood, N., *Chrysler UK: A Corporation in Transition* (New York: Praeger, 1977). xvii 343 pp.

Cockshoot (Joseph) & Co. Ltd

—— *Coachmaking, 1844–1944: The Story of a Century of Service to Travellers by Road* (1944).

Lomax, S. and Norris, J. O. H., *Early Days: Memories of the Beginnings of Automobile Engineering in South Lancashire and Cheshire* (1948).

Cosworth Engineering Co.

Robson, G., *Cosworth: The Search for Power* (Patrick Stephens, 1990). 288 pp.

Cowie (T.) plc

Martin, P., *The Tom Cowie Story: A History of T. Cowie plc* (James & James, 1988). 80 pp.

Crossley Motors Ltd

—— *A Short History of Crossley Motors Ltd* (1950).

Daimler Motor Co.: *see also* Birmingham Small Arms Co. *above*

Davenport-Hines, Richard P. T., *Dudley Docker: The Life and Times of a Trade Warrior* (Cambridge University Press, 1984). 295 pp.

Nixon, St J. C., *Daimler 1896–1946: A Record of Fifty Years of the Daimler Co.* (Foulis, 1946). 232 pp.

De Lorean

Fallon, I. and Strodes, J., *De Lorean: The Rise and Fall of a Dream Maker* (Hamish Hamilton, 1983). 417 pp.

Levin, H., *John de Lorean: The Maverick Mogul* (Orbis, 1983). iii 268 pp.

English Racing Automobiles Ltd

Weguelin, D., *The History of English Racing Automobiles Ltd and the Continuing Story of the Cars 1933–1980* (White Mouse, 1980). 288 pp.

Ferrari

Casucci, Piero, *Enzo Ferrari: 50 Years of Greatness* (Haynes, 1982). 167 pp. [Translated by Simon Pleasance.]

Fiat Auto (UK) Ltd

—— *A Fifty Years' Record* (Verona: Mandadori, 1951). 303 pp.

Kennett, P., *Fiat* (Patrick Stephens, 1980). 88 pp.

Sedgewick, M., *Fiat* (Batsford, 1974).

Shimwell, R., *Fiat* (Luscombe, 1977). 165 pp.

Foden

Kennett, P., *The Foden Story: From Farm Machinery to Diesel Trucks* (Patrick Stephens, 1978). 183 pp.

Ford

Beynon, H., *Working for Ford* (Penguin, 1973). 336 pp.

Herndon, B., *Ford: An Unconventional Biography of the Two Henry Fords and Their Times* (Cassell, 1970). 408 pp.

Lacey, R., *Ford: The Man and the Machine* (Book Club Associates, 1986).

Nevins, A. J. and Hill, F. E., *Ford: Expansion and Challenge 1915–1933* (New York: Scribner, 1957). xviii 714 pp.

Nye, David E., *Henry Ford, 'Ignorant Idealist'* (Kennikat Press, 1979). ix 147 pp.

Ridgeway, *Ford of Britain – The First 75 Years 1911–1986* (Orbis, 1986).

Saunders, H. St G., *Ford At War* (The Firm, 1946). 95 pp.

Seidler, E., *Let's Call it Fiesta: The Autobiography of Ford's Project Bobcat* (Patrick Stephens, 1976). 239 pp.

Sorensen, C. E. and Williamson, S. T., *Forty Years with Ford* (Cape, 1957). vi 345 pp.

Stoney, Barbara, *Ford: The Motor Man* (Hodder & Stoughton, 1981). 128 pp.

Guy Motors

—— *Forty Years of Achievement, 1914–1954* (The Firm, 1954). 65 pp.

Halford Cycle Co. Ltd

Jones, B. A., *The Story of Halfords 1907–82* (The Firm, 1981). 257 pp.

—— *Halfords, 1907–1982* (The Firm, 1982). 72 pp.

Jaguar plc

—— *Case History: The Story of Jaguar Cars Ltd and its Subsidiary Companies* (The Firm, 1964). 57 pp.

Montague of Beaulieu, Lord, *Jaguar: A Biography* (Cassell, 1961). xx, 273 pp.

Underwood, John, *The Will to Win; John Egan and Jaguar* (W. H. Allen, 1989). xii 210 pp.

Whyte, A., *Jaguar: The History of a Great British Car* (Stephens, 1985). 256 pp. (Previous edition, 1980.)

Lanchester Motor Co.

Bird, A. C. and Hutton-Stott, F. H., *Lanchester Motor Cars* (Cassell, 1965). 240 pp.

Kingsford, P. W., *F. W. Lanchester: A Life of an Engineer* (Edward Arnold, 1960). 246 pp.

Lancia

Trow, N., *Lancia: The Shields and Flag* (1980). 270 pp.

Lea-Francis

Price, B., *The Lea-Francis Story* (Batsford, 1978). 144 pp.

Lucas Industries Ltd

Nockolds, Harold, *Lucas: The First 100 Years* (David & Charles, 1976 and 1978). Two volumes.

Matchless

Hartley, P., *Matchless: Once the Largest British Motorcycle Manufacturers* (Osprey, 1980). 208 pp.

Morgan

Bowden, G. H., *Morgan: First and Last of the Real Sports Cars* (Gentry Books, 1972). 191 pp.

Morris Motors

—— *Making Cars: A History of Car Making in Cowley* . . . (Routledge & Kegan Paul, 1985). 131 pp.

Andrews, P. W. S. and Brunner, Elizabeth, *The Life of Lord Nuffield: A Study in Enterprise and Benevolence* (Blackwell, 1955). xvi 356 pp.

Jackson, R., *The Nuffield Story* (Frederick Muller, 1964). 254 pp.

Thomas, W. M. W., *Out on a Wing* (Michael Joseph, 1964).

Napier & Son, Engineers Ltd

Wilson, Charles and Reader, William J., *Men and Machines: A History of Napier & Son, Engineers Ltd 1808–1958* (Weidenfeld & Nicolson, 1958). 187 pp.

Phelon & Moor

Jones, B. M., *The Story of Panther Motorcycles* (Patrick Stephens, 1983). 136 pp.

Plaxtons

Townsin, A., *Plaxtons: An Illustrated History to Mark the Company's Jubilee* (Glossop: Transport Publishing, 1982). 161 pp.

Quicks Group

Brooks, R., *Quicks, the First 75 Years, 1912–1987* (The Firm, 1988). 135 pp.

Raleigh Industries

Bowden, G. H., *The Story of the Raleigh Cycle* (W. H. Allen, 1975). 216 pp.

Millward, A., *The Raleigh Archive: A Detailed List of the Contents* (Birmingham Polytechnic, 1990).

Riley Engine Co.

Birmingham, A. T., *Riley: The Production and Competition History of pre-1939 Riley Motor Cars* (Foulis, 1965). 248 pp.

Rolls-Royce

Bastow, D., *Henry Royce, Mechanic* (Rolls-Royce Heritage Trust, 1989). 214 pp.

Baxter, A., *Olympus The First Forty Years* (Rolls-Royce Heritage Trust, 1990). 179 pp.

Bird, A. C. and Hallows, I. S., *The Rolls-Royce Motor Car* (1972). 328 pp. (3rd edition.)

Bird, D., *Rolls-Royce and the Mustang* (Rolls-Royce Heritage Trust, 1987).

Buist, H. M., *Rolls-Royce Memories: A Coming-of-Age Souvenir* (Cambridge University Press, 1926). 95 pp.

Evans, M., *In the Beginning: The Manchester Origins of Rolls-Royce* (Rolls-Royce Heritage Trust, 1984). 169 pp.

Gray, R. A. S., *Rolls on the Rocks . . .* (Panther/Granada, 1971). 95 pp.

Harker, R. W., *The Engines were Rolls-Royce: An Informal History of that Famous Company* (Collier–Macmillan, 1979). xxi 202 pp.

Harvey-Bailey, A., *Rolls-Royce: The Sons of Martha* (Rolls-Royce Heritage Trust, 1989). 164 pp.

Harvey-Bailey, A. H., *Rolls-Royce: Hives, the Quiet Tiger* (Paulerspury: Sir Henry Royce Memorial Foundation, 1985). 101 pp.

Harvey-Bailey, A. and Evans, M., *Rolls-Royce: The Pursuit of Excellence* (Paulerspury: Sir Henry Royce Memorial Foundation, 1984). 124 pp.

Harvey-Bailey, Alex, *Rolls-Royce: The Formative Years 1906–1939* (Rolls-Royce Heritage Trust, 1982). 95 pp.

Lloyd, I., *Rolls-Royce: The Growth of a Firm; The Merlin at War; The Years of Endeavour* (Macmillan, 1978). Three volumes.

Montague of Beaulieu, Lord, *The Early Days of Rolls-Royce and the Montague Family* (Rolls-Royce Heritage Trust, 1983). 51 pp.

Nockolds, H., *The Magic of a Name* (Foulis, 1950). 283 pp.

Stokes, P., *From Gipsy to Gem with Diversions, 1926–1986* (Rolls-Royce Heritage Trust, 1987). 126 pp.

Rover

Robson, Graham, *The Rover Story: A Century of Success* (Patrick Stephens, 1984). 201 pp.

Royal Enfield Motor Cycles

Hartly, Peter, *The Story of Royal Enfield Motor Cycles* (Patrick Stephens, 1981). 128 pp.

Rudge–Whitworth

Hartley, P., *The Story of Rudge Motor Cycles* (Patrick Stephens, 1985). 128 pp.

Reynolds, B., *Don't Trust It: Rudge It* (Haynes, 1977). 174 pp.

Simms (F. R.)

Adenay, M., *The Motor Makers* (Fontana, 1984).

Nixon, St John C., *The Simms Story from 1891* (privately printed, 1955). 64 pp.

Starley (J. A.) & Co.

Williamson, G., *Wheels within Wheels: The Story of the Starleys of Coventry* (Bles, 1966). 160 pp.

Sunbeam Motor Co.

Cliff, N., *My Life at the Sunbeam 1920–1935* (Ashley James, 1987). 86 pp.

Timms (F.) & Co. (Leigh) Ltd

—— *Thirty Years of Progress 1907–1937* (1937).

Triumph

Langworth, R. and Robson, G., *Triumph Cars: The Complete 75-Year History* (1975). 312 pp.

Louis, H. and Curtiss, R., *The Story of Triumph Motor Cycles* (Patrick Stephens, 1978). 128 pp.

Vandem Plas

Smith, B., *Vandem Plas, Coachbuilders* (Dalton Watson, 1979). 302 pp.

Vauxhall

Darbyshire, L. C., *The Story of Vauxhall, 1857–1946* (1946). 56 pp.

—— *A History of Vauxhall: The Company and its Cars* (The Firm, 1980). 68 pp.

Volkswagen

Etzold, H. R., *The Beetle: The Chronicles of the People's Car* (Haynes Publishing Group).

Nelson, W. H., *Small Wonder: The Amazing Story of the Volkswagen* (Hutchinson, 1967). xiv 304 pp.

Raitton, A., *'The Beetle': A Most Unlikely Story* (The Firm, 1985).

Sloniger, J. E., *The VW Story* (Patrick Stephens, 1980). 216 pp.

Wolsley Tool & Motor Car Co.

Nixon, St J. C., *Wolsley: A Saga of the Motor Industry* (Foulis, 1949). 157 pp.

Office Equipment

General

Moseley, M., *Irascible Genius: A Life of Charles Babbage, Inventor* (1964). 288 pp.

National Archives for the History of Computing: based in the Centre for the History of Science, Technology and Medicine, Manchester University. Funded in 1987 for three years by the Levehulme Trust.

Proudfoot, W. B., *The Origin of Stencil Duplicating* (Hutchinson, 1972). 128 pp.

Tweedale, G., *National Archives for the History of Computing Catalogue* (National Archives, 1990). 114 pp.

Amstrad

Thomas, D., *Alan Sugar: The Amstrad Story* (Century, 1990). 368 pp.

Apple Computer

Rose, F., *West of Eden: The End of Innocence at Apple Computer* (Business Books, 1989). 356 pp.

Brook Street Bureau

Hurst, M., *No Glass Slipper* (Arlington Books, 1967). 176 pp.

Gestetner Holdings Ltd

—— *1854–1934 (Gestetner, 1934).*

Culpan, H. V., *The House of Gestetner* (The Firm, 1951). [70th anniversary souvenir brochure.]

Proudfoot, W. B., *The Origin of Stencil Duplicating* (Hutchinson, 1972). 128 pp.

IBM

Foy, N., *The IBM World* (1973). 234 pp.

Malik, R., *And Tomorrow . . . The World? Inside IBM* (Millington, 1975). xxii 496 pp.

Rogers, W., *Think: A Biography of the Watsons and IBM* (Weidenfeld & Nicolson, 1969). 320 pp.

Sobel, Robert, *IBM: Colossus in Transition* (Sidgwick & Jackson, 1984). 360 pp. [Originally published New York: Times Books, 1981.]

ICL

Campbell-Kelly, M., *ICL. A Business and Technical History: The Official History of Britain's Leading Information Systems Company* (Oxford: Clarendon Press, 1989). 409 pp.

Jones (Percy) (Twinlock) Ltd

—— *Twinlock, 1905–1955: The Story of the Foundation and Progress over 50 Years* (Beckenham: The Firm, 1955). 56 pp.

Lethaby (W.) & Co.

—— *Leda: Fifty Years of Numbering Machines* (The Firm, 1963). 53 pp.

Letraset

Chudley, J. A., *Letraset: A Lesson in Growth* (Business Books, 1974). xi 155 pp.

Olivetti

—— *Olivetti, C. & C., Spa, Olivetti, 1908–1958* (1958). 190 pp.

Pitney Bowes Ltd

Roberts, S. T., *The History of Pitney Bowes Limited* (Harlow, 1975). 144 pp.

Roneo Vickers Ltd

Dorlay, J. S., *The Roneo Story* (Roneo Vickers Ltd, 1978). x 223 pp.

Sinclair

Dale R., *The Sinclair Story* (Duckworth, 1985). 192 pp.

Smith (Arthur C.)

—— *Arthur C. Smith, Typewriter Accessories 1931–1981* (William Sessions, 1981).

Oil

General

Jones, Geoffrey, *The State and the Emergence of the British Oil Industry* (Macmillan, 1981). xi 264 pp. [In association with the Business History Unit.]

Shepherd, P. (compiler), *Oil: A Bibliography Based on Items Held in the Libraries in the North East of Scotland* (Aberdeen, 1974). (2nd edition, 276 pp.)

Yergin, D., *The Epic Quest for Oil, Money and Power* (Simon & Schuster, 1991), 912 pp.

Benzol

Holmes, Graeme M., *Fifty Years of British Benzol: A History of British Benzol and Coal Distillation Ltd* (The Company, 1979). 51 pp.

British Petroleum

—— *Our Industry – Petroleum* (BP, 1977). 600 pp. [5th edition, 1st in 1947.]

—— *Fifty Years in Pictures: A Story in Pictures of the Development of the British Petroleum Group, 1909–1959* (The Firm, 1959). 159 pp.

Anderson, J. R. L., *East of Suez: A Study of Britain's Greatest Trading Enterprise* (Hodder & Stoughton, 1969). 288 pp.

Ferrier, R. W., *A History of the British Petroleum Company*, volume *1: The Developing Years, 1901–1932* (Cambridge University Press, 1982). xxx 801 pp. [The second volume, by Jim Bamberg, will be published by Cambridge University Press in 1994; the third volume is currently being researched.]

Longhurst, H. C., *Adventure in Oil: The Story of British Petroleum* (Sidgwick & Jackson, 1959). 286 pp. [Introduction by Rt Hon. Sir Winston Churchill.]

Burmah Oil Co.

Corley, T. A. B., *Communications, Entrepreneurship and the Managing Agency System: The Burmah Oil Company 1886–1928* (1979). [Unpublished Reading University research paper.]

Corley, T. A. B., *A History of the Burmah Oil Company, 1886–1924* (Heinemann, 1983). xvi 331 pp.

Corley, T. A. B., *A History of the Burmah Oil Company*, volume 2: *1924–1966* (Heinemann, 1988).

Carless, Capel & Leonard Ltd

Liveing, E. G. D., *Pioneers of Petrol: A Centenary History of Carless, Capel and Leonard Ltd 1859–1959* (Witherby, 1959). xviii 94 pp.

Pugh, P., *Carless, Capel & Leonard plc. The Growth of a Family Firm into an International Oil Company* (1986). 128 pp.

Manchester Oil Refinery Ltd

——*The First Ten Years: MOR Group of Companies* (1948).

Mobil

Nash, M. and Keegan, P. (eds), *Mobil into the Second Century 1885–1985* (The Firm, 1985). 152 pp.

National Benzole

Young, E. P., *Forty Years of Motoring 1919–1959: The Story of National Benzole* (Stanley Paul, 1959). 190 pp.

Shell Group

—— *Royal Dutch Petroleum 1890–1950: Diamond Jubilee Book* (The Hague, 1950). 264 pp.

Beaton, Kendall, *Enterprise in Oil: A History of Shell in the United States* (New York: Appleton-Century-Crofts Inc., 1957). 815 pp.

Forbes, R. J. and O'Beirne, D. R., *The Technical Development of the Royal Dutch/Shell 1890–1940* (1957). 670 pp.

Gerretson, F. C., *History of the Royal Dutch* (Leiden, Netherlands: E. J. Brill, 1953–7). Four volumes.

Shell (Transport & Trading Co.)

Henriques, R. D. Q., *Marcus Samuel, First Viscount Bearsted and Founder of the Shell Transport and Trading Company 1853–1927* (Barrie & Rocklift, 1960). xi 676 pp.

—— *The Shell Poster Book* (Hamish Hamilton, 1992). iv 92 pp.

Kerr, G. P., *Time's Forelock: A Record of Shell's Contribution to Aviation in the Second World War* (1948). 100 pp.

Ultramar

Atterbury, P. R. and Mackenzie, J. C. G., *A Golden Adventure: The First Fifty Years of Ultramar* (Hurtwood, 1983). 288 pp.

Wakefield (C. C.) & Co.

—— *The Romance of Wakefields 1899–1949* (1949). 72 pp.

Paper and Packaging

General

Coleman, D. C., *The British Paper Industry, 1495–1860: A Study in Industrial Growth* (Clarendon Press, 1958). xvi 367 pp.

Leif, I. P., *An International Sourcebook of Paper History* (Archon Dawson, 1978). 106 pp.

Shorter, Alfred H., *Paper Making in the British Isles: An Historical and Geographical Study* (David & Charles, 1971).

Thomson, A. G., *The Paper Industry in Scotland 1590–1861* (Scottish Academic Press, 1974). 245 pp.

Balston (W. & R.) Ltd

Balston, T., *William Balston, Papermaker 1759–1849* (Methuen, 1954). xii 178 pp.

Bowater Hall Mills

Reader, W. J., *Bowater: A History* (Cambridge University Press, 1981). xv 426 pp.

Bridge Hall Mills

Tillmanns, M., *Bridge Hall Mills: Three Centuries of Papers and Cellulose Film Manufacture* (Compton Press, 1978). xi 219 pp.

Bunzl plc

—— *The Bunzl Group of Companies 1854–1954: Great Britain, Austria, The United States of America, Switzerland, South Africa, Italy, Germany* (Vienna: Rosenbaum, 1971). 91 pp.

Bushill (Thomas) & Sons Ltd

Howe, E., *The Story of a Coventry Firm of Printers and Boxmakers, 1856–1956* (The Company, 1956). 66 pp.

Coates Brothers

Coates, J. B. M., *A History of Coates Brothers & Company Ltd 1877–1977* (Westerham Press, 1977). 102 pp.

Craig (Robert) & Sons Ltd

—— *A Century of Papermaking* (The Company, 1920). 141 pp.

Culter Paper Mills Co. Ltd

—— *History of Culter Paper Mills: Two Hundred Years of Progress 1751–1951* (The Company, 1951). 63 pp.

Dickinson (John) & Co. Ltd

Evans, Joan, *The Endless Web: John Dickinson & Co. Ltd 1804–1954* (Cape, 1955). xvi 274 pp.

Dray & Drayton

—— *A Century of Service 1856–1956: A Story of G. W. Dray & Son Ltd and the Drayton Paper Works Ltd* (The Firm, 1956). 64 pp.

Duxbury, Yates & Sons Ltd

Green, Tom, *Yates, Duxbury & Sons, Papermakers of Bury* (1963).

East Lancashire Paper Mill Co. Ltd

—— *One Hundred Years of Progress: 1860–1960* (1960). 61 pp.

Fletcher (Robert) & Son

Hampson, C. G., *150th Anniversary of Robert Fletcher & Son Ltd* (Radcliffe, 1973). 69 pp.

Galloway (John) & Co.

Galloway, J., *Galloways of Balerno* (Newman Neame, 1968). 51 pp.

Grosvenor Chater

Chater, Michael, *Family Business: A History of Grosvenor Chater, 1690–1977* (Grosvenor Chater, 1977). 63 pp.

Guard Bridge Paper Company Ltd

Weatherill, L., *One Hundred Years of Papermaking: An Illustrated History of the Guard Bridge Paper Co. Ltd 1873–1973* (The Firm, 1974). vii 122 pp.

Hale Paper Company Ltd

—— *Hale Paper: Jubilee Edition 1921–1971* (The Company, 1971). 60 pp.

Hook (C. Townsend) & Co.

Funnell, K. J., *Snodland Paper Mill, C. Townsend Hook and Company from 1854* (The Company, 1980). 80 pp.

Johnsen & Jorgensen

—— *Johnsen & Jorgensen 1884–1984* (The Firm, 1984). 85 pp.

Lunnon (W.)

Baker, J. H., *History of W. Lunnon: The First 60 Years* (The Firm, 1980). 69 pp.

Mardon, Son & Hall Ltd

—— *Mardon's During the War Years 1939–1945* (Bristol, 1946). 56 pp.

Mardon, H., *Landmarks in the History of a Bristol Firm 1824–1904* (Bristol: The Firm, 1918). 66 pp.

Marsden (Edward)

Whittaker, F. G., *Edward Marsden: The Story of a Company* (The Firm, 1978). 66 pp.

Metal Box plc: *see* 'Metals' (p. 195)

Nash (William)

Shears, W. S., *William Nash of St Paul's Cray, Papermakers* (The Firm, 1950). ix 177 pp.

Shears, W. S., *William Nash of St Paul's Cray, Papermakers* (printed for private circulation, 1950). 184 pp.

Portals

Portal, F. S., *Portals: The Church, the State and the People, Leading to 250 Years of Papermaking* (The Firm, 1962). xii 98 pp.

Reed International plc

Sykes, P., *Albert E. Reed and the Creation of a Paper Business 1860–1960* (The Firm, 1981). viii 493 pp.

Roach Bridge Paper Co. Ltd

Faulds, D., *Roach Bridge Paper Company 1875–1975* (Shearwater Press, 1976). 60 pp.

—— *The Roach Bridge Paper Co. 1876–1936* (The Company, 1936).

Robinson (E. S. & A.)

Darwin, B. R. M., *Robinson of Bristol 1844–1944* (The Firm, 1945). xiii, 72 pp.

Smith Brothers (Whitehaven)

Wigham, L., *Smiths of Whitehaven 1880–1980: A Century of Progress and Development in Flexible Packaging* (The Firm, 1980). 153 pp.

Sommerville (Wm) & Co.

Watson, N., *The Last Mill on the Esk: 150 Years of Papermaking* (Scottish Academic Press, 1987). 148 pp.

Spicers Ltd

—— *The House of Spicer* (The Firm, 1984). 76 pp.

[Spicer, S. D.], *Albert Spicer 1847–1934: A Man of His Times by One of His Family* (Simpkin Marshall, 1938). 85 pp.

Thames Board Mills Ltd

—— *The War and Thames Board Mills* (1952). 60 pp.

—— *This is the Story of Thames at Warrington* (The Company, 1967).

Trinity Paper Mills Ltd

Lyddon, D. and Marshall, P., *Paper in Bolton: A Papermaker's Tale* (Sherratt, 1975). 208 pp.

Tullis (Russell) & Co. Ltd

Ketelbey, C. D. M., *The History of R. Tullis & Company and Tullis Russell & Co. Ltd 1809–1959* (Fife, 1967). xiii 283 pp.

Whatman (J.)

Balston, T., *James Whatman, Father and Son* (Methuen, 1957). 170 pp.

Wiggins Teape & Co. Ltd

—— *Wiggins Teape and Co. (1919) Ltd: Glory Paper Mills, Wooburn Green, High Wycombe, Bucks* (The Firm, 1956).

Willesden Paper & Canvas Works

—— *The Romance of Willesden Dux Oriental: Fabric Proofing, Canvas, Paper, Sandbags, Camouflage* ... (The Firm, 1941). 177 pp.

Yates, Duxbury & Sons

Green, T., *Yates, Duxbury & Sons, Papermakers of Bury 1863–1963* (Newman Neame, 1963). 56 pp.

Pharmaceuticals, Medical and Cosmetics

General

Sheppard, J. and Hall, L., *A Guide to the Contemporary Medical Archives Centre* (The Centre, 1991). 77 pp.

Allen & Hanburys Ltd: *see also* Glaxo Holdings Ltd

Cripps, E. C., *Plough Court, The Story of a Notable Pharmacy, 1715–1927* (1927). xviii 227 pp.

Chapman-Huston, W. D. M. and Cripps, E. C., *Through a City Archway: The Story of Allen & Hanburys, 1715–1954* (Murray, 1954). xv 326 pp.

Tweedale, G., *At the Sign of the Plough: 275 Years of Allen & Hanburys ...* (Murray, 1990). 264 pp.

Aspro–Nicholas Ltd: *see* Nicholas International Ltd, *below*

The Beecham Group plc

—— *Centenary of a Notable Business: A Short History of Messrs Beechams Ltd of St Helens* (1942).

Lazell, H. G., *From Pills to Penicillin: The Beecham Story: Personal Account* (Heinemann, 1975). 208 pp.

Francis, Anne, *A Guinea a Box* (Hale, 1968). 190 pp.

Boots Co. plc

Chapman, S. D., *Jesse Boot of Boots the Chemist: A Study in Business History* (Hodder, 1974). 221 pp.

Roberts, Cecil, *Achievement: A Record of 50 Years Progress* (1938). 94 pp.

Walker, E., *Boots 1877–1977: 100 Years of Shopping at Boots* (1977).

Blatchford (Chas A.) & Sons Ltd

Phillips, G., *Best Foot Forward: Chas A. Blatchford & Sons Ltd
(Artificial Limb Specialists) 1890–1990* (Granta Editions, 1990) xiv,
140 pp.

Cox (A. H.) & Co.

Slinn, Judy A., *Pills and Pharmaceuticals: A. H. Cox & Co.* (privately
printed, 1989). 78 pp.

Bradford Chemists' Alliance

Watson, Nigel, *Bradford Chemists' Alliance – Seventy-Five Years*
(privately printed, 1992). 52 pp.

Dolland and Aitchison

Barty-King, H., *Eyes Right: The Story of Dolland and Aitchison,
Opticians 1750–1985* (Quiller Press, 1986). 264 pp.

King, H. C., *The House of Dolland: Two Hundred Years of Optical
Service 1750–1950* (The Firm, 1950). 35 pp.

Duncan, Flockart & Co.

—— *The History of Duncan, Flockhart & Co.: Commemorating the
Centenaries of Ether and Chloroform*, (The Firm, 1946). 52 pp.

Ethicon Ltd

Bailey, C. A., *On this Slender Thread a Life May Depend: An Authorised
History of Ethicon Ltd* (The Firm, 1977). ix 133 pp.

Evans Medical Supplies Ltd

Smeeton, A. E., *The Story of Evans Medical 1809–1959* (The Firm, 1959). 66 pp.

Glaxo Holdings Ltd

—— *Gold on the Green: Fifty Glaxo Years at Greenford* (The Firm, 1985). 136 pp.

Jephcott, Sir Harry (comp.), *The First 50 Years* (W. S. Cowell, 1969). 118 pp.

Slinn, Judy A. (with Davenport-Hines, R.), *Glaxo: A History to 1962* (Cambridge University Press, 1992). 420 pp.

Hay (William) Ltd

—— *William Hay Limited* (Hull: The Firm, 1948?). 78 pp.

Imperial Chemical Industries: *see* 'Chemical Industries' (p. 70)

Jeyes Group

Palfreyman, D., *John Jeyes: The Making of a Household Name* (The Firm, 1977). 127 pp.

May & Baker

Slinn, Judy, *A History of May & Baker* (Hobsons, 1984). 191 pp.

Nicholas International Ltd

Morgan, B., *Apothecary's Venture: The Scientific Quest of the International Nicholas Organisation* (Aspro–Nicholas Ltd, 1959) 60 pp.

Smith, Robert Grenville and Barrie, A., *Aspro: How a Family Business Grew Up* (Nicholas International, 1976). x 181 pp.

Pears (A. & F.)

Dempsey, M. (ed.), *Bubbles: Early Advertising Art from A. & F. Pears* (Fontana, 1978). 72 pp.

Pro-Care

Watson, Nigel, *Serving the Dentist: From Baxters of Bradford to Pro-care 1841–1991* (privately published, 1991). 50 pp.

Reckitt & Sons Ltd

—— *The Welfare Work of Reckitt and Sons Ltd* (The Company, 1924). 96 pp.

Reckitt, Basil N., *The History of Reckitt and Sons Ltd* (Brown, 1951). xvi 113 pp. [2nd and revised edition 1958.]

Robinson & Sons Ltd

Porteous, C., *Pill Boxes and Bandages ... Biography of the First Two Generations of Robinsons of Chesterfield* (The Firm, 1960). 188 pp.

Robinson, P. M., *The Robinson Family of Bolsover and Chesterfield* (Chesterfield: The Firm, 1961). 320 pp.

Savory & Moore

Savory, A. C. S., *The Savorys of Savory and Moore* (Lymington: The Author, 1962). 80 pp.

Smith & Nephew Associated Companies

Bennett, R. and Leavey, J. A., *A History of Smith and Nephew 1856–1981* (The Firm, 1981). 76 pp.

Swann–Morton

—— Swann–Morton, *The First 50 Years* (The Firm, 1984). 110 pp.

British Business History

Unilever Ltd: *see* 'Food' (p. 135) and 'Chemicals' (p. 74)

Wellcome Foundation Ltd

Hall, A. R. and Bemridge, B. A., *Physic and Philanthropy: A History of the Wellcome Trust* (1986).

MacDonald, G., *In Pursuit of Excellence: One Hundred Years, Wellcome 1880–1980* (Wellcome Foundaton, 1980). 120 pp.

Parish, H. J., 'History of Wellcome Physiological Research Laboratories' (1980). [Unpublished manuscript, c. 1980, property of the author.]

Turner, H. E., *Henry Wellcome: The Man, His Collection and His Legacy* (Wellcome Trust, 1980). 96 pp.

Yardley & Co. Ltd

Thomas, E. Wynne, *The House of Yardley 1770–1953* (Sylvan Press, 1953). 102 pp.

Precision Instruments

Baird & Tatlock (London) Ltd

Longdon-Davies, J., *Measuring the Future: Scientific Progress ... Wartime Experience of Messrs Baird & Tatlock* (London) Ltd (The Firm, 1947). 51 pp.

Barr & Stroud

Moss, M. and Russell, I., *Range and Vision: The First Hundred Years of Barr and Stroud* (Mainstream Publishing, 1988). 256 pp.

Cambridge Instrument Co. Ltd

Cattermole, M. J. G. and Wolfe, A. F., *Horace Darwin's Shop: A History of the Cambridge Scientific Instrument Company, 1878–1968* (Adam Hilger, 1987). 285 pp.

Churchill Machine Tool Co. Ltd

—— *The Story of Churchill Machine Tool Co. Ltd: A History of Precision Grinding (Golden Jubilee, 1906–1956)* (1956). 54 pp.

Cooke, Troughton & Simms

McConnell, A., *Instrument Makers to the World: A History of Cooke, Troughton & Simms* (William Sessions, 1992). 120 pp.

Cossor (A. C.) & Son (Surgical) Ltd

—— *1859–1959 (A. C.) Cossor & Son (Surgical) Ltd* (1959).

Flatters & Garnett Ltd

—— *50 Years' Service to Microscopy 1901–1951* (The Company, 1952).

Frodsham

Mercer, V., *The Frodshams: The Story of a Family of Chronometer Makers* (Antiquarian Horological Society, 1981). xvii 458 pp.

Griffin & Tatlock Ltd

Mayer, H. C., 'The History of Griffin & George Ltd' (unpublished, Alperton, Wembley, 1980).

Kent (George) Ltd

—— *George Kent Limited 1838–1938* (The Firm, 1938). 100 pp.

Longworth Scientific Instrument Co. Ltd

Jephcott, Sir A., *A History of Longworth Scientific Instrument Co. Ltd* (Regency Press, 1988). 202 pp.

Mercer (Thomas) Ltd

Mercer, T., *Mercer Chronometers: Radical Tom Mercer and the House He Founded* (Brant Wright, 1978). xxiv 251 pp.

Munro (R. W.)

—— *R. W. Munro Centenary 1864–1964: A Century of Instrument Making and Precision Engineering* (The Firm, 1964). 57 pp.

Stanley (W. F.) & Co. Ltd

Allen, Cecil J., *A Century of Scientific Instrument Making 1853–1953* (1953). 63 pp.

Printers and Publishers

[See separately Leisure and Media; Bookselling, Newsagents and Stationers; Papers and Packaging]

General

—— *Dictionary of Literary Biography, vol. 106, inc. British Literary Publishing Houses 1820–1880* (Detroit: Gale Research, 1991).

—— *Dictionary of Literary Biography, vol. 112, inc. British Literary Publishing Houses 1881–1965* (Detroit: Gale Research, 1991).

Haines, J., *Maxwell* (Macdonald, 1988). ix 525 pp.

Aberdeen University Press

Keith, A., *Aberdeen University Press: An Account of the Press from its Foundation in 1840 until its Occupation of New Premises in 1963* (private circulation, 1963). 72 pp.

Allen (George) & Unwin (Publishers) Ltd: *see also* Unwin Brothers

Mumby, F. A. and Stallybrass, F. H. S., *From Swan Sonnenschein to George Allen & Unwin Ltd* (Allen & Unwin, 1955). 100 pp.

Unwin, Sir Stanley, *The Truth about a Publisher* (1960). 455 pp.

Allens (David)

Allens, W. E. D., *The History of a Family Firm 1857–1957* (Murray, 1957). 322 pp.

Arnold (E. J.) & Son Ltd

—— *A Service to Education: The Story of the Growth of E. J. Arnold & Sons Ltd of Leeds and a Study of Some of the Present Trends in Teaching Methods and Equipment* (1963). 64 pp.

Arnold, Edward

Bennett, B. and Hamilton, A., *Edward Arnold: 100 Years of Publishing* (The Firm, 1990). 122 pp.

Atkinson (James)

—— *100 Years of Steady Progress: Centenary of the Famous Firm of Ulverston Booksellers, Printers and Stationers 1837–1937* (1937).

Austin (Stephen) & Sons Ltd

Moran, James, *Stephen Austin's (Printers) of Hertford: A Bicentenary History* (Stephen Austin, 1968). 72 pp.

Ballantyne Press

—— *The Ballantyne Press and its Founders 1796–1908* (Edinburgh: Ballantyne, Hanson, 1909). 191 pp.

Owens, L. T., *J. H. Mason, 1875–1975, Scholar-Printer* (Muller, 1976). xvi 192 pp.

Bartholomew & Son Ltd

Gardiner, L., *Bartholomew, 150 Years* (Bartholomew, 1976). 112 pp.

Batsford (B. T.) Ltd

Bolitho, H. H., *The Batsford Century: A Record of a Hundred Years of Publishing* (1943). 148 pp.

Baxter (W. E.) Ltd

Mitzman, Max E., *George Baxter and the Baxter Prints* (The Firm, 1978).

Lewis, C. T. Courtney, *George Baxter – The Picture Printer* (1920).

Beaumont Press

Beaumont, C. W., *The First Score: An Account of the Foundation and Development of the Beaumont Press and its First Twenty Publications* (Beaumont, 1927).

Bemrose & Sons

Bemrose, H. H., *The House of Bemrose 1826–1926* (Bemrose, 1926). 160 pp.

Hackett, Dennis, *The History of the Future: The Bemrose Corporation 1826–1976* (Scolar Press for Bemrose, 1976). 144 pp.

Benn Brothers

Battison, P. (ed.), *Benn Centenary Magazine 1980* (The Firm, 1980). 64 pp.

Bentley (Richard) & Son

Gettman, R. A., *A Victorian Publisher: A Study of the Bentley Papers* (Cambridge University Press, 1960). xi 272 pp.

Black (A. & C.) Ltd

Newth, J. D., *Adam and Charles Black 1807–1957: Some Chapters in the History of a Publishing House* (Black, 1957). xi 116 pp.

Blackie Publishing Group

Blackie, A. A. C., *Blackie & Son 1809–1959: A Short History of the Firm* (Blackie, 1959). viii 78 pp.

—— *John Blackie Senior* (1933). viii 78 pp.

—— *Walter Graham Blackie* (1936). ix 170 pp.

Blackwell Publishing Group

Norrington, A. L. P., *Blackwell's 1879–1979: History of a Family Firm* (Blackwell, 1983). 191 pp.

Blackwood (William) & Sons Ltd

Tredrey, F. D., *The House of Blackwood 1804–1954: The History of a Publishing Firm* (Blackwood, 1954). ix 282 pp.

Bodley Head

Lambert, J. W. and Ratcliffe, M., *The Bodley Head, 1887–1987* (The Firm, 1988). 365 pp.

Bradshaw's Guides

Smith, G. R., *The History of Bradshaw: A Centenary Review* (1939). 76 pp.

Burall Brothers

Burall, K. M., *Douglas Burall: His Wartime Letter with an Account of His Life* (Wisbech: The Firm, 1951). 185 pp.

Burgess & Son (Abingdon) Ltd

Stopps, L. B., *Burgess & Son (Abingdon) Ltd 1827–1980: A Short History* (The Firm, 1980). 63 pp.

Burn (James) & Co. Ltd

Darley, L. S., *Bookbinding Then and Now: A Survey of the First Hundred and Seventy-Eight Years of James Burn & Company* (Faber & Faber, 1959). 126 pp.

Butterworths & Co. (Publishers) Ltd

Jones, H. Kay, *Butterworths: A History of a Publishing House* (Butterworths, 1980). x, 285 pp.

Cadell & Davies

Besterman, T., *The Publishing Firm of Cadell & Davies 1793–1836* (Oxford University Press, 1938). 189 pp.

Cambridge University Press

Black, M. H., *Cambridge University Press 1584–1984* (Cambridge University Press, 1984). xvii 343 pp.

McKitterick, David, *Four Hundred Years of University Printing and Publishing in Cambridge 1584–1984* (Cambridge University Press, 1984). 192 pp.

Roberts, S. C., *A History of Cambridge University Press 1521–1921* (Cambridge University Press, 1921).

Roberts, S. C., *The Evolution of Cambridge Publishing* (1956). 66 pp.

Cape (Jonathan) Ltd

Howard, M. S., *Jonathan Cape, Publisher: Herbert Jonathan Cape, G. Wren Howard* (Cape, 1971). 351 pp.

Lusty, R., *Bound To Be Read* (Jonathan Cape, n.d.). 314 pp.

Cassell Ltd

Nowell-Smith, S., *The House of Cassell* (1958). x 299 pp.

Catnach Press

Hindley, C., *The History of the Catnach Press at Berwick-upon-Tweed ...* (The Firm, 1886). 308 pp.

Chapman & Hall Ltd

Waugh, A., *A Hundred Years of Publishing* (1930). 326 pp.

Chappell & Co. Ltd

Mair, C. (comp.), *The Chappell Story, 1811–1961* (Chappell, 1961).
89 pp.

Cheney (John) & Sons

—— *John Cheney and Sons and His Descendants* (Cheney, 1936). 81 pp.

Clay (Richard) & Co. Ltd

Moran, J., *Clays of Bungay* (Richard Clay & Co. Ltd, 1978). 160 pp.

Clowes (William) & Sons Ltd (now a subsidiary of Norton Opax plc)

Clowes, W. B., *Family Business 1803–1953* (Clowes, 1953). 81 pp.

Coates Brothers

Coates, J. B. M., *A History of Coates Brothers & Co. Ltd 1877–1977*
(Westerham Press Ltd, 1977). 103 pp.

Collins (William)

Keir, D. E., *The House of Collins: The Story of a Scottish Family of
Publishers from 1789 to the Present Day* (Collins, 1952). 303 pp.

Kent, D., *The Story of a Scottish Family: Collins from 1789 to Present
Day* (1952). 303 pp.

Constable & Co.

Arnold, R., *Orange Street & Brickhole Lane* (Hart-Davis, 1963). 190 pp.

Curwen Press Ltd

Simon, H., *Songs and Words: A History of the Curwen Press* (Allen & Unwin, 1973). 261 pp.

David & Charles

—— *Good Books Come from Devon: The David & Charles Twenty-First Birthday Book* (David & Charles, 1981). 104 pp.

De La Rue Co. Ltd

Houseman, L., *The House that Thomas Built: The Story of De La Rue* (Chatto & Windus, 1968). xi 207 pp.

Dent (J. M.) & Sons Ltd

Dent, J. M., *The House of Dent 1888–1939* (J. M. Dent, 1938). xvii 334 pp.

Derry & Sons

—— *Derry's: A Century in Print 1867–1967* (The Firm, 1967). 84 pp.

Duckworth (Gerald) & Co. Ltd

—— *Fifty Years 1898–1948* (1948). 51 pp.

East Midland Allied Press

Newton, D., *Men of Mark: Makers of East Midland Allied Press* (The Firm, 1977). 254 pp.

Fishburn Printing Ink Co. Ltd

Leach, R., *Let the Ink Flow: The History of the First Fifty Years of Fishburn Ink* (Fishburn, 1980). 100 pp.

Fortune Press

D'Arch Smith, G., *R. A. Caton and the Fortune Press: A Memoir and a Handlist* (Rota, 1983). 92 pp.

Friedheim (Oscar) Ltd

Brewer, R., *Friedheim: A Century of Service 1884–1984* (Oscar Friedheim Ltd, 1984). 66 pp.

Glasgow University Press

Maclehose, J., *The Glasgow University Press 1638–1931* (Glasgow University Press, 1931). xx 285 pp.

Gollancz (Victor) Ltd

Edwards, Ruth Dudley, *Victor Gollancz* (Gollancz, 1987). 640 pp.

Hodges, Sheila, *Gollancz: The Story of a Publishing House 1928–1978* (Gollancz, 1978). 256 pp.

Gregynog Press

Harrop, D., *A History of the Gregynog Press* (Private Libraries Association, 1980). xv 266 pp.

Gresham Press: *see* Unwin Brothers

Harrap Ltd.

Harrap, G. G., *Some Memories 1901–1935: A Publisher's Contribution to the History of Publishing* (Harrap, 1935). 172 pp.

Haworth (John S.)

—— *James Haworth & Company: A Family in Print* (The Firm, 1989). iv 208 pp.

Haynes Publishing Group

Clew, Jeff, *Haynes Publishing: The First 25 Years* (Haynes, 1985). 120 pp.

Hazell, Watson & Viney Ltd

Keefe, H. J., *A Century in Print: The Story of Hazell's 1839–1939* (1939). 224 pp.

—— *Hazell's in Aylesbury 1867–1967: A Scrapbook* ... (The Firm, 1968). 188 pp.

Heinemann (William)

St John, John, *William Heinemann: A Century of Publishing 1890–1990* (Heinemann, 1990). xiv 689 pp.

Heywood (Abel) & Son Ltd

Heywood, G. B., *Abel Heywood, Abel Heywood & Son, Abel Heywood & Son Ltd 1832–1932* (1932).

Hodder & Stoughton Ltd

Attenborough, J., *A Living Memory: Hodder & Stoughton, Publishers, 1868–1975* (Hodder & Stoughton, 1975). 287 pp.

England, E. O., *An Unfading Vision: The Adventure of Books* (Hodder & Stoughton, 1982). 159 pp.

Hogarth Press

Kennedy, R., *A Boy at the Hogarth Press* (Penguin Books, 1978). 99 pp.

Woolmer, J. H. (comp.), *A Checklist of the Hogarth Press, 1917–1938* (Hogarth Press, 1976). xi 177 pp.

Horsell Group

Brewer, R., *A Sharper Image: A History of the Horsell Group 1885–1989* (James & James, 1989). 64 pp.

Kitcat (G. & J.) Ltd

Adams, J., *The House of Kitcat: A Story of Bookbinding 1798–1948* (Kitcat, 1948). 64 pp.

Liverpool University Press

Droop, J. P., *Liverpool University Press of Liverpool: A Record of Progress, 1899–1946* (University of Liverpool Press, 1947). 78 pp.

Livingstone (E. & S.)

Junor, I., *Footprints on the Sands of Time 1863–1963: The Story of the House of Livingstone, Medical, Scientific & Dental Publishers* (Edinburgh: Livingstone, 1963). 71 pp.

Longman Group Ltd

Briggs, Asa, *Essay in the History of Publishing: In Celebration of the 250th Anniversary of the House of Longman 1724–1974* (Longmans, 1974). viii 468 pp.

Longman, C. J., *The House of Longman 1724–1800* (Longmans, 1936). xv 488 pp.

Wallis, P., *At the Sign of the Ship: Notes on the House of Longman 1724–1974* (The Firm, 1974). 85 pp.

Macmillan

Morgan, Charles, *The House of Macmillan 1843–1943* (Macmillan, 1943). xxi 248 pp.

Mardon, Son & Hall Ltd: *see under* 'Paper'

Methodist Publishing House

Cumbers, F. H., *The Book Room: The Story of the Methodist Publishing House and Epworth Press* (1956). 153 pp.

Minerva Press

Blakey, D., *The Minerva Press 1790–1820 (And its Founder William Lane)* (Bibliographical Society, 1939). 339 pp.

Netherwood & Dalton

—— *Netherwood and Dalton, History: vols 1–3, 1868–1951* (Microfilm).

Newbery Press (London) Ltd

Roscoe, S., *John Newbery and His Successors 1740–1814: A Bibliography* (Five Owls Press, 1975). xxxi 460 pp.

Nonesuch Press

Dreyfus, John, *A History of the Nonesuch Press* (Nonesuch Press, 1981). 320 pp.

Novello & Co. Ltd

—— *A Century and a Half in Soho: A Short History of the Firm of Novello 1811–1961* (1961). 85 pp.

Hurd, M., *Vincent Novello – And Company* (Granada, 1981). 163 pp.

Odhams

Minney, R. J., *Viscount Southwood* (Odhams, 1954). 384 pp.

Odhams, W. J. B., *The Business and I* (Secker, 1935). xii 193 pp.

Ottley (Charles) & Landon

Carter, J. and Pollard, H. G., *The Firm of Charles Ottley, London: Footnote to an Enquiry* (Hart-Davis, 1948). 95 pp.

Oxford University Press

—— *Some Account of the Oxford University Press 1468–1921* (1922). 111 pp.

Barker, N., *The Oxford University Press and the Spread of Learning, 1478–1978. An Illustrated History* (Clarendon Press, 1978).

Carter, H., *A History of the Oxford University Press. Volume 1: To The Year 1789* (Clarendon Press, 1975). xxxi 640 pp.

Sutcliffe, Peter, *The Oxford University Press: An Informal History* (Clarendon Press, 1978). xxviii, 303 pp.

Parsons (J. F.) Ltd

—— *100 Years of Fine Printing* (1954).

Penguin Books Ltd

—— *Penguin's Progress* (Penguin, 1960). 86 pp.

Morpurgo, Jack, *Allen Lane, King Penguin: A Biography* (Hutchinson, 1979). 406 pp.

Segrave, E., *Ten Years of Penguins* (Penguin, 1945).

Williams, Sir W. E., *The Penguin Story 1935–1956* (1956). 125 pp.

Jones, L. L., *Fifty Penguin Years* (Penguin, 1985). 142 pp.

Petty & Sons Ltd

Murray, C. C., *Petty & Sons Limited 1865–1965* (1965). 55 pp.

Philip (George) & Son Ltd

Philip, George, *The Story of the Last Hundred years – A Geographical Record 1834–1934* (1934). 108 pp.

Pitman (Sir Isaac) & Sons Ltd

Pitman, A., *Half a Century of Commercial Education and Publishing* (c. 1935). 154 pp.

—— *The House of Pitman 1930* (Pitman, 1930). 63 pp.

—— *The Life of Sir Isaac Pitman* (1908, reprinted 1980). 402 pp.

Raithby Lawrence & Co.

Brewer, R., *Raithby Lawrence & Co.: 1776–1876: Raithby Lawrence & Co.; 1876–1976: De Montfort press* (The Firm, 1976). 90 pp.

Rationalist Press Association Ltd

Gould, F. J., *The Pioneers of Johnson's Court: A History of The Association from 1899* (1929). 160 pp.

Reed (Thomas)

Benn, D., *Thomas Reed, the First 200 Years: A Brief History 1782–1982* (The Firm, 1982). 64 pp.

Rivington

Rivington, S., *The Publishing Family of Rivington* (1919). 182 pp.

Routledge & Kegan Paul Ltd

Mumby, F. A., *The House of Routledge, 1834–1934* (1934). 232 pp.

Secker & Warburg Ltd

Warburg, Frederick, *An Occupation for Gentlemen* (Hutchinson, 1959). 287 pp.

Warburg, F. J., *All Authors are Equal: The Publishing Life of Frederic Warburg 1936–1971* (1973). 323 pp.

Seed (R.) & Sons

—— *Fifty Years' Service in the Printing Industry of Preston 1877–1927* (The Company, 1927).

Sessions (William)

Sessions, W., *Sessions of York and their Printing Forebears* (William Sessions, 1985). x 69 pp. (2nd revised edition.)

Smart (L. A.) & Son Ltd

—— *A Century of Progress in Printing 1850–1950* (1950?). 60 pp.

Smith Elder

—— *The House of Smith Elder* (The Firm, 1923). 249 pp.

Smith (S.) & Son Ltd

—— *12 Essays by a Process-Engraving and Printing Firm* (1956). 55 pp.

Society for Promoting Christian Knowledge

Clarke, W. K. L., *A History of the SPCK* (1959). 244 pp.

The Society of London Bookbinders

Howe, Ellic and Child, John, *The Society of London Bookbinders* (Sylvan, 1952). 288 pp.

Spottiswoode, Ballantyne & Co. Ltd

Leigh, R. A. A., *The Story of a Printing House: Being a Short Account of the Strahans and Spottiswoodes* (1912). 61 pp. (2nd edition.)

Sweet & Maxwell Ltd

Sayle, R. T. D., *Notes on the South East Corner of Chancery Lane 1919–1929* (1929). x 70 pp.

—— *Sweet & Maxwell, Then and Now 1799–1974, Commemorating 175 Years of Bookselling and Publishing* (Sweet & Maxwell, 1974). xii 219 pp.

Taylor & Francis

Brock, W. H., and Meadows, A. J., *The Lamp of Learning: Taylor and Francis and the Development of Science Publishing* (Taylor & Francis, 1984). xv 240 pp.

Temple Press Ltd

Armstrong, A. C., *Bouverie Street to Bowling Green Lane: Fifty-Five Years of Specialised Publishing* (Hodder, 1946). 224 pp.

Tillotson & Son Ltd

Singleton, F., *Tillotsons, 1850–1926* (Tillotson, 1926). 94 pp.

Singleton, Frank, *Tillotsons 1850–1950: Centenary of a Family Business* (Bolton, 1950). x, 94 pp.

Unwin Brothers Ltd: *see also* Allen & Unwin, *above*

—— *Unwins: A Century of Progress: Being a record of the rise and present position of The Gresham Press 1826–1926* (1926). 67 pp.

Unwin, Philip S., *The Publishing Unwins* (Heinemann, 1972). x 182 pp.

Unwin, Philip S., *The Printing Unwins: A Short History of Unwin Brothers, The Gresham Press, 1826–1976* (Allen & Unwin, 1976) 159 pp.

Waddie & Co.

Mackie, A. D., *A Centenary History of Waddie & Co. Limited, Edinburgh & London* (The Firm, 1960). 78 pp.

Waide (Thomas) & Sons

Clay, E. W., *Waide's 100 Years 1878–1978 . . . Printers and Carton Manufacturers* (Leeds: The Firm, 1978). 60 pp.

Ward Lock Educational Co. Ltd

Liveing, E. G. D., *Adventure in Publishing: The House of Ward Lock 1854–1954* (Ward Lock, 1954). 108 pp.

Warne (Frederick)

King, A. and Stuart, A. F., *The House of Warne: One Hundred Years of Publishing* (The Firm, 1965). x 107 pp.

Willmer Brothers & Haram Ltd

Willmer, E. W., *Family Business: The Story of Willmer Brothers & Haram Ltd* (The Firm, 1961). 87 pp.

Wright & Sons Ltd

—— *125 Years of Printing and Publishing, 1825–1950* (The Stonebridge Press, 1950).

Yelf

Daish, A. N., *Printer's Pride: The House of Yelf at Newport, Isle of Wight, 1816–1966* (The Firm, 1967). 92 pp.

Rubber

General

Woodruff, William, *The Rise of the British Rubber Industry During the Nineteenth Century* (Liverpool University Press, 1958). xvii 246 pp.

Angus (George) & Co.

—— *Angus: A Story of Progress in Industry* (The Firm, 1963?). 53 pp.

Avon Rubber Co.

—— *A Romance of Rubber: The Avon and Rubber Works 1886–1927* (The Firm, 1927).

Social Audit, *Social Audit on the Avon Rubber Co. Ltd* (The author, 1976). 91 pp.

Dick, (R. & J.)

Chalmers, T., *100 Years of Guttapercha* (The Firm, n.d.). 53 pp.

Dunlop Rubber Co. Ltd

Du Cros, Sir A. P., *Wheels of Fortune* (1938). 316 pp.

—— *1939–45: The Part Player in these Momentous Years of the Dunlop Organisation* (The Firm, 1945). 100 pp.

Dunlop, Kathleen E., *A History of the Dunlop Rubber Co. in England 1888–1939* (1948). (USA: University of Illinois Ph.D. thesis.)

—— *Dunlop Research Centre, Fort Dunlop, Birmingham* (The Firm, 1955). 77 pp.

Jennings, Paul, *Dunlopera: The Works and Workings of the Dunlop Rubber Company* (privately printed, 1961). 157 pp.

McMillan, J., *The Dunlop Story* (Weidenfeld & Nicolson, 1989). 240 pp.

Storrs, Sir Ronald, *Dunlop in War and Peace* (Hutchinson, 1946). xii 147 pp.

North British Rubber Co.

—— *North British Rubber and Gorgie-Dairy Living Memory Project: Stretch a Mile* (The Firm, 1985). Two volumes.

Spencer Moulton

—— *1848–1949: A Hundred Years of Rubber Manufacture* (The Firm, 1948).

Shipping and General Merchants

[Includes Shipbuilders, Shipowners, Agents, etc.]

There is a vast amount of material on shipping and I could not possibly include each and every title within the confines of this bibliography: so please take a good look at the general titles for further information.

General

Davies, P. N., *Sir Alfred Jones. Shipping Entrepreneur Par Excellence* (Europa, 1978). lxii 162 pp.

Hope, R., *A New History of British Shipping* (Murray, 1990). xiii 533 pp.

Hume, J. R. and Moss, M. S., *Clyde Shipbuilding from Old Photographs* (Batsford, 1975).

Knight, R. J. B. (ed.), *Guide to the Manuscripts in the National Maritime Museum,* vol. 2 (Mansell, 1980). 216 pp.

Mathias, Peter and Pearsall, A. W. H. (eds), *Shipping: A Survey of Historical Records* (David & Charles, 1971). 162 pp. [In association with the Business Archives council.]

Ritchie, L. A., *Modern British Shipbuilding: A Guide to Historical Records* (National Maritime Museum, 1980). 72 pp.

Ritchie, L. A., *The Shipbuilding Industry: A Guide to Historical Records* (Manchester University Press, 1992). vi 206 pp.

Walker, Fred M., *Song of the Clyde: A History of Clyde Shipbuilding* (Stephens, 1984).

Abbey Line

Heaton, P. M., *The Abbey Line: History of a Cardiff Shipping Venture* (Starling Press, 1983). 151 pp.

Aberdeen Line

Cornford, L. C., *The Sea Carriers 1825–1925: The Aberdeen Line* (The Firm, 1925). iii 79 pp.

Anchor Line Ltd

McLellan, R. S., *Anchor Line, 1856–1956* (Anchor Line Ltd, 1956). 184 pp.

Asiatic Steam Navigation Co.

Laxon, W.A., *Asiatic Steam Navigation Co. Ltd 1878–1963* (Kendall, 1963).

B & B Line plc

Smyth, H. P., *The B & B Line: A History of the British and Irish Steam Packet Company* (Gill & MacMillan, 1984). 246 pp.

Baltic Mercantile & Shipping Exchange Ltd

Barty-King, Hugh, *The Baltic Exchange: The History of a Unique Market* (Hutchinson Benham, 1977). xx 431 pp.

Findlay, J. A., *The Baltic Exchange: Being a Short History, 1744–1927* (1927). 55 pp.

Bank Line

—— *Seventy Adventurous Years: The Story of the Bank Line 1885–1955* (Liverpool: Shipping Telegraph, 1956). 136 pp.

Appleyard, H. S., *Bank Line and Andrew Weir and Company* (World Ship Society, 1985). 176 pp.

Ben Line

Blake, G., *The Ben Line: The History of a Merchant Fleet 1825–1955* (1956). ix 222 pp.

Bennett (D.) & Co.

Jones, Alfred Godfrey E., *Daniel Bennett & Co.* (The Company, 1960). Typewritten.

Bibby Line Ltd

—— *Bibby Line 1807–1957* (The Company, 1957). 64 pp.

Paget-Tomlinson, E. W., *The History of the Bibby Line* (The Firm, 1969). 78 pp.

Paget-Tomlinson, E. W., *Bibby Line: 175 Years of Achievement* (The Firm, 1982). 69 pp.

Plight, J., *History of the Bibby Line* (1949).

Watson, N., *The Bibby Line 1807–1990: A Story of Wars, Booms and Slumps* (James & James, 1990). 74 pp.

Bolston (J.) & Son

Chalk, D. L., *Any More for the Skylark? The Story of Bournemouth's Pleasure Boats* (Bournemouth: The Author, 1980). 54 pp.

Booth (Alfred) & Co.

John, A. H., *A Liverpool Merchant House: The History of Alfred Booth & Co. 1863–1958* (Allen & Unwin, 1959). 197 pp.

Boston Deep Sea Fisheries Ltd

—— *The Boston Saga: 1885–1968 (1968).* [Trawler owners.]

Bowring (C. T.) & Co.

Keir, D. E., *The Bowring Story* (Bodley Head, 1962). 448 pp.

Wardle, A. C., *Benjamin Bowring and His Descendants* (Hodder, 1940). 229 pp.

Bristol Shipping Line

Hill, J. C. G., *Shipshape and Bristol Fashion* (Liverpool: Journal of Commerce and Shipping Telegraph, 1952). viii 110 pp.

British India Steam Navigation Co. Ltd

Blake, G., *Bl Centenary 1856–1956: The Story of the British India Steam Navigation Company* (Collins, 1956). 272 pp.

British South Africa Company

Galbraith, J. S., *Crown and Charter: The Early Years of the British South Africa Company* (University of California Press, 1974).

Malcolm, Sir D. O., *The Company 1889–1939* (1939). 73 pp.

Brocklebank & Co. Ltd

Gibson, J. F., *Brocklebanks: 1770–1950* (Young, 1953). Two volumes.

Hollett, D., *From Cumberland to Cape Horn: The Complete History of the Sailing Fleet of Thomas and John Brocklebank of Whitehaven and Liverpool* (Fairplay Publications, 1984). 204 pp.

Brown (John) & Co. Ltd: *see also* 'Engineering' (p. 109) *and* 'Iron and Steel' (p. 169)

Grant, Sir A., *Steel and Ships: The History of John Brown's* (1950). 97 pp.

—— *John Brown, Atlas Works, Sheffield: Shipyard and Engineering Works, Clydebank* (1903). 118 pp.

Burnyeat Ltd

Rolt, L. T. C., *Mariners' Market: Burnyeat Ltd: Growth Over a Century* (Newman Neame, 1961). 62 pp.

Butterfield & Swire

Cooke, C., *The Lion and the Dragon: British Voices from the China Coast* (Elm Tree Books, 1985). 184 pp.

Drage, C., *Taikoo* (Constable, 1970). 320 pp.

Caledon Shipbuilding Co.

—— *An Illustrated Brochure* ... (William Kidd, n.d.). 110 pp.

Caledonian Steam Packet Co.

MacArthur, I. C., *The Caledonian Steam Packet Co.* (Clyde River Steamers Club, 1971).

Cammell Laird & Co.: *see also* **Wilson Cammell** in 'Iron and Steel' (p. 177)

—— *Builders of Great Ships* (1959). 79 pp.

Cayzer Irvine & Co.

Muir, A. and Davies, M., *A Victorian Shipowner. A Portrait of Sir Charles Cayzer, Baronet of Gartmore* (Cayzer Irvine & Co., 1978). 320 pp.

Chapman of Newcastle

Lingwood, J. and Appleyard, H., *Chapman of Newcastle: The Story of a Tyneside Shipping Company* (World Ship Society, 1985). 80 pp.

Clan Line

Hurd, Sir Archibald Spicer, *The Clan Line in the Great War* (192?).
viii 134 pp.

Clarkson (H.) & Co. Ltd

—— *The Clarkson Chronicle 1852–1952* (1953). 115 pp.

—— *H. Clarkson & Co. Ltd 1852–1952* (1952). 166 pp.

Clyde Shipping Co. Ltd

Cuthbert, A. D., *Clyde Shipping Company Limited: A History*
(The Firm, 1956). 125 pp.

Collins Line

Armstrong, W., *The Collins Story* (Robert Hale, 1957). 192 pp.

Constantine Holdings

Appleyard, H. S., *The Constantine Group* (World Ship Society, 1983).
56 pp.

Cook (Walter) & Son

Cook, C. J., *A Barge on the Blocks: A Short History of Walter Cook and
Son, Boatbuilders, Maldon, Essex 1894–1970* (The Firm, 1980?).
64 pp.

Cosens & Co.

Cox, B. F., *The Buff Funnel Handbook: A Fully Illustrated Guide to the
Steamers, Their Routes and Services* (Bournemouth: The Firm, 1959).
51 pp.

Crawford (Andrew) & Co.

—— *The 'Vales' of Glasgow: Andrew Crawford & Co. Ltd 1895–1955*
(The Firm, 1955). 77 pp.

Cunard Steam-ship Co. Ltd

—— *A History of the Cunard Line from 1840–1902* (privately printed,
1902).

—— *Triumph of a Great Tradition: Official Souvenir of the Cunard Line*
(The Firm, 1990). 80 pp.

Coldey, D. (ed.), *The Cunarders, 1840–1969: A Transatlantic Story
Spanning 129 Years* (Peter Barker, 1969). 127 pp.

Grant, H. K., *Samuel Cunard: Pioneer of the Atlantic Steamship* (Abelard
Schuman, 1967). 192 pp.

Hyde, F. E., *Cunard and the North Atlantic 1840–1973: A History of
Shipping Management* (Macmillan, 1975). xx 382 pp.

Johnson, H., *The Cunard Story* (Whittet Books, 1987). 204 pp.

Denny (William) & Bros

—— *Denny Dumbarton 1844–1932* (Dumbarton: The Firm, 1932).
114 pp.

—— *Denny's Dumbarton Souvenir 1908* (The Firm, 1908). 155 pp.

—— *Souvenir of One Thousand Venues* (The Firm, 1913). 155 pp.

Devitt & Moore

Course, A. G., *Painted Ports: The Story of the Ships of Devitt & Moore*
(Hollis & Carter, 1961). x 230 pp.

Jones, C. W., *Sea Trading and Sea Training: Being a Short History of the
Firm of Devitt and Moore* (Arnold, 1936). 192 pp.

Dodwell & Co. Ltd

Warde, E., *The House of Dodwell: A Century of Achievement, 1858–1958* (1958). xiii 160 pp.

Donaldson Lines

Dunnett, A. M., *The Donaldson Line: A Century of Shipping 1854–1954* (Jackson, 1960). x 125 pp.

Telford, P. J., *Donaldson Line of Glasgow* (World Ship Society, 1989). 127 pp.

Duncan (Walter) & Goodricke Ltd

—— *The Duncan Group: Being a Short History 1859–1959* (1959). 184 pp.

Dunstan (Richard) Ltd

Dunstan, R., *Richard Dunstan Ltd, Shipbuilders, Thorne Near Doncaster* (1958). 62 pp.

Eagle Fleet

Lucas, W. E., *Eagle Fleet: The Story of a Tanker Fleet in Peace and War* (Weidenfeld & Nicolson, 1955). 149 pp.

Earles Shipbuilding & Engineering Co. Ltd

Credland, A. G., *Earles of Hull, 1853–1932: Iron and Steel Shipbuilding on the Humber* (Kingston-upon-Hull: City Museums and Galleries, 1982). 70 pp.

East India Company

Bellasis, M., *Honourable Company* (1952). 285 pp.

Chandhuri, K. N., *The English East India Company: The Study of an Early Joint-Stock Company* ... (Cass, 1965). 245 pp.

Keay, J., *The Honourable Company: A History of the English East India Company* (Harper Collins, 1991).

Sutherland, L. S., *The East India Company in Eighteenth-Century Politics* (Clarendon Press, 1952). 430 pp.

Elder Dempster & Co.

Davies, P. N., *The Trade Makers: Elder Dempster in West Africa 1852–1972* (Allen & Unwin, 1973). 526 pp.

Ellerman Lines Ltd

—— *The Development of British Shipping Throughout the Ages* (Gustav Schueler, 1924). 63 pp. [Refers especially to the Ellerman Lines 1839–1924.]

Taylor, James, *Ellermans: A Wealth of Shipping* (Wilton House Gentry, 1976). 320 pp.

Erlebach

Paul, Philip, *City Voyage: The Story of Erlebach & Co. Ltd 1867–1967* (Harley Publishing Co., 1967). 84 pp.

Escombe, McGrath & Co. Ltd

Escombe, W. M. L., *Full and Down: The History of Escombe, McGrath & Co.* (1953). 90 pp.

Escombe, W. M. L., *The History of Escombe, McGrath & Company Limited* (The Firm, 1969). vii 131 pp.

Fairfield Shipbuilding & Engineering Co. Ltd

—— *Fairfield Shipbuilding & Engineering Co. Ltd 1860–1960.* [Commemorative booklet.] 100 pp.

Alexander, K. J. W. and Jenkins, C. L., *Fairfields: A Study of Industrial Change* (Allen Lane, Penguin, 1970). 285 pp.

Paulden, S. P. L. and Hawkins, W., *Whatever Happened at Fairfields?* (Gower Press, 1969). x 214 pp.

Federal Steam Navigation Company

Holman, G., *In the Wake of Endeavour* (1973). 241 pp.

Finlay (James) & Co. Ltd

—— *James Finlay & Co. Ltd: Manufacturers and East India Merchants 1750–1950* (Jackson, 1951). 276 pp.

France (William), Fenwick & Co. Ltd

—— *Wm France, Fenwick & Co. Ltd: Its History* (1954). ix 83 pp.

Gellatly, Hankey & Co. Ltd

Blake, G., *Gellatly's 1862–1962. A Short History* (Blackie, 1962). 178 pp.

General Steam Navigation Co. Ltd

Cornford, L. C., *A Century of Sea Trading 1824–1924* (A. & C. Black, 1924). xi 182 pp.

Hancock, H. E., *Semper Fidelis: The Saga of the 'Navvies' (1924–1948)* (The Firm, 1949). 155 pp. [Continuation of *A Century of Sea Trading 1824–1924*.]

Graig Shipping plc

Williams, D. Y., *Seventy Years in Shipping: Special Reminiscences of the History of Graig Shipping plc* (The Firm, 1989). 119 pp.

Grayson, Rollo & Clover Docks Ltd

Brooks, C., *'Grayson's of Liverpool': A History of Grayson, Rollo and Clover Docks Ltd* (Henry Young, 1956). 97 pp.

Hammond (George) plc

Watson, Nigel, *The History of George Hammond plc 1767–1992* (Granta Editions, 1993). 104 pp.

Harland & Wolff

Moss, M. and Hume, J. R., *Shipbuilders to the World: 125 Years of Harland and Wolff 1861–1986* (Blackstaff Press, 1986). 640 pp.

Pearson, J. G., *Great Shipbuilders or the Rise of Harland & Wolff* (The Firm, 1935).

Harrisons & Crosfield plc

—— *One Hundred Years as East India Merchants* (1943). 69 pp.

Hyde, F. E., *Shipping Enterprise and Management 1830–1939: Harrisons of Liverpool* (Liverpool University Press, 1967). 208 pp.

Pugh, P. and others, *Great Enterprise: A History of Harrisons & Crosfield* (The Firm, 1990). 272 pp.

Harrison (T. & J.)

Hyde, F. E. and others, *Shipping Enterprise and Management 1830–1939: Harrisons of Liverpool* (Liverpool University Press, 1967). xx 208 pp.

Hawthorn Leslie (R. & W.) & Co.: *see* 'Engineering' (p. 115)

Henderson (P.) & Co.

Laird, D., *Paddy Henderson: A History of the Scottish Shipping Firm P. Henderson & Co. ... 1834–1961* (Glasgow: George Ontram, 1961). 230 pp.

Henley (Michael) & Son

Currie, A., *Henleys of Wapping: A London Shipowning Family, 1770–1830* (National Maritime Museum, 1988). 76 pp.

Hogarth (H.) & Sons

McAlister, A. A. and Gray, L., *A Short History of H. Hogarth & Sons Limited and Fleet List* [Baron Line] (World Ship Society, 1976). 56 pp.

Holland America Line

Schaap, D., *A Bridge to the Seven Seas* [a centenary celebration] (PSL, 1973). 119 pp.

Holt (Alfred) & Co.

—— *The Blue Funnel Line* (1938).

Falkus, M., *The Blue Funnel Legend: A History of the Ocean Steam Ship Company 1865–1973* (Macmillan, 1990). 432 pp.

Hyde, F. E. and Harris, J. R., *Blue Funnel: A History of Alfred Holt & Company of Liverpool 1865 to 1914* (Liverpool University Press, 1956). 201 pp.

Le Fleming, H. M., *Ships of the Blue Funnel Line* (1961).

Roskill, S. W., *A Merchant Fleet at War, Alfred Holt & Co. 1939–1945* (1962). 352 pp.

Holt (John) & Co. (Liverpool) Ltd

—— *Merchant Adventure: John Holt & Co. (Liverpool)* (The Firm, 1947). 80 pp.

—— *Diary of John Holt* (The Company, 1951). 279 pp.

Houlder Bros & Co. Ltd

—— *Sea Hazard (1939–1945). A Record of the Engagements Between Enemy Submarines and the Ships of Houlder Bros* (1947). 105 pp.

Stevens, E. F., *One Hundred Years of Houlders: A Record of the History of Houlder Bros from 1849–1850* (1951). 101 pp.

Hughes Bolckow

White, H. *Battleship Wharf* (Blyth: The Firm, 1961). vi 68 pp.

Hull, Blyth & Co.

Woodhouse, G. B., *Hull, Blyth & Company Limited: A Short History* (The Firm, 1979). 60 pp.

Imperial British East Africa Co.

Hodge, E. R. V., *Imperial British East Africa Company* (1960). 95 pp.

Inchcape plc

Cater, W., *Inchcape & Co. Limited* (The Firm, 1977). 60 pp.

Griffiths, Sir P., *A History of the Inchcape Group* (1977). 211 pp.

Jones, Stephanie, *Two Centuries of Overseas Trading: The Origins and Growth of the Inchcape Group* (Macmillan, 1986). 328 pp.

—— *The Inchcape Group including Inchcape & Co. Ltd and Subsidiary and Associated Companies* (The Firm, 1963). 86 pp.

Isle of Man Steam Packet Co. Ltd

Caine, P. W. (ed.), *The Isle of Man Steam Packet Co. Ltd: Centenary 1830–1930* (1930).

Moore, A. W., *The Isle of Man Steam Packet Co. Ltd 1830–1904* (1904).

Ismay Line

Oldham, W. J., *The Ismay Line: The White Star Line and the Ismay Family Story* (1961). xviii 283 pp.

Jardine, Matheson & Co.

—— *'Jardines' and EWO Interests* (1947). 52 pp.

—— *Jardine Matheson & Co. – An Historical Sketch* (The Firm, 1969). 64 pp.

Greenberg, M., *British Trade and the Opening of China, 1800–42* (1951). 238 pp. [Based mainly on the papers of Jardine, Matheson & Co.]

Keswick, M. (ed.), *The Thistle and the Jade: A Celebration of Jardine Matheson & Co.* (Octopus, 1982). 272 pp.

Jenkins Brothers

Jenkins, D., *Davis Brothers of Cardiff: A Ceredigion Family's Shipping Ventures* (Cardiff: National Museum of Wales, 1985). 112 pp.

Killick, Martin & Co. Ltd

MacGregor, D. R., *The China Bird: The History of Captain Killick and One Hundred Years of Sail and Steam* (Chatto, 1961). xvii 366 pp.

King Line

Mallett, A. S., *Idyll of the Kings, 1889–1979: The Story of the King Line, its Ships and the Men Who Sailed and Managed Them* (World Ship Society, 1980). 64 pp.

Lamey (J. H.) Ltd

Hallam, W., *Fifty Years of Mersey Towage 1916–1966: The History of J. H. Lamey Ltd* (1966).

Lithgow

Reid, J. M., *James Lithgow, Master of Work* (Hutchinson, 1964). 254 pp.

Lloyd's Register of Shipping

—— *Annals of Lloyd's Register* (1934). 274 pp.

Blake, G., *Lloyd's Register of Shipping 1760–1960* (1960). 194 pp.

Lockwood & Carlisle Ltd

Simons, E. N., *Lockwood and Carlisle Ltd of Sheffield: A Chapter of Marine History* (The Firm, 1962). 62 pp.

London Graving Dock Co. Ltd

Hurd, E., *Eighty-six Years Plus: The Story of the London Graving Dock Co. Ltd 1890–1976* (The Firm, 1976). 95 pp.

Lyle Shipping Co.

Orbell, J. and others, *From Cape to Cape: The History of the Lyle Shipping Company* (Harris, 1973). xii 239 pp.

MacCallum (P.) & Sons Ltd

Hume, J. R. and Moss, M. S., *A Bed of Nails: The History of P. MacCallum & Sons Ltd of Geenock 1781–1981: A Study in Survival* (Lang & Fulton, 1983). x 148 pp.

Mitchell (Charles)

McGuire, D. F., *Charles Mitchell, 1820–1895: Victorian Shipbuilder* (Newcastle-upon-Tyne: City Libraries & Arts, 1988). 74 pp.

Morel (Cardiff)

Gibbs, J. M., *Morels of Cardiff: The History of a Family Shipping Firm* (National Museum of Wales, 1982). 183 pp.

Neills of Bangor

Wilson, D., *Neills of Bangor* (The Firm, 1982). 82 pp.

Norton (John) & Sons

Mason, F. N. (ed.) *John Norton & Sons Merchants of London and Virginia* (1937). 573 pp. [Reprinted 1968.]

Ocean Steam Ship Co.: *see* Holt (Alfred) & Co., *above*

Orient Line

Morris, C. F., *Origins, Orient and 'Oriana'* (Teredo Books, 1980). xx 491 pp.

Overend, Gurney & Co.

Xenos, S., *Depredations for Overend, Gurney & Co. and the Greek & Oriental Steam Navigation Co.* (The Author, 1869). 377 pp.

Palmers of Jarrow

Davidson, J. F., *From Collier to Battleships: Palmers of Jarrow 1852–1933* (Durham, 1946).

Dillon, M., *Some Account of the Works of Palmers Shipbuilding & Iron Co.* (Franklin, 1900). 55 pp.

Peninsular & Oriental Steam Navigation Co. (P. & O.)

Cable, B., *A Hundred Year History of the P. & O.* (Nicolson & Watson, 1937). x 289 pp.

Divine, A. D., *These Splendid Ships: The Story of the Peninsular and Oriental Line* (Muller, 1960). 255 pp.

Donaldson, G., *Northwards By Sea* (Paul Harris, 1978). 162 pp.

Ewart, E. A., *A Hundred-Year History of P. & O.* (Nicolson, 1937). x 289 pp.

Gordon, M. R., *From Chusan to Sea Princess. The Australian Services of the P. & O. Lines* (Allen & Unwin, 1985). 184 pp.

Howarth, D. and Howarth, S., *The Story of P. & O.: The Peninsular and Oriental Steam Navigation Company* (Weidenfeld & Nicolson, 1986). 224 pp.

Kerr, G. F., *Business in Great Waters: The War History of P. & O. 1939–1945* (Faber, 1951). 196 pp.

Kirk, R., *The P. & O. Bombay & Australian Lines 1852–1914* (Proud-Bailey, 1982). 166 pp.

Kirk, R., *The P. & O. Lines to the Far East* (Proud-Bailey, 1982). 224 pp.

Padfield, P., *Beneath the House Flag of the P. & O.* (Hutchinson, 1981). 147 pp.

—— *P. & O. in the Falklands* (The Firm, 1982). 86 pp.

Port Line

McMillan, S., *Port Line Story: A Short History of the Company* (The Firm, 1964). 75 pp.

Radcliffe (Evan Thomas) & Co.

Jenkins, J. G., *Evan Thomas Radcliffe: A Cardiff Shipowning Company* (National Museum of Wales, 1982). 92 pp.

Rathbones

Marriner, S., *Rathbones of Liverpool 1845–1873* (Liverpool University Press, 1961). 258 pp.

Reardon Smith Line

Heaton, P. M., *Reardon Smith Line: The History of a South Wales Shipping Venture* (Starling Press, 1984). 133 pp.

Richards (Shipbuilders) Ltd

Goodey, C., *The First Hundred Years: The Story of Richards Shipbuilders* (Boydell Press, 1976). 111 pp.

Ropner plc

Dear, I., *The Ropner Story* (Hutchinson Benham, 1986). 165 pp.

Royal Africa Company

Davies, K. G., *The Royal Africa Company* (Longmans, 1957). ix 390 pp.

Royal Mail Lines Ltd

Brooks, C., *The Royal Mail Case* (Hodge, 1933).

Bushell, T. A., *'Royal Mail': A Centenary History of the Royal Mail Line 1839–1939* (Trade & Travel Publications, 1939). xvi 270 pp.

Bushell, T. A., *Eight Bells: Royal Mail Lines War Story 1939–45* (1950). xv 207 pp.

Dowden, P., *Ships of the Royal Mail Lines* (Adlard Coles, 1953). 79 pp.

Green, Edwin and Moss, Michael, *A Business of National Importance: The Royal Mail Shipping Group 1902–1937* (Methuen, 1982). xii 291 pp.

Griffiths, Denis, *Brunel's 'Great Western'* (Patrick Stephens, 1985). 160 pp.

O'Connor, G. W., *The First Hundred Years: The Royal Mail Steam Packet Co. Ltd* (The Firm, 1961). 107 pp.

Vice, A., *Financier at Sea: Lord Kylsant and the Royal Mail* (Merlin Books, 1985). 124 pp.

Royden (Thomas) & Sons

Royden, Sir Ernest B., *Thomas Royden & Sons, Shipbuilders, Liverpool, 1818–1893* (privately printed, 1953). 56 pp.

Russia Company

Willan, T. S., *The Early History of the Russia Company* (Manchester University Press, 1956). ix 295 pp.

Saint Line

Heaton, P. M., *The South American Saint Line: History of a Welsh Shipping Line* (Starling Press, 1985).

Salvesen (Christian)

Somner, G., *From 70 North to 70 South: A History of the Christian Salvesen Fleet* (The Firm, 1984). 142 pp.

Vamplew, W., *Salvesen of Leith* (Scottish Academic Press, 1975). xii 311 pp.

Scotts of Greenock

—— *Two Hundred & Fifty Years of Shipbuilding by the Scotts of Greenock* (The Firm, 1961). xx 279 pp.

Scruttons Ltd

Jeffery, A. E., *The History of Scruttons: Ship Brokers and Shipowners 1801–1926; Stevedors, Master Porters and Cargo Superintendents 1890–1967* (privately printed, 1971). ix 164 pp.

Shaw Savill & Albion Co. Ltd

—— *Sail to New Zealand: The Story of Shaw, Savill & Co. 1858–1985* (Hale, 1986). 192 pp.

Bowen, F. C., *The Flag of the Southern Cross: The History of Shaw Savill & Albion Co. Ltd 1858–1939* (The Firm, 1939). 122 pp.

Mitchell, A., *Splendid Sisters: A Story of the Planning, Construction and Operation of the Shaw Savill Liners* (Harrap, 1960). 192 pp.

Shipping Federation Ltd

Powell, L. H., *The Shipping Federation 1890–1950* (1950). 149 pp.

Staley Radford & Co.

Archer, J. F., *A History of Staley Radford & Co. Ltd 1875–1975* (Staley Radford & Co., 1975). 374 pp.

Stephen (Alexander) & Sons Ltd

—— *Alexander Stephen & Sons, 1750–1932* (Aberdeen, 1932). 212 pp.

Carvel, J. L., *Stephen of Linthowe: A Record of Two Hundred Years of Shipbuilding 1750–1950* (The Firm, 1950), 211 pp.

Lingwood, J. and Gay, L., *Stephens, Sutton Limited* (World Ship Society, 1983). 68 pp.

Stephenson Clarke Ltd

Carter, C. J. M., *The Stephenson Clarke Fleet Story, 1730–1958* (1958). 52 pp. [Reprinted from 'Sea Breezes' 1958.]

Carter, C. J. M., *Stephenson Clarke Shipping: A Brief Chronology and History* (World Ship Society, 1981). 62 pp.

Stewart (John) & Co.

Course, A. G., *The Wheel's Kick and the Wind's Song: The Story of John Stewart Line of Sailing Ships 1877–1928* (David & Charles, 1968). xiv 264 pp. (3rd edition).

Swire (John) & Sons

Cook, C. (ed.), *The Lion and the Dragon* (1982).

Hook, E., *A Guide to the Papers of John Swire & Sons Ltd* (London University, School of Oriental & African Studies, 1977). 176 pp.

Marriner, Sheila and Hyde, E., *The Senior John Samuel Swire 1825–98: Management in Far Eastern Shipping Trade* (Liverpool University Press, 1967). vv 224 pp.

—— *The Swire Group* (The Firm, 1975). 60 pp.

Tatham, Bromage & Co. Ltd

—— *Tatham's Log 1859–1958: The Centenary of Tatham, Bromage & Company Limited* (The Firm, 1958). 100 pp.

Tees Towing Co.

Proud, J. H., *Seahorses of the Tees: The Story of Tees Towing Company Limited* (The Firm, 1985). 189 pp.

Thomson (William) & Co.: *see* Ben Line, *above*

Thorneycroft (John I.) & Co. Ltd

Barnaby, K. C., *100 Years of Specialised Shipbuilding and Engineering: John I. Thorneycroft Centenary, 1964* (Hutchinson, 1964). 263 pp.

Turnbull Scott & Co.

Appleyard, H. S., *Turnbull Scott and Company* (World Ship Society, 1978). 52 pp.

Long, A., and Long, R., *A Shipping Venture: Turnbull Scott and Company 1872–1972* (Hutchinson Benham, 1974). xix 326 pp.

Tyrer (Henry) & Co. Ltd

Davies, P. N., *Henry Tyrer: A Liverpool Shipping Agent and his Enterprise 1879–1979* (Croom Helm, 1979). 159 pp.

Uganda Company Ltd

Erlich, C., *The First Fifty* (1953). 68 pp.

Union-Castle Mail Steamship Co. Ltd

Knight, E. F., *The Union-Castle and the War 1914–1919* (The Company, 1920). 63 pp.

Mitchell, W. H. and Sawyer, L. A., *The Cape Run: The Story of Union-Castle Service to South Africa* (Terrance Dalton, 1984). 214 pp.

Murray, M., *Union-Castle Chronicle 1853–1953* (Longmans, 1953). xvii, 392 pp.

Porter, A., *Victorian Shipping, Business and Imperial Policy: Donald Currie, the Castle Line and Southern Africa* (Boydall Press, 1986). 332 pp.

Upper Clyde Shipbuilders

McGill, J., *Crisis on the Clyde: The Story of Upper Clyde Shipbuilders* (Davis-Poynter, 1973). 144 pp.

Usk Ships

Heaton, P. M., *The Usk Ships: History of a Newport Shipping Venture* (Newport: Starling Press, 1982). 88 pp.

Vickers-Armstrong (Shipbuilders) Ltd: *see also* **Armstrong Whitworth** *and* **Vickers** *in* 'Arms for War and Peace' (p. 13) *and* 'Engineering' (p. 125)

—— *Launching Out* (Newcastle-upon-Tyne, 195?). 66 pp.

Warren, K., *Armstrongs of Elswick: Growth in Engineering and Armaments to the Merger with Vickers* (1989). 302 pp.

Vickers Sons & Maxim

—— *Vickers Sons & Maxim Ltd: Their Works and Manufactures* (Engineering, 1902). 200 pp.

Wallace Brothers & Co. (Holdings) Ltd

Pointon, A. C., *Wallace Brothers* (1974). 120 pp.

Watkins (William) Ltd

Bowen, F. C., *A Hundred Years of Towage: A History of William Watkins Ltd 1833–1933* (1933). 215 pp.

The Weir Group

Reader, W. J., *The Weir Group: A Centenary History* (Weidenfeld & Nicolson, 1971). x 230 pp.

West Hartlepool Steam Navigation Co.

Spaldin, B. G. and Appleyard, H. S., *The West Hartlepool Steam Navigation Company Limited and Talisman Trawlers Limited* (World Ship Society, 1980). 56 pp.

Westcotts

Merry, I. D., *The Westcotts and their Lines* (National Maritime Museum, 1977). x 149 pp.

Westray (J. B.) & Co. Ltd

Fagg, Alan, *Westrays: A Record of J. B. Westray & Co. Ltd* (Westrays, 1957). 117 pp.

White (J. Samuel) & Co.

—— *Whites of Cowes, Shipbuilders* (Cowes: The Firm, 195?). 104 pp.

White Star Line: *see also* Ismay Line, *above*

Anderson, R., *White Star* (Stephenson, 1964). 236 pp.

Williams (Samuel) & Sons Ltd

—— *A Company's Story in its Setting* (1855–1955) (1955). 88 pp.

Wilson, Sons & Co. Ltd [now Ellerman's Wilson Line Ltd]: *see* Ellerman Lines Ltd *above*

Yarrow & Co. Ltd

Borthwick, A., *Yarrow and Company Limited: The First Hundred Years 1865–1965* (The Company, 1965). 135 pp.

—— *Yarrow and Company Limited 1865–1977* (The Firm, 1977). 158 pp.

The Stock Exchange and Stockbrokers

General

Duguid, C., *The Story of the Stock Exchange* (Grant Richards, 1901). x 463 pp.

Michie, R. C., *Money, Mania and Markets: Investment, Company Formation and the Stock Exchange in 19th Century Scotland* (Donald, 1981). ix 287 pp.

Morgan, E. V. and Thomas, W. A., *The Stock Exchange* (Elek, 1962). 293 pp.

Thomas, W. A., *The Provincial Stock Exchange* (Cass, 1973).

Capel (James) & Co.

—— *List of Partners 1801–1951 in the Form of a Christmas Card* (1951). [In Guildhall Library.]

Reed, M. C., *A History of James Capel & Co.* (privately printed, 1975). xiii 129 pp.

Cazenove & Co.

Hornby, A., *My Life at Cazenove's* (privately published, 1971). 96 pp.

Kynaston, D., *Cazenove & Co.: A History* (Batsford, 1991). 359 pp.

De Zoete & Gorton

Janes, Henry Hurford (comp.), *De Zoete & Gorton: A History* (Harley, privately printed, 1963). 80 pp.

Foster & Braithwaite

Reader, W. J., *A House in the City: A Study of the City and of the Stock Exchange, Based on the Records of Foster & Braithwaite 1825–1975* (Batsford, 1979). 198 pp.

Liverpool Stock Exchange

Dumbell, S., *The Centenary Book of the Liverpool Stock Exchange 1836–1936* (The Firm, 1936). 68 pp.

Nathan & Rosselli

—— *Time and Adams Court* (1937). 86 pp.

Panmure Gordon & Co.

MacDermot, B. H. D., *Panmure Gordon & Co. 1876–1976: A Century of Stockbroking* (The Firm, 1976). iv 70 pp.

Sheppards & Chase

Hennessy, E., *Stockbrokers for 150 Years: A History of Sheppards & Chase 1827–1977* (The Firm, 1978). x 63 pp.

Stock Exchange

[There are many books and journals about the Stock Exchange. Only a selection has been listed.]

Stock Exchange Year-Books

Armstrong, F. E., *The Book of the Stock Exchange* (Pitman, 1934). ix 405 pp.

Ellinger, A. G., 'The Post-War History of the Stockmarket 1945–(1975)', Cambridge Investment Research, 1973–6. Two volumes, typewritten script in Guildhall Library.

Jenkins, A., *The Stock Exchange Story* (Heinemann, 1973). x 212 pp.

Morgan, E. V. and Thomas, W. A., *The Stock Exchange: Its History and Functions* (Elek Books, 1969). 295 pp.

S. G. Warburg Ackroyd Rowe & Pitman Mullens Securities Ltd

Wainright, D., *Government Broker: The Story of an Office and of Mullens & Co.* (Matham Publishing, 1990). 142 pp.

Textiles

[*Includes Bleaching, Carpets, Cotton, Drapers, Dyeing, Silk, Textile Machinery, Wool, etc.*]

General

Baines, E., *History of the Cotton Manufacture in Great Britain* (Cass, 1966). [2nd edition with W. H. Chaloner's bibliographic introduction, reprint of original edition 1835.]

Bartlett, J. Neville, *Carpeting the Millions: The Growth of Britain's Carpet Industry* (Donald, 1977). xiv 296 pp.

Boyson, Rhodes, *The Ashworth Cotton Enterprise* (Clarendon Press, 1970). 285 pp.

Edwards, Michael M., *The Growth of the British Cotton Trade 1780–1815* (Manchester University Press, 1967).

Farnie, D. A., *The English Cotton Industry and the World Market 1815–1896* (Clarendon Press, 1979). xiii 399 pp.

Gill, C., *The Rise of the Irish Linen Industry* (1925). (Reprinted 1964.)

Gulvin, Clifford, *The Tweedmakers: A History of the Scottish Fancy Woollen Industry 1600–1914* (David & Charles, 1973). 240 pp.

Gulvin, Clifford, *The Scottish Hosiery and Knitwear Industries: 1680–1980* (Donald, 1984). ix 163 pp.

Harte, N. B. and Ponting, K. G. (eds), *Textile History and Economic History* (Manchester University Press, 1973).

Howe, A., *The Cotton Masters 1830–1960* (Clarendon Press, 1984). 359 pp.

Hudson, P., *The West Riding Wool Textile Industry: A Catalogue of Business Records from the 16th to the 20th Century* (Pasold, 1975). 560 pp.

Kerridge, E., *Textile Manufacturers in Early Modern England* (Manchester University Press, 1985). 428 pp.

Robson, R., *The Cotton Industry in Britain* (Macmillan, 1957). xx 364 pp.

Robson, R., *The Man-Made Fibres Industry* (Macmillan, 1958). vii 135 pp.

Slinn, Judy A., *The Textile Industry* (Batsford Working Lives, 1986).

Wells, F. A., *The British Hosiery and Knitwear Industry: Its History and Organisation* (David & Charles, 1972). 256 pp.

Amalgamated Cotton Mills Trust Ltd

—— *Concerning Cotton: A Brief Account of the Aims and Achievements of the Amalgamated Cotton Mills Trust and its Component Companies* (192?). 152 pp. [In Manchester Central Reference Library.]

Arthur (J. F.) & Co. Ltd

Barclay, J. F., *One Hundred Years of Textile Distribution* (The Firm, 1953). xii 172 pp.

Axminster Carpet Co.

Jacobs, Bertram, *Axminster Carpets 1755–1957* (Lewis, 1970). 80 pp.

Baxter Brothers

Cooks, A. J., *Baxter's of Dundee* (Dundee University Press, 1980). 80 pp.

Berisfords Ltd

Sebire, C. B., *Berisfords, the Ribbon People: The Story of 100 Years 1858–1958* (Sessions, 1966). (2nd edition) xiv 154 pp (3rd edition, 1976.)

Sebire, J. F., *A Reputation in Ribbons* (The Firm, 1985). 107 pp.

Birtwistle (William) Group

Brothers, J. A., *W. B. Centenary 1851–1951* (1951).

Blackwood Morton & Sons Ltd & Cooke, Sons & Co.

—— *From Loom to Lathe – and Back Again: The Story of a Wartime Achievement* (1946). 61 pp.

Bodden (William) & Son Ltd

—— *Centenary 1858–1958* (The Company, 1958).

Bowers Mills

Muir, A., *In Blackburn Valley: The History of Bowers Mills* (Heffer, 1969). 90 pp.

Brettle (George) & Co. Ltd

Harte, N. B., *A History of George Brettle & Co. Ltd 1801–1964* (The Company, 1974). 165 pp.

Brierfield Mills Ltd

—— *Brierfield Mills Ltd 1904–1925* (Brierfield, 1925).

Brocklehurst-Whiston

—— *Brocklehurst–Whiston: The Story of its Activities* (The Firm, n.d.). 64 pp.

Calvert (I. & I.) Ltd

Garnett, W. O., *Wainstalls Mills: The History of I. and I. Calvert Ltd 1821–1951* (1951). x 153 pp.

Carrington Vyella plc: *see* **Hollins & Vyella,** *below*

Cooper (I., J. & G.) Ltd

—— *Cooper's of Manchester: The Home of Fancies 1823–1923* (1923).

Corah (N.)

Jopp, K., *Corah of Leicester: 1815–1965* (Newman Neame, 1965). 60 pp.

Webb, C. W., *An Historical Record of N. Corah & Sons Ltd, St Margaret's Works, Leicester* (The Firm, 1947?). 120 pp.

Courtaulds

—— *The Textile Development Unit* (Arrow Mill, Rochdale, 1956).

—— *Courtaulds: The Anatomy of a Multinational* (General Federation of Trade Unions, 1975). 112 pp.

Coleman, D. C., *Courtaulds: An Economic and Social History* (Clarendon Press 1969–80). Three volumes.

Coleman, D. C., *A Brief History of Courtaulds* (Clarendon Press, 1969). [Condensed from author's *Courtaulds: An Economic and Social History* as described above.]

Courtauld, Sir Stephen Lewis, *The Huguenot Family of Courtauld* (privately printed, 1957–67). Three volumes.

Knight, A. W., *Private Enterprise and Public Intervention: The Courtaulds Experience* (Allen & Unwin, 1974). 223 pp.

Supple, B., *Essays in British Business History* (Clarendon Press, 1977). [Chapter 5: 'Courtaulds and the Beginning of Rayon', D. C. Coleman.]

Warde-Jackson, C. H., *The 'Cellophane' Story: Origins of a British Industrial Group* (privately printed, 1977). 144 pp.

Warde-Jackson, C. H., *A History of Courtaulds: An Account of the Origin and Rise of the Industrial Enterprise of Courtauld Ltd* (privately printed, 1941). ix 177 pp.

Crombie Knowles & Co.

Allen, J. R. (ed.), *Crombies of Grandholm and Cothal 1805–1960: Records of an Aberdeenshire Enterprise* (Central Press, n.d.). 139 pp.

Dawson International

Moore, J., *Rich and Rare: The Story of Dawson International* (Melland, 1986). 110 pp.

Dickinson (William) Ltd

—— *Record of One Hundred Years 1826–1926* (The Company, 1926).

Dobson & Barlow Ltd

—— *Dobson & Barlow Ltd, Textile Machinists: 134 Years in Progress 1790–1924* (The Firm, 1924). 119 pp.

Crompton, Samuel, *The Inventor of the Spinning Mule: A Brief Survey of his Life and Work, with which is Incorporated a Short History of Messrs Dobson & Barlow* (The Company, 1927). 147 pp.

Domithorpe

Ellis, S., *A Mill on the Soar: A Personal and Company Narrative* (The Author, 1978). 147 pp.

Drew (Alexander) & Sons Ltd

—— *Seventy-Five Years of Textile Progress 1872–1947: A Souvenir Booklet* (1947).

Eadie Brothers

—— *Eadie Brothers, 1871–1971* (Newman Neame, 1971). 71 pp.

Early (Charles) & Marriott (Witney) Ltd

Plummer, A. and Early, R. E., *The Blanket Makers 1669–1969: A History of Charles Early and Marriott Witney Ltd* (Routledge & Kegan Paul, 1969). xii 205 pp.

English Sewing Cotton Company

Blyth, H. E., *Through the Eyes of a Needle: The Story of the English Sewing Cotton Company 1897–1947* (1947). 111 pp.

Harrison, Sir Cyril E., *A Company's Policy in the Ten Post-War Years* (1955).

Ferguson Brothers

—— *Centenary: Ferguson Brothers, Carlisle, 1824–1924* (Charles Thurnam, 1924). 68 pp.

Fletcher (William) & Sons

Fletcher, S. B., *The Fletcher House of Lace and its Wider Family Associations* (The Firm, 1957). xvi 307 pp.

Ford, Ayrton & Co. Ltd

Pafford, E. R. and John, H. P., *Employer and Employed: Ford, Ayrton & Co. Ltd, Silk Spinners . . . 1870–1970* (Pasold Research, 1974).

Foster (John) & Son Ltd

Sigsworth, Eric M., *A History* (Liverpool University Press, 1958). xvii 385 pp.

Fox Brothers & Co.

Fox, H., *Quaker Homespun: The Life of Thomas Fox at Wellington, Serge Maker and Banker 1747–1821* (Allen & Unwin, 1958). 136 pp.

Fox, J. H., *The Woollen Manufacture at Wellington, Somerset* (Humphreys, 1914). viii 121 pp.

Garnett (G.) & Sons Ltd

Dobson, E. P., *The Garnett Story 1831–1962: The History of a Yorkshire Worsted and Woollen Business through Four Generations* (1962). 112 pp.

Gourock Ropework Co. Ltd

Blake, G., *'The Gourock'* (The Firm, 1963). 200 pp.

Greg (R.) & Co. Ltd

—— *The Story of Greg: A Study in Yarn* (The Firm, 1957).

Greg (Samuel) & Co.

Rose, M. B., *The Gregs of Quarry Bank Mill: The Rise and Decline of a Family Firm, 1750–1914* (Cambridge University Press, 1986). 169 pp.

Heap (Samuel) & Son Ltd

Harte, N. B., *A History of Samuel Heap & Sons Ltd 1823–1964* (privately published, 1967). 69 pp.

Heathcoat & Co. Ltd

—— *John Heathcoat and His Heritage* (1958). 222 pp.

Hirst (C. & J.) & Sons Ltd

Hirst, G. C., *History of C. & J. Hirst & Sons Ltd* (1942). 59 pp.

Hinde (Fras.) & Sons Ltd

—— *The Story of Norwich Silks: Being a Short Account of Silks by Fras. Hinde & Sons Limited from 1810 to the Present Day* (The Firm, 1948). 64 pp.

Hitchcock, Williams & Co.

Walden, H. A., *'Operation Textiles': A City Warehouse in Wartime. A Short History of the Firm of Hichcock, Williams & Co.* (1946). 89 pp.

Holdsworth & Gibb Ltd

—— *1860–1960: The History of Holdsworth & Gibb Ltd* (1961).

Holland & Webb

Weston-Webb, W. F. M., *The Autobiography of a British Yarn Merchant* (Cayme Press, 1929). 247 pp.

Hollins & Vyella

Pigott, Stanley, *Hollins: A Study of Industry with Hollins & Co.* (1949). 151 pp.

Wells, F. A., *Hollins & Vyella: A Study in Business History* (David & Charles, 1968). 264 pp.

Holt (Thomas) Ltd

Dwyer, F. J., *The Atlas Ironworks: The History of Thomas Holt Ltd 1855–1959, Textile Machinists* (1960). viii 102 pp.

Hooley Bridge Cotton Mills

Stott, W., *The Hooley Bridge Estate* (1970).

Horrockses, Crewdson & Co. Ltd

—— *History of Origin and Development of the Firm of Horrockses, Crewdson & Co. Ltd 1791–1912* (1913).

—— *The Story of the Evolution of the Cotton Boll and History of the Origin and Development of the Firm of Horrockses, Crewdson & Co. Ltd* (The Company, 192?).

Brown, Sir Charles, *Origin and Progress of Horrockses, Crewdson & Co., the Manufacturers of 'Horrockses Long Cloth'* (1925).

Pedrick, Gale, *The Story of Horrockses* (1950). 68 pp.

International Federation of Cotton & Allied Textile Industries

—— *Historic Sketch 1904–1960* (1960). 72 pp.

Ives (James)

Dobson, E. P. and Ives, J. B., *A Century of Achievement: The History of James Ives & Co., 1848–1948* . . . (William Sessions, 1948). 103 pp.

Keighley Fleece Mills Co. Ltd

—— *The Keighley Fleece Mills Co. Ltd 1865–1965* (privately printed, 1965).

Kelsall & Kemp Ltd

—— *1815–1965* (The Company, 1965).

Kenyon (James) & Son Ltd

Muir, Augustus M., *The Kenyon Tradition: The History of James Kenyon & Son Ltd 1664–1964* (Heffer & Sons, 1964). 112 pp.

—— *The House of Kenyon 1714–1930* (The Firm, 1938).

—— *Kenyons of Bury: Cotton and Woollen Manufacturers* (1950). (3rd edition, 1958.)

—— *Two Hundred and Twenty Years of the House of Kenyon 1714–1934* (1935).

Ladybird

Pasold, E. W., *Ladybird, Ladybird: A Story of Private Enterprise* (Manchester University Press, 1977). 668 pp.

The Lancashire Cotton Corporation Ltd

—— *The Mills and Organisation of the Cotton Corporation Ltd* (1950).

Lee (William)

Lowe, D. and Richards, J., *William Lee and Lace* (Nottingham Lace Centre, 1989). 116 pp.

Lester (C. & T.)

Buck, Anne, *Thomas Lester, His Lace and the East Midlands Industry 1820–1905* (Ruth Bean, 1981). x 108 pp.

Linen Thread Co. Ltd

Sinclair, R. G., *The Faithful Fibre: The Story of the Development of the Linen Thread Company Limited* (The Company, 1956). 68 pp.

Lister & Co. plc

Keighley, M., *A Fabric Hinge: The Story of Listers* (James & James, 1989). 95 pp.

The London Weavers' Co.

Plummer, A., *The London Weavers' Co. 1600–1970* (1972).

Lowthian, Drake & Co. Ltd

—— *Across the Globe, Eighteen-Forty-Eight–Nineteen-Forty-Eight* (The Firm, 1948).

Macnab (A. & J.)

—— *A. & J. Macnab: A Company History* (The Firm, 1960). 62 pp.

McConnel & Kennedy Co. Ltd

McConnel, J. W., *A Century of Fine Cotton Spinning 1790–1906* (1906). (2nd edition, 1913).

Lee, C. H., *A Cotton Enterprise 1795–1940* (Manchester University Press, 1972). 188 pp.

Marshalls of Leeds

Rimmer, W. G., *Marshalls of Leeds: Flax Spinners 1788–1886* (Cambridge University Press, 1960). xiii 342 pp.

Morley (I. & R.)

Finch, R., *The Flying Wheel: I. & R. Morley* (The Firm, 1924). 89 pp.

Thomas, F. M., *I. & R. Morley: A Record of a Hundred Years* (Chiswick Press, 1900). x 103 pp.

Morris & Co.

Gere, C., *Morris & Company 1861–1939* [In exhibition catalogue, 1979] (Fine Art Society, 1979). 56 pp.

Morton (Alexander) & Co.

Morton, J., *Three Generations in a Family Firm* (Routledge & Kegan Paul, 1971). xxi 481 pp.

Mossley Wool Combing & Spinning Co.

Dupont-Lhotelain, H., *The Story of the Mossley Wool Combing and Spinning Company Ltd 1932–1982* (The Firm, 1982). 71 pp.

Nairn (Michael) & Co. Ltd

Muir, A., *Nairns of Kirkcaldy: A Short History of the Company 1547–1956* (Heffer, 1956). vii 158 pp.

Nelson (James) Ltd

Nelson, J., *Nelsons of Nelson: The Story of James Nelson Ltd 1881–1951* (Harley, 1951). 53 pp.

Openshaw (Charles) & Sons (Manchester) Ltd

——— *150 Years of Service 1805–1955* (1955).

Pasold

Pasold, E. W., *Ladybird, Ladybird: A Story of Private Enterprise* (Manchester University Press, 1977). xvi 668 pp.

Pearl Mill

Russell, L. and Holden, R. N., *Pearl Mill 1907–1929: A Stockport Cotton Spinning Company* (1987).

Platt Bros & Co. Ltd

——— *Progress of the Cotton Industry and Textiles Machinery Making* (The Company, 1929).

——— *Souvenir: 1821–1926* (The Company, 1926). (2nd edition.)

Playne (William) & Co.

Playne, A. T. and Long, A. L., *200th Anniversary: A History of Playne & Longfords Mills* (The Firm, 1959). 64 pp.

Potter (Edmund) & Co. Ltd

Hurst, J. G., *Edmund Potter and Dinting Vale* (The Company, 1948). xiii 89 pp.

Readson Ltd

Beaver, P., *Readson Limited 1932–1982* (Melland, 1982). 64 pp.

Royton Spinning Co. Ltd

—— *Eightieth Anniversary 1871–1951* (The Company, 1951).

Salt (Titus)

Suddards, R. W., *Titus of Salts* (Watmough, 1976). 64 pp.

Sanderson & Murray

MacLaren, D. D. S., *Sanderson & Murray: Fellmongers and Wool Merchants 1844–1954* (The Firm, 1955). 83 pp.

Shiloh Mills Ltd

—— *The Shiloh Story 1874–1974* (Shiloh Spinners Ltd, 1974). 52 pp.

Simon, May & Co. Ltd

—— *1849–1949: Century of Achievement: The Simon & May Story* (The Firm, 1948). 63 pp.

Simpson (Stephen) Ltd

Simpson, Stephen, *History of the Firm of Stephen Simpson (Preston) 1829–1929* (The Firm, 1929). 74 pp.

Smith (Joshua) (1908) Ltd

—— *British Piece Goods* (1947).

Stoddard (A. F.) & Co. Ltd

—— *The Carpet Makers: 100 Years of Designing and Manufacturing Carpets of Quality* (The Firm, 1962). 72 pp.

Storey Brothers & Co. Ltd

Christie, Guy, *Storeys of Lancaster 1848–1964* (Collins for Storey Bros, 1964). 256 pp.

Symington (R. & W. H.) & Co.

—— *In Our Own Fashion 1856–1956: The Story of R. and W. H. Symington & Co. Ltd, Market Harborough* (Harley, 1956). 104 pp.

Tatham (William) Ltd

—— *Tatham: A Centenary History 1866–1966* (The Firm, 1966).

Tatton (William) & Co.

Tatton, M. A. and others (comp.), *A Staffordshire Centenary: William Tatton of Leek 1869–1969* (The Firm, 1969). 60 pp.

Taylor of Batley

Greenwood, G. A., *Taylor of Batley: A Story of 102 Years* (Max Parrish, 1957). 188 pp.

Taylor (J. T. and J.) Ltd

Taylor, T. C., *One Hundred Years: Records, Recollections and Reflections* (Whitehead & Miller, 1946). 69 pp.

Templeton (James) & Co.

Young, A. H., *A Century of Carpet Making 1839–1939* (The Firm, 1943). 80 pp.

Textile Institute

Sondhelm, W. and Denyer, R., *Jubilee: The Textile Institute 75th Anniversary Souvenir Publication* (The Firm, 1985). 116 pp.

Thompson (William) & Co. Ltd

—— *Time Marches On: 150 Years of Silk Spinning 1792–1942* (The Company, 1942).

Turnbull & Stockdale Ltd

—— *Jubilee Souvenir 1881–1931* (The Firm, 1931).

Turner (W. & R.) & Co.

Aspin, Christopher, *The Turners of Helmshore and Higher Mill* (The Company, 1970).

Wade (Mark Thornhill)

Dagley, D. B., *Mark Thornhill Wade, Silk Dyer* (1961). 157 pp.

Warner & Sons

Goodale, Sir Ernest William, *Weavers and the Warners 1870–1970* (F. Lewis, 1971). 58 pp.

Goodale, Sir E. W., *The Evolution of Warners: An Account of One Hundred Years of Weaving (1870–1970)* . . . (private circulation from typewritten copy). 150 pp.

Schoeser, M., *The May Silks* (1983).

Schoeser, M., *Fifties Printed Textiles* (1985).

Schoeser, M., *Marianne Straub* (1984).

—— *A Choice of Design 1850–1950, Fabrics by Warner & Son Ltd* (The Firm, 1981). 113 pp.

White, Child & Beney

Godwin, G. (ed.), *A Century of Trading: The Story of the Firm of White, Child & Beney* (The Firm, 1943). 32 pp.

Whitehead (David) & Sons (Holdings) Ltd

—— *A Short History of the Firm 1815–1943* (1943).

Thompson, T. and others, *Johnny and Joan: Drawn by T. J. Bond* (1946).

Whitehead, Harry, *David Whitehead & Sons Ltd 1815–1909* (1909).

Wigston Hosiers Ltd

Greening, E. O., *A Democratic Co-partnership Successfully Established by the Wigston Hosiers Ltd* (Co-op Printing Society, 1921). 125 pp.

Wilson Brothers Bobbin Co.

—— *Wilson Brothers Bobbin Co.: One Hundred Years 1823–1923* (The Firm, 1923). 77 pp.

Yates (William) & Sons Ltd

—— *The Happy Mill: William Yates & Sons Ltd, 160th Anniversary* (1954). (1954).

Timber

Alsford (J.) Ltd

Beaver, Patrick, *The Alsford Tradition: A Century of Quality Timber 1882–1982* (Melland, 1982). 100 pp.

Anderson (C. F.) & Son Ltd

Muir, A., *Andersons of Islington: The History of C. F. Anderson & Son Ltd 1863–1963* (The Firm, 1963). xii 52 pp. [New edition 1988.]

Bambergers Ltd

Bamberger, Louis, *Memories of Sixty Years in the Timber and Pianoforte Trades* (Sampson Low, 1930). xviii 270 pp.

Brownlee & Co. Ltd

Carnegie, J. F., *Brownlee 125: The History of Brownlee & Co. Ltd 1949–1974* (The Company, 1977). 80 pp. [A sequel to *One Hundred Years of Timber* (1950) as described below.]

Carvel, J., *One Hundred Years of Timber 1848–1949* (The Company, 1950). 168 pp.

Burbidge (H.)

Clarke, L. J. and Burbidge, H. L., *An Account of the Development of the Business of H. Burbidge, Woodturner, Founded in Conventry 1867* (1984). 57 pp.

Burt, Boulton & Haywood Ltd

—— *A Century of Progress 1848–1948* (The Firm, 1948). 66 pp.

Churchill & Sim

Muir, A., *Churchill & Sim 1813–1963: A Short History* (Newman Neame
   for The Firm, 1963). 84 pp.

Denny, Mott & Dickson Ltd: *see also* **Mallinson (William) & Denny
Molt** *below.*

—— *DMD: 1875–1952* (1952).

Fleming (John) & Co.

Perren, R., *John Fleming & Company Limited 1877–1977* (The Firm,
   1977). 96 pp.

Howard's

Howard, H. M., *Howard's for Timber: A Family Document 1876–1976*
   (1976). 84 pp.

Howarth Timber Group

Watson, Nigel, *The Story of the Howarth Timber Group 1840–1990*
   (Garland Press, 1990). xi 52 pp.

Latham (James)

Latham, E. B., *Timber: Its Development and Distribution. . . Includes
   1757–1957, The Story of James Latham* (Harrap, 1957). 305 pp.

Mallinson (William) & Sons Ltd

Potter, W. C., *The House of Mallinson 1877–1947* (1947). 175 pp.

Mallinson (William) & Denny Mott

Mackie, W. E., *The Mallinson Story 1877–1977* (The Firm, 1977).
   109 pp.

May (R.) & Son Ltd

—— *R. May & Son Ltd, Timber Merchants. . . 1855–1955* (n.d.).

Pollock, Gilmour & Co.

Rankin, John, *A History of Our Firm: Some Account of Pollock, Gilmour & Co. and its Off-shoots and Connections* (1908). (2nd edition revised, 1921.) ix 1 330 pp.

Ritchie (Andrew) & Son Ltd

House, J., *A Century of Box-Making: A History of Andrew Ritchie and Son Ltd from 1850 to 1950* (The Firm, 1950). 77 pp.

Tobacco

General

Corina, M., *Trust in Tobacco: The Anglo-American Struggle for Power* (Michael Joseph, 1975). 320 pp.

Devine, T. M., *The Tobacco Lords: A Study of the Tobacco Merchants of Glasgow* (John Donald, 1973).

Durden, R. F., *The Dukes of Durham 1865–1929* (Durham, North Carolina, 1975).

Mullen, C., *Cigarette Pack Art* (Hamlyn, 1979). 128 pp.

Supple, B. (ed.), *Essays in British Business History* (Clarendon Press, 1977). [Chapter entitled 'Penny Cigarettes, Oligopoly and Entrepreneurship in the UK Tobacco Industry in the late Nineteenth Century' by B. W. E. Alford.]

Chalmers (Andrew) & Co.

Mack, P. H., *The Golden Weed: A History of Tobacco and of the House of Andrew Chalmers 1865–1965* (Newman Neame, 1965). 64 pp.

Cunningham (W.) and Co.

Devine, T. M., *A Scottish Firm in Virginia 1767–1777* (Clark Constable, 1984). 255 pp.

Dunhill (Alfred) Ltd

Balfour, M., *Alfred Dunhill: One Hundred Years and More* (Weidenfeld & Nicolson, 1992). 240 pp.

Dunhill, Mary, *Our Family Business* (Bodley Head, 1979). 146 pp.

Fribourg & Treyer

Arlott, J., *The Snuff Shop* (1974). 61 pp.

Evans, G., *The Old Snuff House of Fribourg & Treyer 1720–1920* (1921). 50 pp.

Gallaher Ltd

—— *Gallaher Ltd and Subsidiary Companies 1857–1956* (Gallaher, 1956).

Imperial Group plc

Basu, C., *Challenge and Change: The ITC Story, 1910–1985* (Sangam Books, 1988). 367 pp.

Davies, W. T., *Fifty Years of Progress: An Account of the African Organisation of the Imperial Tobacco Company 1907–1957* (The Firm, 1957). 92 pp.

Dempsey, M. (ed.), *Pipe Dreams: Early Advertising Art from the Imperial Tobacco Company* (Pavilion Books, 1982). 96 pp.

Dickinson, S. V., *The First Sixty Years: A History of the Imperial Tobacco Company (G. B. & Ireland) Ltd in the U.S.A., 1902–1962* (The Firm, 1965). 134 pp.

Lewis (Robert) (St James's)

Scarlet, I., *A Puff of Smoke* (The Firm, 1987). 64 pp.

Wills (W. D. & H. O.)

—— *Tobacco: Its History, Culture and Manufacture* (1958). 53 pp.

Alford, B. W. E., *W. D. & H. O. Wills and the Development of the UK Tobacco Industry 1786–1965* (Methuen, 1973). xv 500 pp.

Till, R., *Wills of Bristol 1786–1901* (The Firm, n.d.). 74 pp.

Wilsons & Co. (Sharrow) Ltd

Chayton, M. H. F., *The Wilsons of Sharrow: The Snuff Makers of Sheffield* (privately printed, 1962). xii 191 pp.

Transport and Road Haulage

[See separately Motor Industry and Bicycles]

General

[For Railways see Ottley, George (comp.), *Bibliography of British Railway History* (HMSO, 1983), (2nd edition).]

Bagwell, Philip S., *The Transport Revolution from 1770* (Batsford, 1974).

Barker, T. C. and Savage, C. I., *An Economic History of Transport in Britain* (Hutchinson, 1974).

Alexanders

—— *Alexanders the Great* (The Firm, 1947). 60 pp.

Alexandra Towing Co.

Hallam, W. B., *Blow Five: A History of the Alexandra Towing Company Limited* (Liverpool: Journal of Commerce and Shipping Telegraph, 1976). 107 pp.

Allen (Thomas) Ltd

—— *The First Hundred Years of Thomas Allen Ltd* (1954). 63 pp.

Associated Equipment Company

Thomas, Alan and Aldridge, John, *AEC: 'Builders of London's Buses'* (Henry, 1979). 63 pp.

Birmingham & Midland Motor Bus Co.

Gray, P. and others, *Midland Red: A History of the Company and its Vehicles from 1940–1970* (Glossop: Transport Publishing, 1978–79). Two volumes.

Bishop & Sons

—— *Bishop and Sons, Furniture Removing and Warehousing Establishments: Prospectus* (The Firm, 1907). 84 pp.

British Electric Traction Co.

Brown, S. J., *N.B.C.: Antecedents and Formation* (Ian Allen, 1983). 128 pp.

Fulford, R., *The Sixth Decade, 1946–1956* (BET House History, privately printed, 1956). 86 pp.

Fulford, R., *Five Decades of B.E.T.: The British Electric Traction Company Limited* (The Firm, 1946). 84 pp.

Mingay, G. E., *Fifteen Years On, 1956–1971* (1973). 118 pp.

Brown, Atkinson & Co.

Janes, H., *Full Ahead: The Story of Brown, Atkinson & Co. Ltd* (Harley, 1960). 71 pp.

Crosville Motor Services

Anderson, R. C., *A History of Crosville Motor Services* (David & Charles, 1981). 192 pp.

Crosland-Taylor, W. J. C., *State Owned Without Tears: The Story of Crosville 1948–1953*, 2nd edition (Liverpool: Transport Publishing, 1987). 272 pp.

Dennis Brothers

Kennet, Pat, *Dennis* (Patrick Stephens, 1979).

Twelvetrees, Richard and Squire, P., *Why Dennis and How?* (privately printed, 1945). 106 pp.

Eastern Coach Works

Doggert, M., *Eastern Coach Works; vol. 1: A History of the Coachbuilding Activities at Lowestoft 1919–1946* (Glossop: Transport Publishing, 1987). 160 pp.

Gammons (Walter) Ltd

Gammons, W., *Forty Years in Transport* (1931). 163 pp.

Gattie (Alfred)

Jenkins, P. R., *The Other Railway Clearing House* (Dragonwheel Books, 1987). 96 pp.

Gilbert (John & Thomas)

Lead, P., *Agents of Revolution: John and Thomas Gilbert, Entrepreneurs* (University of Keele, Centre for Local History, 1989). 183 pp.

Hay's Wharf Cartage Co. Ltd

—— *Transport Saga 1646–1947* (1947). 63 pp. [Includes history of Pickfords & Carter Paterson.]

Hoults Ltd

—— *A Story of 50,000,000 Miles* (1967).

Hunting Group

Hunting, Sir P., *The Group and I: An Account of the Hunting Group. . .* (The Firm, 1968). xi 136 pp.

Jempson (John) & Son

Barker, T. C., *The Transport Contractors of Rye: John Jempson & Son: A Chapter in the History of Road Haulage* (Athlone Press, 1982). 88 pp.

King Alfred Motor Services

Freeman, J. D. F. and others, *King Alfred Motor Services: The Story of a Winchester Family Business* (Kingfisher, 1984). 208 pp.

London General Omnibus Co.

—— *One Hundred Years of the London Omnibus, 1829–1929* (1929).

London Transport

Barker, T. C. and Robbins, Michael, *A History of London Transport: Passenger Travel and Development of the Metropolis* (Allen & Unwin, 1963 and 1974). Two volumes.

Barker, T. C., *Moving Millions: A Pictorial History of London Transport* (London Transport Museum, 1992). 132 pp.

McNamara & Co. Ltd

—— *A Historic Review* (1977).

Midland Red

Anderson, R. C., *A History of the Midland Red* (David & Charles, 1984). 192 pp.

National Bus Company

Birks, J. A. and others, *National Bus Company 1968–1989: A Commemorative Volume* (Glossop: Transport Publishing, 1989). xxiv 728 pp.

National Freight Corporation

Thompson, Peter, *Sharing the Success: The Story of NFC* (Fontana, 1991). 224 pp.

Silcock Express

Watson, Nigel, *Excellence by Caring – The Continuing Story of Silcock Express* (James & James, 1991). 64 pp.

SPD Ltd

Reader, W. J., *Hard Roads and Highways: SPD Limited 1918–1968: A Study in Distribution* (Batsford, 1969). 152 pp.

Tilling (Thomas) Ltd

Tilling, J., *Kings of the Highway* (1957). 126 pp.

United Automobile Services

Watson, N., *'United': A Short History of the United Automobile Services Ltd 1912–1987* (The Firm, 1987). 97 pp.

United Counties Omnibus Co.

Warwick, R. M., *An Illustrated History of the United Counties Omnibus Limited*, parts 1–8 (Northampton, The Author, 1977–87).

United Towing

Ford, A., *United Towing 1920–90: A History* (Hutton Press, 1990). 156 pp.

Wines and Spirits

General

Barty-King, H. and Massel, Anton, *Rum Yesterday and Today* (Heinemann, 1983). (Foreword by Hammond Innes.)

Moss, Michael and Hume, John R., *The Making of Scotch Whisky: The History of the Scotch Whisky Distilling Industry* (James & James, 1981). 303 pp.

Ballantine (George) & Son

Mantle, J., *A History of George Ballantine & Sons* (James & James, 1992). 64 pp.

Bell (Arthur) & Sons Ltd

House, Jack, *Pride of Perth: The Story of Arthur Bell & Sons Ltd, Scotch Whisky Distillers* (Hutchinson Benham, 1976). 135 pp.

Berry Brothers & Rudd Ltd

Allen, H. W., *Number Three Saint James's Street: A History of Berry's The Wine Merchants* (Chatto, 1950). 269 pp.

Bollinger

Ray, C., *Bollinger: Tradition of a Champagne Family* (Peter Davies, 1971). (2nd edition, Heinemann, 1981). 217 pp.

Ray, C., *Bollinger: Tradition of a Champagne Family*, 3rd edition (Heinemann Kingwood, 1988). 217 pp.

Booth's Distilleries Ltd

Balfour, J. P. D., *The Kindred Spirit: A History of Gin and the House of Booth* (Newman Neame, 1959). xi 93 pp.

Buchanan (James) & Co.

Spiller, B., *The Chameleon's Eye: James Buchanan & Co. Ltd, 1884–1984* (The Firm, 1984). 148 pp.

Bulmer (H. P.) & Co.

Wildinson, L. P., *Bulmers of Hereford: A Century of Cider-making* (David & Charles, 1987). 215 pp.

Bushmills Distillery

McCreary, A., *Spirit of the Age: The Story of 'Old Bushmills'* (Belfast: The Firm, 1983). 232 pp.

Cardhu

Spiller, B., *Cardhu: The World of Malt Whisky* (John Walker & Sons, 1985). 80 pp.

Cognac

Faith, N., *Cognac* (Hamish Hamilton, 1986). 190 pp.

Cotswold Cider Co.

White, F. J., *The Hargreaves Story: Including a Full History of the 'Cotswold Cider Company'* (Bodley Head, 1953). 192 pp.

Dallas Dhu Distillery

Hume, J., *Dallas Dhu Distillery* (HMSO, 1988).

Deinhard & Co. Ltd

Bruce, George, *A Wine Day's Work: 150th of Deinhard, London* (Clark Constable, 1985). 160 pp.

Dewar (John) & Sons

—— *The House of Dewar 1846–1946* (The Firm, 1946). 68 pp.

Gilbey (W. A.) Ltd

Gold, A. H., *Four-in-Hand: A History of W. A. Gilbey Ltd 1857–1957* (Gilbey, 1957). 83 pp.

Maxwell, Sir H. E., *Half a Century of Successful Trade: Being a Sketch of the Rise and Development of the Business of W. A. Gilbey & Co. 1857–1907* (1907). 85 pp.

Waugh, A. R., *Merchants of Wine: Being a Centenary Account of the Fortunes of the House of Gilbey* (Cassell, 1957). vii 135 pp.

Glenfiddich Scotch Whisky

Reeve-Jones, *A Dream like This* (Elm Tree Books, 1974). 122 pp.

Gonzalez Byass (UK) Ltd

—— *Old Sherry: The Story of the First Hundred Years of Gonzalez Byass & Co. Ltd 1835–1935* (The Firm, 1935). 155 pp.

Grant (William) & Sons Ltd

Collinson, F., *The Life & Times of William Grant* (The Firm, 1979). 102 pp.

Haig (John) & Co. Ltd

Laver, James, *The House of Haig* (1958). vii 75 pp.

Harvey (John) & Sons Ltd

Harrison, G., *Bristol Cream (History of a Firm of Wine Merchants)* (Batsford, 1955). 162 pp.

Henry, T., *Harveys of Bristol* (1986).

Justerini Brothers

Wheatley, D., *1749–1949: The Seven Ages of Justerini's* (Riddle Books, 1949). 85 pp.

Krug

Arlott, John, *Krug: House of Champagne* (David Poynter, 1976). 224 pp.

North British Distillery Co. Ltd

Gardiner, L., *The North British Distillery Co. Ltd: The First Hundred Years* (The Firm, 1985).

Sandeman (Geo. G.) Sons & Co. Ltd

—— *Port and Sherry: The Story of Two Fine Wines* (1955). 63 pp. (2nd revised edition, 1964). 55 pp.

—— *The House of Sandeman: A Story of Fine Wines and Spirits* (Sandeman Sons & Co. Ltd, 1972). 61 pp. (4th revised edition, 1978).

Halley, N., *Sandeman: Two Hundred Years of Port and Sherry* (Granta Editions, 1990). 152 pp.

Sanderson (Wm) Ltd

Wilson, Ross, *The House of Sanderson* (William Sanderson Ltd, 1963). 108 pp.

Southard & Co. Ltd

—— *An Outline of the Foundation and Development of the House of Southard's* (1945). 112 pp. (2nd edition).

Stone's Finsbury Distillery

Janes, H., *Stone's 1740–1965: The Story of the Finsbury Distillery* (Harley, 1965). 55 pp.

Wainwright, D., *Stone's Ginger Wine: Fortunes of a Family Firm 1740–1990* (Quiller, 1490). 124 pp.

Teacher (William) & Sons

—— *William Teacher & Sons* (1985).

Cousins, G. E., *A Family of Spirit: William Teacher and His Descendants in the Scotch Whisky Trade 1830–1975* (The Firm, 1975). 174 pp.

Victoria Wine Co. Ltd

—— *Here's How* (Victoria Wine Co. Ltd, 1965). 80 pp. [Published to mark the centenary of the Firm.]

Briggs, Asa, *Wine for Sale: Victoria Wine and the Liquor Trade 1860–1984* (Batsford, 1985). 199 pp.

Yates Brothers Wine Lodges

—— *Yates Brothers Wine Lodges Ltd 1884–1984* (The Firm, 1984). 71 pp.

Books of General Use to the Business Historian

Aldcroft, Derek H. *The Development of British Industry and Foreign Competition* (Allen & Unwin, 1968).

Allen, G. C. *British Industries and Their Organisation* (Allen & Unwin, 1938). (5th edition, 1970.)

Allen, G. C. *The Industrial Development of Birmingham and the Black Country 1860–1927* (Longmans, 1929). (Reprinted by Cass, 1966.) 479 pp.

Allen, G. C. *The Structure of Industry in Britain: A Study in Economic Changes* (Longmans, 1961). (3rd edition, 1970.)

Allen, G. C. *Monopoly and Restrictive Practices* (Allen & Unwin, 1968).

Armstrong, J. *Directory of Corporate Archives* (Business Archives Council, 1985) 59 pp.

Armstrong, J. and Jones, S. *Business Documents: Their Origins, Sources and Uses in Historical Research* (Mansell, 1987) vi 251 pp.

Atkins, P. J. *The Directories of London 1672–1977* (Mansell, 1990) 744 pp.

Barker, T. C., Campbell, R. H., Mathias, P. and Yamey, B. S. *Business History* (Debrett's Business History Research, 1984).

Beable, W.H. *Romance of Great Businesses* (Heath Cranton, 1926) Two volumes.

Bellamy, Joyce M. *Yorkshire Business Histories: A Bibliography* (Bradford University, 1970) 457 pp.

Boswell, Jonathan S. *The Rise and Decline of Small Firms* (Allen & Unwin, 1973).

Business Archives Council *The First 500* (1959). (Available from the BAC and in the Guildhall Reference Library.)

Business History   *Britain and the Dominions: A Guide to Business and Related Records in the United Kingdom Concerning Australia, Canada, New Zealand and South Africa* (Boston, Mass.: G. K. Hall, 1978) 253 pp.

Button, H. G. and Lampert, A. P. (eds)   *The Guinness Book of the Business World* (Guinness Superlatives, 1976) 256 pp.

Buxton, Neil K. and Aldcroft, Derek H.   *British Industry between the Wars* (Scolar Press, 1979).

Bythell, Duncan   *The Sweated Trades: Outwork in Nineteenth Century Britain* (Batsford, 1978).

Campbell, R. H.   *The Rise and Fall of Scottish Industry 1707–1939* (John Donald, 1980).

Chaloner, W. H. and Richardson, R. C. (comps)   *British Economic and Social History: A Bibliographical Guide* (Manchester University Press, 1976). (2nd edition, 1984.) 208 pp.

Chapman, S   *Merchant Enterprise in Britain from the Industrial Revolution to World War II* (Cambridge University Press, 1992).

Church, Roy (ed.)   *The Dynamics of Victorian Business* (Allen & Unwin, 1980).

Cottrell, P. L.   *Industrial Finance 1830–1914: The Finance and Organisation of English Manufacturing Industry* (Methuen, 1980) xii 298 pp.

Crouzet, François   *The First Industrialists* (Cambridge University Press, 1985).

Davenport-Hines, R. P. T. (ed.)   *Speculators and Patriots: Essays in Business Biography* (Frank Cass, 1986) viii 139 pp.

Derdak, T. and Hast, A. (eds)   *International Directory of Company Histories, vols I–V* (St James Press, 1988–1992).

Dinning, R.   *Leviathan: The Business Who's Who* (Leviathan House, 1972) 501 pp.

Foster, J and Sheppard, J.   *British Archives: A Guide to Archive Resources in the United Kingdom* (Macmillan, 1982) 533 pp. (Second edition, 1989.)

Fraser, W. Hamish *The Coming of the Mass Market 1850–1914* (Macmillan, 1981).

Goodall, F. *A Bibliography of British Business Histories* (Gower, 1987) 638 pp.

Green, J. and others *Business in Avon and Somerset: A Survey of Archives* (Business History Centre, Bristol Polytechnic, 1991) 209 pp.

Guildhall Reference Library *London Business Histories: A Handlist* (1964).

Hannah, Leslie *Management Strategy and Business Development: An Historical and Comparative Study* (Macmillan, 1976).

Hannah, Leslie *The Rise of the Corporate Economy* (Methuen, 1976). (2nd edition, 1983.)

Hertner, P. and Jones, G. *Multinationals: Theory and History* (Gower, 1986) vii 200 pp.

Honeyman, K. *Origins of Enterprise. Business Leadership in the Industrial Revolution* (St Martin's, 1983).

Hood, N. and Young, S. *Multinationals in Retreat: The Scottish Experience* (Edinburgh University Press, 1982).

Horrocks, Sidney *Lancashire Business Histories* (Manchester University, Joint Committee on the Lancashire Bibliography, 1971) 116 pp.

Howard, A. and Newman, E. *British Enterprise* (1952) 255 pp.

Jeremy, D. *Dictionary of Business Biography: A Biographical Dictionary of Business Leaders Active in the Period 1860–1980* (Butterworths, 1984–5). Five vols. Supplement: 1986, 120 pp.

Jones, G. *British Multi-Nationals: Origins, Management and Performance* (Gower, 1986) 200 pp.

Kinross, John *Fifty Years in the City: Financing Small Business* (John Murray, 1982) ix 238 pp.

Marriner, Sheila (ed.) *Business and Businessmen. Studies in Business Economic and Accounting History* (Liverpool University Press, 1978) xiv 300 pp.

Musson, A. E. *The Growth of British Industry* (Batsford, 1978).

Orbell, M. J.   *A Guide to Tracing the History of a Business* (Business Archives Council, 1987) x 116 pp.

Ottley, George (comp.)   *Bibliography of British Railways* (HMSO, 1983). (2nd edition.) 683 pp.

Ottley, George (comp.)   *Supplement to Bibliography of British Railway History* (HMSO, 1988) 544 pp.

Payne, P. L.   *The Early Scottish Limited Companies, 1856–1895: Historical & Analytical Survey* (Academic Press, 1980) 140 pp.

Payne, P. L.   *Studies in Scottish Business History* (Frank Cass, 1967) 453 pp.

Prais, J. G.   *The Evolution of Giant Firms in Britain 1909–70* (Cambridge University Press, 1976).

Richmond, Lesley and Stockford, Bridget   *The Survey of the Records of 1000 of the First Registered Companies in England and Wales* (Gower, 1986) 616 pp.

Rowe, D. J.   *Northern Business Histories: A Bibliography* (The Library Association, 1979) 191 pp.

Sanderson, M.   *The Universities and British Industry* (Routledge, 1972).

Sheppard, D. K.   *The Growth and Role of UK Financial Institutions 1880–1962* (Methuen, 1971).

Slaven, A. and Aldcroft, D. H. (eds)   *Business, Banking and Urban History* (John Donald, 1982) 235 pp.

Slaven, A. and Checkland, S. G. (eds)   *The Dictionary of Scottish Business Biography* (Aberdeen University Press, 1986–90). Two volumes.

Supple, B. E. (ed.)   *Essays in British Business History* (Clarendon Press, 1977) viii 267 pp.

The Times 1000 annual from 1971 (Times Books) printed by *The Times 300* (1965–1970).

Tucker, K. A. (ed.)   *Business History: Selected Readings* (Cass, 1977) xvi 442 pp.

Turner, Graham   *Business in Britain* (Eyre & Spottiswoode, 1969) 451 pp.

Turton, Alison (ed.)   *Managing Business Archives*
(Butterworth–Heinemann in association with the Business Archives
Council, 1991) xv 462 pp.

Wilcox, M.   *The Confederation of British Industry Predecessor Archive*
(University of Warwick, 1984) 51 pp.

Index of Companies